THE OAKWOOD LIBRARY OF RAILWAY

The Wisbech & Upwell Tramway

by
Peter Paye

THE OAKWOOD PRESS

© Oakwood Press & Peter Paye 2009

British Library Cataloguing in Publication Data
A Record for this book is available from the British Library
ISBN 978 0 85361 689 4

Typeset by Oakwood Graphics.
Repro by PKmediaworks, Cranborne, Dorset.
Printed by Cambrian Printers, Aberystwyth, Ceredigion.

An Upwell to Wisbech train hauled by a 'G15' class 0-4-0 tram locomotive has followed the winding course from Goodman's Corner beside the River Nene (Old Course) and is approaching Outwell Village depot. In the foreground is Church Terrace open level crossing No. 12 and Isle bridge spanning the waterway. The line diverging to the right served Water siding. The windmill in the background is Outwell Corn Mill.

Author's Collection

Title page: 'G15' class 0-4-0 tram locomotive No. 134 standing at Upwell with a train for Wisbech formed of bogie composite tramcar No. 7, a four-wheel tramcar and passenger brake van No. 16. This was the usual loading for passenger trains.   *Author's Collection*

Front cover: 'J70' class 0-6-0 tram locomotive No. 68217 enters Elm Bridge depot with an Upwell to Wisbech freight working in 1950.   *Malcolm Root*

Rear cover: The close proximity of the tramway to housing in Elm High Road is well illustrated as Drewry 204 hp 0-6-0 diesel-mechanical locomotive No. D2202 heads for Upwell with the 1.30 pm from Wisbech just beyond the Duke of Wellington Junction on 18th August, 1964.   *Ken Paye*

Published by The Oakwood Press (Usk), P.O. Box 13, Usk, Mon., NP15 1YS.
E-mail: sales@oakwoodpress.co.uk
Website: www.oakwoodpress.co.uk

Contents

Wisbech from a period postcard. *Author's Collection*

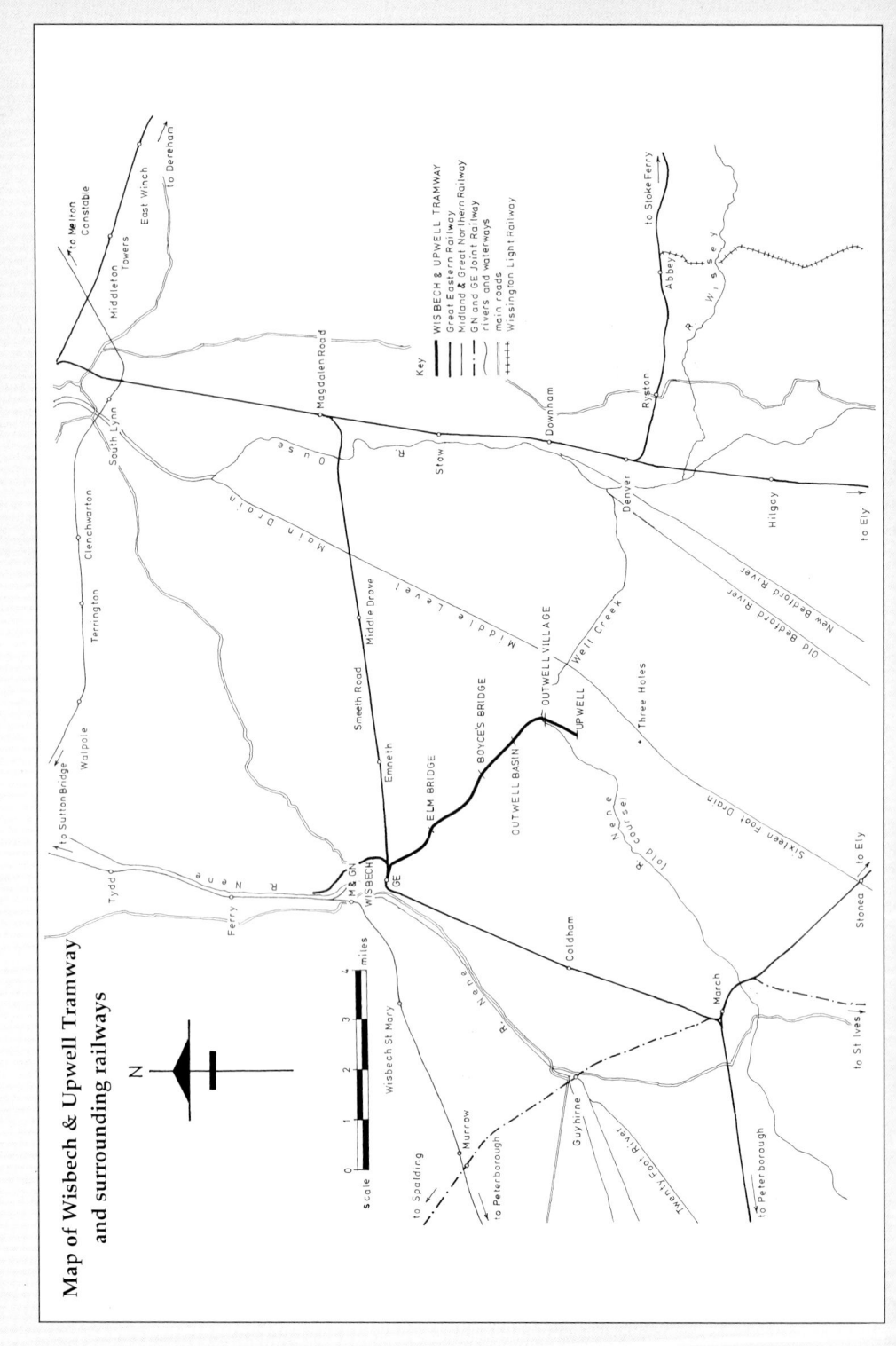

Map of Wisbech & Upwell Tramway and surrounding railways

Introduction

Unsuspecting passengers arriving by the Great Eastern Railway (GER) for the first time at the fenland port of Wisbech in the years before the Great War, and intending to travel on business or visit relatives in the canal side villages to the south-east of the town, could be forgiven for initially disbelieving the sight which greeted them. As porters busied themselves transferring luggage and parcels off the arriving train, travellers were cajoled to join the service standing in the back platform, which was unlike any other they had encountered. The first impressions of the locomotive at the head of the formation, was that it resembled the guard's van of a goods train. A second glance would reveal wisps of steam emanating from its interior, whilst the exterior was highly polished teak livery. The 'guard's van' was in fact a diminutive tank engine with its boiler encased in the wooden body and the motion enclosed behind a side skirting, which reached almost to rail level. To the front and rear of the skirting was a cowcatcher, whilst a bell was mounted on the roof. Behind the locomotive the passenger vehicles were an assortment of four-wheel and bogie tramway coaches, with balconies and steps at each end, and a drop plate above the couplings to permit the conductor-guard to proceed from one coach to another, whilst *en route*, to check the tickets and collect the fares. Having joined this unusual train for the onward journey the travellers were made to sit facing inwards as the seats were all located longitudinally with backs to the windows within the coaches. The guard's 'right away' signal soon heralded departure and after an acknowledging whistle from the 'boxed' locomotive the train rumbled into motion.

Any hopes of speed were dashed for the 'Wisbech and Upwell' tram was restricted to a top speed of 12 mph so progress was sedate. Restrictions when crossing main roads brought speed down to 8 mph and this was further reduced to 4 mph through all facing points. The train ambled alongside the main line to Kings Lynn for almost a third of a mile before swinging to the right through a gate across a main road and alongside the Wisbech canal. In its infant years the train could be stopped at any point as well as the official stopping places, but this caused severe delays and on this journey halts were made at the numerous official stopping points as well as the depots at Elm Bridge, Boyce's Bridge, Outwell Basin and Outwell Village before terminating at Upwell. There were no platforms at these stopping places and passengers were required to use the steps at the end of each of the tramcar coaches to alight and join the train. Except for two short sections of reserved railway company-owned track, the tramway followed and ran alongside public highways on the 5 miles 72 chains journey from Wisbech to Upwell.

Such was the Wisbech & Upwell Tramway in its heyday. Devised by the GER as an experiment, with Board of Trade approval, to act as feeder to the main line system, its genesis lay with the 1870 Tramways Act as a cheap alternative where expenditure did not justify the outlay on a heavily-engineered branch line. Opened in 1883 it enjoyed a full passenger service until the last day of 1927, when road competition provided alternative and quicker means of transport on the roads paralleling the line. Goods traffic continued to flourish, especially in the fruit growing season for which the area was renowned but after World War II and the removal of petrol rationing, competitive road transport made ever increasing inroads into the surviving rail traffic and, despite the introduction of diesel traction from 1952, the last train ran on 20th May, 1966.

Upwell terminus, 5 miles 72 chains from Wisbech, with a passenger train formed of passenger brake van No. 16, a bogie tram and four-wheel tram hauled by 'G15' class 0-4-0 tram locomotive standing at the ground level platform. Behind the fencing is a line of GER open wagons. *Author's Collection*

The Tramway enjoyed success in its own right but the GER never ventured into providing similar lines and tramway working was confined to the docks at Ipswich and Yarmouth as well as Hythe Quay near Colchester. With the passing of the Light Railways Act in 1896 the provision of secondary feeder railways to assist agriculture was to follow a far different criteria but that is another story. I have attempted in this volume to provide the complete story of this unique experiment in rural transport from conception to closure and details have been checked with available documents, but apologies are offered for any errors which may have occurred.

Peter Paye
Bishop's Stortford

Postscript

Generations of children have been nurtured on the stories of Thomas the Tank Engine by the Reverend Wilbert Awdry. As Vicar of Emneth from 1953 until his retirement in 1965, Awdry a keen railway enthusiast, quickly became acquainted with the Wisbech & Upwell Tramway, its quaint steam tram locomotives and with many of the staff who became personal friends. With his love of the unique line, begun a few years earlier with the encouragement of the Reverend Teddy Boston, he could not resist introducing a tram engine to his stories. In 1952, No. 7 in the Railway Series of books, *Toby the Tram Engine* with his companion four-wheel tram coach *Henrietta*, began a series of adventures, which continued in subsequent volumes. Modernity came in 1972 when diesel-mechanical shunting locomotive *Mavis* was introduced in Volume 26 *Tramway Engines*. The Tram engines of the Upwell line live on in these stories and in the minds of millions of readers thus ensuring the ghost of the tramway will never be laid to rest.

Chapter One

Advent of the Tramway

The River Nene rising near Naseby in Northamptonshire follows a meandering course in its 90 miles passage to the sea. South and east of Peterborough the stream found no easy outlet through the silt lands, which lay as wide barriers and the river made several wide loops, the sluggish stream forming broad meres. During the Middle Ages John Moreton, Bishop of Ely authorized the cutting of Morton's Leam, a canal 40 feet wide and 40 miles long from the River Nene at Peterborough through Guyhirne and Wisbech where it joined the original stream to provide access to the North Sea, with the result Wisbech acquired the waters of the Nene in exchange for those of the Ouse. Later a more direct waterway North Bank was built running almost parallel and to the north of Morton's Leam. The Nene Old Course had two outlets, one via Popham's Eau, passing by Three Holes where it intersected with the Middle Level Main Drain and then Nordelph, before joining the River Ouse and ultimately the Wash at King's Lynn. The second outlet was via the Ouse, later the Wisbech canal at Outwell for the onward journey to Wisbech and the sea. Wisbech, derived from Ousebec, mouth of the Ouse or river, up to the 13th century was the outfall of several fen rivers and an important seaport. However, over the years as the estuary silted up the waters found a fresh outlet at Lynn. This was disastrous for the prosperity and trade of the town but the silt and sand that had formed later produced the alluvial silt that was some of the richest farming soil in Britain.

With the object of reclaiming land many more cuts were subsequently constructed, the land drained leaving a vast acreage of rich agricultural land criss-crossed by navigational and irrigational waterways. Over three centuries the Nene was converted in stages north of Wisbech, into a long almost straight embanked channel allowing for the passage of ships. Thus by the early Georgian era the town had recovered from its relative obscurity and a 'great and constant trade' flourished with a good proportion brought to the town for onward transit, along the 11 miles of the Nene to the coastal waters of the Wash and ultimately to British and Continental ports. Wisbech, with its grand three- and four-storey houses on the thoroughfares of North Brink and South Brink facing each other in Dutch mode across the narrow tidal river, became a port with a large and prosperous hinterland, and facilities were enlarged to accommodate vessels of up to 225 feet in length and 1,500 tons unladen weight.

The construction of the Wisbech canal was proposed at meeting on 19th July, 1793 and an authorizing Act obtained the following year, the aim being to reopen the Well Creek and restore navigation between the Ouse and the Nene. The dredging and construction of the five miles of waterway was completed at the end of 1795 and opened between Wisbech and Outwell in January 1796, thus connecting indirectly with further systems of fenland waterways. The £14,000 capital authorized by the Act was exceeded and at meeting on 22nd September, 1796 was increased by £3,300. As well as goods plying the canal, in later years a passenger service was operated by Mr Whybrow of Nordelph and known as 'Whybrow's Packet', the horse-drawn boat had a cover of sorts, and the fare was 2*d*. from Wisbech to Outwell.

With the coming of the railway age Wisbech had much to offer developers and businessmen, and traders of the town were keen to take advantage of the new mode of transport so the community was not isolated from the rest of the country. The gestation period was contracted, however, for East Anglian railways began with the incorporation of the Eastern Counties Railway (ECR) on 4th July, 1836, with a share capital of £1,600,000, to build a 126 mile line from Shoreditch in East London to Norwich and Yarmouth via Colchester, Ipswich and Eye. Construction began late in March 1837 at the London end only, as incomplete negotiations with landowners prevented a concurrent start planned between Norwich and Yarmouth. Severe financial difficulties precluded any progress beyond Colchester and the first public train ran from a temporary terminus at Mile End to Romford on 20th June, 1839 with extensions at each end to Shoreditch and Brentwood opening for traffic on 1st July, 1840. Eventually the line was opened to Colchester for goods traffic on 7th March, 1843 and for passenger trains on 29th March. The 51-mile line had taken seven years to construct at a cost of nearly £2½ million. The decision to terminate well short of the intended destination was a matter of grave concern to the merchants of Ipswich and Norwich, but in 1842 local factions in the cathedral city promoted their own railway linking Norwich and Yarmouth, with an extension the following year westwards to Brandon. These developments caused consternation in Ipswich trading and business circles, which were further aggravated by a revitalised ECR planning a possible extension to join up with the Norwich and Brandon line at Thetford. The outcome was the incorporation of the Eastern Union Railway (EUR) on 19th July, 1844 to connect Ipswich and Colchester and this opened for goods traffic on 1st June, 1846 and to passenger traffic on 15th June. In the meantime on 21st July, 1845 the Act authorizing the nominally independent Ipswich & Bury St Edmunds Railway, but effectively an extension of the EUR, paved the way for a northerly extension from Ipswich and this line was officially opened on 7th December, 1846 with passenger services commencing on Christmas Eve. The proposed ECR extension from Colchester to Thetford was thus abandoned. From 1st January, 1847 the EUR and Ipswich & Bury had entered into a working agreement whereby the whole system was worked as one undertaking, and ratified by Act of Parliament on 8th June, 1847. The southern approach to Norwich was built by the EUR and ran from a junction with the Bury St Edmunds line at Haughley, north-west of Stowmarket and opened in stages, finally reaching Norwich on 7th November, 1849. Initially the relationship between the EUR and ECR was good but then soured and by March 1851 the rift was extreme. Eventually the workings of the EUR was taken over by the ECR from 1st January, 1854 under a tripartite agreement, also involving the Norfolk Railway, made on 13th December, 1853 and the arrangements were ratified by Act of Parliament dated 7th August, 1854 (17 and 18 Vict. cap. ccxx).

By terminating at Colchester in 1843 the ECR had not abandoned its goals of Norwich and Yarmouth and had taken steps to reach Norfolk via an alternative route. On the same day as the ECR was incorporated in 1836, a rival company the Northern & Eastern Railway (N&E) received the Royal Assent to build a line over the 53 miles from Islington to Cambridge, with a share capital of £1,200,000. Like the ECR, the N&E ran into financial and purchasing difficulties and it was not until 1839 that construction commenced and only then with the sanction of the ECR. To save money the N&E route was diverted from Tottenham via Stratford, where running powers were granted into the ECR terminus at Shoreditch. Like the ECR the new line was built to a gauge of 5 feet and despite the abandonment of the route north of Bishop's Stortford by Act of Parliament in 1840, the railway had reached the Hertfordshire town on 16th May, 1842 at a cost of £25,000 per mile. In 1843, the N&E secured an extension Act for the line to Newport, some 10 miles nearer Cambridge. On 23rd December of that year, however, the ECR agreed with the company a 999 years lease from 1st January, 1844. Once the lease was in force the ECR obtained powers on 4th July, 1844, for a line linking Newport to the Norwich & Brandon Railway at Brandon via Cambridge and Ely. The N&ER, as with the ECR, was converted to the standard gauge of 4 feet 8½ inches in the late summer of the same year and, after a formal opening the previous day, the entire line from Bishop's Stortford to a temporary terminus at Norwich Trowse commenced public service on 30th July, 1845. A whole number of schemes were produced in this period of Railway Mania to fill unoccupied spaces in East Anglia and the *Norfolk Chronicle* reported in April 1845 that amongst other towns and cities, Wisbech was the nucleus of seven proposed railways.

In the interim in 1844 the ECR planned a route from Ely to Peterborough via March, and despite numerous problems during construction, because of the marshy soil, the line was opened to goods traffic on 9th December, 1846, and for passenger traffic from 14th January, 1847. Considerable freight traffic soon developed in association with the London & Birmingham Railway, later the London & North Western Railway, line from Blisworth to Peterborough and the Midland Railway, Syston to Peterborough branch. In 1845 the ECR obtained powers for a line from Chesterton Junction, north of Cambridge to the Huntingdonshire market town of St Ives and this opened on 17th August, 1847, the same day as the Ely and Huntingdon line opened from St Ives to Godmanchester, and over which the ECR had running powers.

Then in 1846 authority was given for the construction of the Wisbech, St Ives & Cambridge Junction Railway (WStI&CJR) (9 and 10 Vict. cap. ccclvi), promoted by local landowners and growers especially to enable the cattle and corn traffic from St Ives market to be conveyed to the harbour at Wisbech. Captain J. Coddington carried out the Board of Trade (BoT) inspection of the short 7 miles 58 chains branch from March to the South Brink terminus at Wisbech on 30th April, 1847 and the line opened to traffic on 3rd May, initially with no intermediate station but Pear Tree Hill, later renamed Coldham, was subsequently added. The southern section of the line from March to St Ives, effectively making a through route from Chesterton Junction, was opened on 1st February, 1848, by which time the WStI&CJR had been absorbed by the all powerful ECR, that company working the line from the outset.

The authorization of the ECR lines to Brandon and Peterborough in 1844 had caused panic amongst the business fraternity in the Norfolk port of King's

Lynn. Whilst it enjoyed a lucrative trade with commodities arriving and departing by sea for onwards transit via the Great Ouse and its tributaries to and from destinations in an area stretching from Bedford, Cambridge, Northampton, Peterborough, Bury St Edmunds and Thetford, complacency had set in. The harbour was neglected and Wisbech was providing a challenge for supremacy. A cartel of wealthy Lynn merchants reigned supreme but the threat of continuous rail connections from Yarmouth to the Midlands would result in the loss of over half the town's trade at a stroke. The ECR was approached and would offer no more than a branch railway from Wisbech, a totally unacceptable solution. With the Corporation unwilling or unable to take control of affairs a local solicitor J.C. Williams had a leading role in the formation of three railways to rescue Lynn from its threatened economic stagnation: the Lynn & Ely, with a branches to Lynn Harbour and to Wisbech, incorporated on 30th June, 1845 (8 and 9 Vict. cap. lv), the Lynn & Dereham, incorporated on 21st July, 1845 (8 and 9 Vict. cap. cxxvi) and the Ely & Huntingdon, the latter running from St Ives to Godmanchester. The trio was amalgamated on 27th July, 1847 as the East Anglian Railway (EAR). The intention of the first named was to link King's Lynn to the ECR at Ely and although traffic was to be mainly agricultural, it was hoped large quantities of coal would be brought to Lynn Harbour by sea for onward rail transit. A further Bill for the extension of the Wisbech branch to March and Spalding passed through all stages of the House of Commons but was withdrawn to save costs, when it was hoped the ECR would allow running powers over the former WStI&CJR line.

On 29th December, 1847 Captain George Wynne duly conducted the Board of Trade inspection of the East Anglian Railway (formerly Lynn & Ely Railway) Wisbech branch, which extended the 9 miles 51 chains from the junction at Watlington to the fenland town with one intermediate station at Emneth. All was in order and the line opened for freight traffic on 1st February, 1848 and for passengers to a temporary timber station at Wisbech on 1st March. Thus Wisbech enjoyed two railway systems with a physical connection between the EAR line from Watlington and the branch from March, authorized by the ECR Directors on 22nd June, 1848, but few trains were worked through. In complicated political manoeuvrings early in 1851 the Great Northern Railway (GNR) was making the arrangements to take over the EAR, as the company was keen to extend its system into Norfolk. In February GNR officers inspected the EAR line and rolling stock and a traffic agreement for a period of 21 years was signed on 16th May, 1851, with the GN taking at least 40 per cent of the receipts in return for maintaining the infrastructure. The EAR for its part agreed to make permanent bridges on the Wisbech branch. Agreement was reached for the GNR to work general traffic from 1st July and the GN gave notice to the ECR of its intention to work over its line from Peterborough to Wisbech, under the provision of an agreement made between the ECR, the Boston, Stamford & Birmingham Railway and the GNR on 29th May, 1849; the ECR then granting the GNR running powers, in return for the GN abandoning its powers to construct a direct line from Stamford via Peterborough to Wisbech. The ECR accepted the notice as it was irrational to have two parallel lines from Peterborough to Wisbech, but when the first GN train *en route* from

Peterborough to Lynn and the first train from Lynn to Peterborough approached Wisbech they found vehicles chained to the rails blocking the connecting line between the ECR and the EAR.

The dispute was placed before the Railway Commissioners, with the ECR claiming the EAR had departed from its authorized line during construction; that it had no right to form a junction with the ECR at its present location and that in granting powers to the GNR it expected the GNR to use the ECR Wisbech station before travelling over the junction. Lastly the junction had only been provided to give EAR trains a shorter route to their isolated St Ives to Huntingdon section. The Commissioners might have ordered the removal of the obstructions but refused to arbitrate when it was realized the junction had not received BoT inspection or approval.

Further arguments ensued including the GNR applying to the Court of Chancery for an injunction to compel the ECR to keep to the agreement and remove the obstructions and even contemplation of building their own station. Vice Chancellor Turner was disposed to find in favour of the GN using the connecting line but found the EAR/GNR agreement was a lease and therefore invalid without Parliamentary sanction and refused the injunction. Captain Wynne had, however, returned to Wisbech on 9th August, 1851 to inspect the physical junction between the two railways and although no such junction was shown on the Parliamentary plans of either the EAR or ECR companies, clause 44 of the ECR Act sanctioned a junction being made. Wynne found the double track connecting line on a 10 chains radius curve commenced a short distance south of the ECR station and joined the EAR line at its Wisbech station and, noting nothing amiss, sanctioned use of the connection.

The Kings Cross management were by now tiring of the problems of the EAR and after a further few months' ramifications the EAR proprietors bowed to the inevitable and their company was leased to and worked by the ECR from 1st January, 1852. Despite all the arguments and counter arguments, until 1855 the ECR passenger services continued to use their own station before transferring to the new Wisbech station in Victoria Road on the site of the EAR station. Unfortunately, except at Wisbech, the route of both branches by-passed the main centres of habitation and passenger receipts were abysmal, the chief use was therefore for freight traffic to and from Wisbech Harbour. With no direct access to the river, problems were soon encountered transferring commodities from river to rail and much traffic was lost. On 6th July, 1859 plans for a harbour tramway at Wisbech were considered at an ECR Traffic Committee meeting and rights of way discussed as well as benefits. The costs were estimated at £2,500, land purchase £1,800, other land sold for £1,000 and cost of constructing the line at £1,500. Plans were finalized and the Eastern Counties Railway Act of 1861 (24 and 25 Vict. cap. ccxxxi) duly authorized the construction of the 2½ miles Wisbech St Peter branch, which commenced at a junction with the Wisbech to Watlington branch and ran to the banks of the River Nene.

Having leased or taken over the working of all major railways in East Anglia, the Eastern Counties Railway was the principal party to a scheme being prepared for the amalgamation of the Eastern Counties, Eastern Union, East Anglian, Newmarket and Norfolk Railways into a new undertaking to be known as the Great Eastern Railway. The Act sanctioning the amalgamation, the Great Eastern Railway Act 1862 (25 and 26 Vict. cap. ccxxiii) received the Royal Assent on 7th August, 1862 but took effect retrospectively from July of that year. Few initial changes were made by the new regime but within months Richard Young, the Mayor, officially opened the Wisbech Harbour branch (then referred to as the Wisbech Tramway) on 19th February, 1863, although the first train had run across the branch on 11th November, 1862. He later wrote to the GER Board he '… hoped through the current season to arrange for the shipping of Derby coal through to the Baltic'. The members of the GER Board were, however, looking for more than coal traffic to sustain the new branch and develop trade from the environs of Wisbech.

The alluvial area especially to the south and east of Wisbech was good for fruit growing and vegetable cultivation. It had been realized for some time that it was essential to get soft fruits and vegetables to markets as quickly as possible to obtain the best prices and certainly before the produce rotted. The existing roads and waterways were considered too slow for the conveyance of commodities to the railhead at Wisbech, especially in periods of adverse weather when the roads were muddy quagmires with horse-drawn waggons sinking up to their axles in the mire or the waterways were frozen solid with ice. It was thought by some that additional railways could provide the answer. The first intimation of a railway to Upwell was made as early as June 1864 when a Mr Dale of Upwell wrote to the GER suggesting the construction of a single track railway from Pear Tree Hill station on the March to Wisbech line to a terminal between the parishes of Upwell and Outwell, a distance of between four and five miles. The GER Board and the Traffic Committee considered the application on 22nd June, 1864 and Sinclair, the company Engineer was asked to report on the feasibility of the scheme and potential traffic. Little came of the proposal but on 8th November, 1865 a deputation comprising George Dewbarn, Mayor of Wisbech, and several council members together with the Town Clerk met with the GER Board to draw attention to several points, including the possibility of a joint passenger station with the embryonic Peterborough, Wisbech & Sutton Bridge Railway then being built on the north bank of the River Nene and arrangements for working trains along the quay lines. At the same meeting the deputation also enquired whether the GER would oppose any third party seeking Parliamentary approval for a railway to Upwell but were informed the Directors could not give a pledge on the subject. The Peterborough, Wisbech & Sutton Bridge Railway Company subsequently opened its line on north bank of the Nene on 1st August, 1866, remaining totally independent of the GER, and later became part of the Midland & Great Northern Joint Railway.

Little progress was made on the possible construction of feeder lines until on 21st June, 1871 the GER Way & Works Committee discussed plans for a tramway at Wisbech costing £4,350, but again there was lethargy on the part of the officers of the main line company and it was left to private individuals to promote a scheme. In an effort to obviate the problem, early in 1873 W.L. Ollard and others proposed a railway from the best crop producing areas of Upwell and Outwell to Wisbech. G.B. Bruce, the Engineer of the embryonic concern, approached the GER asking if the main line company would be prepared to work the line and if so on what terms. The GER Directors considered the matter at their meeting on 10th February, 1873 and replied that the company would be willing to work the railway at cost price but would provide no rebate on traffic other than that provided for under Railway Clearing House rules.

The Upwell, Outwell & Wisbech Railway Act (36 and 37 Vict. cap. clxxxiv) received the Royal Assent on 21st July, 1873 and authorized the company to construct a railway 6 miles, 2 furlongs, 4 chains and 10 yards in length or thereabouts, commencing by a junction with the Great Eastern Railway at a point 72 yards or thereabouts measured in an easterly direction from the east end of the platform of the passenger station at the town of Wisbech in the parish of Wisbech St Peter, and terminating at the north side of the turnpike road leading from Wisbech to Ely about 95 yards west from Three Holes Bridge in the parish of Upwell. To finance the works the company was authorized to raise £40,000 in £10 shares and from time to time borrow on mortgage a sum not exceeding £13,000 once the capital had been issued and accepted and £20,000 actually paid up. The issue of debenture stock was sanctioned and the three initial Directors were John Farmery Ollard, Issac Donnithorne Walker and William Milner Crowe. Clause 22 of the statute granted the company powers to cross the undermentioned public roads on the level:

Road	Parish
23	Wisbech St Peter
36, 59, 70, 94 and 107	Elm
10, 11 and 36	Outwell
141	Upwell, Cambridgeshire
24, 47 and 110	Upwell, Norfolk

By clause 23, the junction with the GER at Wisbech was to be effected according to the limits shown on the deposited plans and to the satisfaction of the GER company Engineer. The GER was also permitted to erect signals for the protection of its railway at the junction and charge the Upwell Company the cost of providing signalmen or pointsmen for such protection, the account being submitted every six months. As the new line intended to cross over the Middle Level of the Fens in its course between Wisbech and Upwell, all works were required to be completed to the satisfaction of the Middle Level Commissioners or their Engineer and any land taken was subject to drainage tax. When crossing any earth banks, protecting dykes or drainage channels, banks had to be strengthen by a thickness of not less than two yards for a distance of not less than 20 yards each side of the proposed railway. Clause 30 required the company to carry the railway over the River Nene in the parish of Upwell by a substantial bridge having one square span not less than 25 feet in width, with the soffit or underside of the structure not less than 18 feet 6 inches clear above the Middle Level datum line. Towing paths alongside rivers or streams were to be kept clear and widened if required and after construction of the railway, kept in good order. The railway was to be completed within a period of four years from the passing of the Act.

Little progress was made in the initial months and early in November 1873 G.B. Bruce again wrote to the GER Directors stating he was the Engineer of the

Upwell, Outwell & Wisbech Railway (UO&WR) line, which had obtained its Act in the previous Parliamentary session, and asked whether the GER would agree to work the line; suggesting as terms 50 per cent of the gross receipts. He further advised the debentures of the company were to be the first charge against the gross receipts and suggested that a rebate was to be allowed the smaller company upon all traffic passing from that line to the GER or coming from the GER to the Upwell line. The Traffic Committee considered the letter on 19th November, 1873 but were not enamoured by the application and the General Manager was instructed to reply that the GER was not prepared to work the line on the proposed terms.

There was no advancement in the construction of the railway for over a year and during the first week of February 1875 Messrs Heinke and Davis, the new Engineers of the UO&WR again asked the GER authorities whether the company was willing to work their line when completed and if so what percentage of the gross receipts they would allow? They also asked if a rebate would be granted on goods traffic passing from and to the Upwell and Wisbech line to the GER at Wisbech. The GER Board discussed the matter on 10th February and the Secretary reiterated that the GER would work the line at cost price once the railway was constructed to the satisfaction of the GER Engineer. They declined to negotiate on the other points raised. And there matters rested with no progress, as the promoters were experiencing difficulty raising the necessary finance. In the meantime on 1st September, 1876 Pear Tree Hill station on the March to Wisbech line was renamed Coldham, for Pear Tree Hill, whilst from 4th May, 1877 the spelling of Wisbeach station was altered to Wisbech.

The GER Directors were continually seeking ways of engendering additional traffic to increase receipts and the promotion of the UO&WR was considered an interesting variation to the usual railway, where sparse tracts of agricultural country might be tapped with cheaply built lines. Nothing had been heard of the scheme for almost five years and the date allowed for completion in the Parliamentary Act was almost expired. In the spring of 1880 the GER Directors dusted down the papers and requested a feasibility study; on 16th June, 1880 the GER Board considered a report from the Chairman and C.S. Read regarding the provision of steam tramways in Norfolk. The Directors duly noted the findings and requested proposals for specific areas. It was fortuitous that on 20th July, 1880 the Traffic Committee considered a report from the Acting General Manager regarding the proposed Upwell, Outwell and Wisbech Railway. The report enclosed correspondence and plans submitted by J.G. Parson, the solicitor of the proposed line, again asking if the GER would consent to operate the undertaking when the railway was completed and to enquire to the terms of any future agreement. By now the GER management was seriously considering promoting a scheme for a railway serving the district and following almost the same route. After due discussion the Secretary was instructed to notify the UO&WR that the GER considered their proposed line would not pay and therefore any request for assistance would be declined.

On 18th August, 1880 C.H. Parkes, the GER Chairman, reported at the Board meeting on the proposal for the steam tramway in Norfolk. After investigation it was considered the district west of Ely and March would not bear a railway but Stonea with a population of 200 to 300 souls producing 11,000 tons of produce per annum could support a steam tramway. The estimated cost of £20,000 to £25,000 included the provision of two bridges. However, there were more lucrative pastures than Stonea and in view of the failure of the UO&WR to get its scheme off the ground the GER Board at their meeting on 14th September, 1880 finally resolved the company would make its own tramway from Wisbech to Outwell and Upwell as an experiment and with Board of Trade support, to bring rail transport to places which it would not be economic to serve by normal line. John Wilson, the company's consulting engineer, was delegated to act with the solicitor on local questions regarding legalities, land purchase and consent of road authorities. The proposed tramway was the first of its kind to be made and worked by steam traction alongside the ordinary highway. The line was to be designed by John Wilson and to reduce costs most of the construction work would be carried out by the company's own civil engineering staff. Thus at a stroke the failing UO&W scheme was rendered obsolete.

At a special Board meeting on 2nd November, 1880 C.H. Parkes announced Wilson had yet to prepare estimates or meet road authorities but as they were in an advanced state the solicitor was to prepare the necessary Parliamentary notices. By 17th November, 1880 the local road authorities had been consulted and appeared satisfied with the scheme. It was duly noted that the canal was to be crossed at Outwell as the street through Upwell was very narrow. The necessary plans and estimates were included in the GER Bill presented to the Parliamentary Private Bill Office in December with copies to Clerks of the Peace for the Isle of Ely, Cambridgeshire and Norfolk respectively and to the relevant parish councils, through which the line was to pass. No opposition was encountered.

The making and working of 'tramways in and between the town of Wisbech and the villages of Outwell and Upwell in the Isle of Ely in the county of Cambridge and in the county of Norfolk, to acquire lands for the purposes in connection with and to have other powers in relation to the tramways', was included in the Great Eastern Railway Act 1881 (44 and 45 Vict. cap. cxxxiv) which received the Royal Assent on 18th July, 1881. Clause 24 sanctioned the company to form, lay down, work, use and maintain the five tramways according to levels shown on the deposited plans but could not take up or purchase any public road.

Tramway No 1: 4 miles 1 furlong and 4 chains in length commencing in the parish of Wisbech St Peter, in the Isle of Ely in the County of Cambridge at a point upon the west side of the Wisbech and Lynn branch of the Company about 30 yards distant from the booking office at Wisbech station and proceed thence along and by the side of the railway into and along the road leading from Wisbech to Elm, Outwell and Upwell and terminating in the parish of Emneth in the County of Norfolk upon the towing path on the east side of the Wisbech canal at a point thereon 46½ chains or thereabouts measured in a southerly direction along the said towing path from the mile post on the said road indicating 4 miles from Wisbech.

Tramway No. 2: 6 furlongs and 3.50 chains in length commencing by a junction with Tramway No 1 at its termination and terminating in the parish of Outwell in the Isle of

Ely, County of Cambridge at a point upon the west bank of the Old Welney River about 100 yards measured in a south-westerly direction from the footbridge over the Outwell Sluice.

Tramway No. 3: 6 furlongs and 9 chains in length commencing by junction with Tramway No. 2 at its termination and terminating in the parish of Upwell in the County of Norfolk in a field known as Five Acre Piece belonging to or reputed to belong to Charles Chapman and occupied by John Bowers at a point on the western boundary about 16 yards from the point where the boundary joins the northern boundary.

Tramway No. 4: 7.50 chains in length wholly in the parish of Elm in the Isle of Ely, in the County of Cambridge commencing by a junction with Tramway No. 1 at a point on the said road from Wisbech to Elm, Outwell and Upwell, distant about 73 yards measured in a westerly direction from the milestone indicating 2 miles from Wisbech and terminating by a junction with Tramway No. 1 at a point on the road about 113 yards measured in a southerly direction from the 2 mile milestone.

Tramway No 5: 7.60 chains in length wholly situated in the parish of Elm commencing by a junction with Tramway No. 1 at a point upon the Wisbech to Upwell road about 31 chains measured along the centre of the road in a northerly and north-westerly direction from the mile stone indicating 4 miles from Wisbech and terminating at a point on the road about 23 chains measured along the centre of the road in a northerly direction from the milestone.

The railway was to be single track, to a gauge of 4 feet 8½ inches and had to be laid and maintained in such a manner as to be level with the existing surface of the road or surface of the road as altered by the building of the line. Clause 26 stipulated where a double track line was permitted:

Tramway No. 1 in the parish of Emneth between a point opposite the milestone indicating 1 mile from Wisbech and a point 110 yards to the south of the mile post.

Tramway No. 1 in the parish of Elm between a point opposite the northern end of the Duke of Wellington public house and a point 110 yards measured in a northerly direction from the end of the public house.

Tramway No. 1 in the parish of Emneth between a point about 31½ chains measured in a southerly direction from the milestone indicating 2 miles from Wisbech and a point 36½ chains measured in the same direction from the milestone.

Tramway No. 1 in the parish of Elm between a point about 5 chains measured in a south-easterly direction from the milestone indicating 3 miles from Wisbech and a point about 10 chains measured in the same direction from the milestone.

Tramway No. 1 in the parish of Elm between a point about 3 chains measured in a north-westerly direction from the milestone indicating 4 miles from Wisbech and a point about 2 chains measured in a south-westerly direction from the milestone.

Tramway No. 2 in the parish of Outwell in the Isle of Ely between a point about 1 chain to the north-west of the footbridge over Outwell Sluice and a point about 4 chains to the south-west of the footbridge.

Clause 27 permitted Tramway No. 2 in the parish of Outwell in the Isle of Ely on the western side of the road running along the western side of the canal in Outwell between a point about 24 chains north of the footbridge at Outwell Sluice and a point on the same road opposite the footbridge, to be less than 10 feet 6 inches from the footpath. The following clause required the GER to give one month's notice to the road authority in the parish of Elm before commencing any works, and if deemed necessary by the authority to construct the line on the western side of the road instead of the eastern side, between the boundary of the parish north of the Duke of Wellington public house to the southern boundary of the parish. If the road authority objected to the installation of the double line of rails as mentioned in the Act, the GER was to construct the double line of rails at an alternative site in the parish, but if the two parties failed to agree the exact location the matter was to be adjudicated by an arbiter appointed by the BoT.

Clause 29 of the statute required the company to construct a new bridge over the Wisbech canal with increased width for the accommodation of road and tramway traffic and a towing path on the eastern side of the waterway in place of the existing Newcommon bridge on Tramway No. 1. A bridge was also to be constructed where Tramway No. 2 crossed the canal with room for a towing path on each bank. The bridges were to be constructed to the reasonable satisfaction of the Engineer of the canal company according to the specification previously submitted by the GER Engineer; the construction to occasion no impediment to the navigation along the canal and with a clear waterway 18 feet wide under each bridge and clearance of 7 feet 6 inches above the ordinary level of the water and 7 feet above each towing path. The GER was to maintain the bridges.

As Tramways Nos. 2 and 3 intended to pass over certain parts of the Middle Level of the Fens the construction and maintenance of the tramways was to be carried out with the agreement of and to the satisfaction of the Middle Level Commissioners. The railway company was to ensure that no work was to be carried out within 20 yards from the land side of any bank except as necessary to construct bridges or culverts. In the course of construction no waterway was to be combined and land taken or used by the company from the Middle Level was subject to drainage tax. In crossing the River Nene in the parish of Outwell, clause 35 required Tramway No. 3 to be carried over 'a good and substantial bridge' having one span of no less than 25 feet square span with the line of the direction of the river and the soffit or underside of the girder no less than 18 feet clear height above the Middle Level datum line. A safe and sufficient platform, properly fenced, 6 feet wide at least and 11 feet 6 inches in height above the Middle Level datum line was to be constructed on the same side of the river as the existing towing path so as to give a clear height of at least 6 feet 6 inches between the towing path and soffit or underside of the arch or girder of the bridge and allow the free passage for horses towing vessels, to prevent the necessity of detaching the horses from the towing lines. The bridges were to be maintained by the company.

The BoT reserved the right to require the company to adopt any improvements having regard to the greater security of the public. In addition to Section 26 of the Tramways Act 1870, the GER was required to provide plans and seek the approval of the BoT and the local authorities before modifying or extending the authorized tramway. The BoT had also to approve the type of rails used on the construction and required the line to be fully inspected before opening to the public. If any local authority altered the level of the road surface the railway company was to maintain the rails level with the altered road surface. Clause 48 gave the sewer authorities free access to all drains and sewers whilst clause 49 gave the GER consent, with agreement of the local and road authorities, to maintain, alter and remove such crossings, curves, passing places, sidings, loops, junction and other works for the efficient working of the tramways or for providing access to any premises of the company or into any buildings, yards or other premises near to or abutting on any street or road providing during the construction no rail was laid less than 10 feet 6 inches from the outside of the footpath on each side of the road. Also during the course of construction temporary tramways were allowed but these had to be removed once the authorized line was constructed.

Clause 54 allowed the tramway to be used for passenger and goods traffic hauled by locomotives, or other mechanical power or horse power, with carriages and trucks adapted for use on main line railways. The following clause authorized the use of steam locomotives subject to strict regulations and with the consent of the BoT with inspection every seven years. Clause 57 elaborated the bye-laws regulating the use of bell, whistle or other warning on the locomotive, the emission of smoke and steam, stopping places, the entrance and exit from passenger vehicles.

Clauses 61 and 62 of the statute required the company to give at least two months' notice of intention to the local road authorities to use steam-powered locomotives and to enter into contract for payment or part payment for the upkeep of the route, the contract being for a maximum period of two years before renewal. Schedule A attached to the Act provided the BoT Regulations and Bye-Laws for working the tramway and these are quoted in full in Chapter Seven.

At the GER Board meeting on 4th October, 1881 the Chairman C.H. Parkes considered the Wisbech & Upwell Tramway experiment should be made as early as possible. The type of rail and kind of engine, electric or Kitson's steam locomotive was to be evaluated and an early decision agreed. Land was to be purchased but works were not to commence until the New Year. On 1st November it was agreed the GER Bill for the 1881-2 Session would include provision for the extension of the tramway into Wisbech town centre and essential land purchases.

At a special meeting of the GER proprietors on 27th January, 1882 the Bill for the general works including the tramway was unanimously adopted. On 6th February, 1882 it was agreed any additional land was to be bought and tenders invited for railway No. 1, 4 miles in length on which the proposed tramway motive power could be practically tested. Messrs Edward Wilson, engineers responsible for the plans and specifications, were to discuss the points with Sir Henry Tyler, former Chief Inspector of Railways and Conservative MP for Harwich, and report to the next meeting. At the gathering on 7th March, 1882 the construction of the tramway of 5 miles in length, including turnouts and sidings, was estimated at £16,000: £6,000 for rails, chairs and sleepers, £2,000 for bridges, the highest cost being Newcommon bridge, and £8,000 for excavations and rail laying. It was approved subject to details of the contracting which would be left to the engineers Messrs Wilson.

Jonathan Wilson, consultant engineer to GER had duly prepared the plans, and the local authority accepted the envisaged construction alongside roads for most of the length. The resident engineer was Henry (Harry) Jones who had commenced his career as a pupil of Edward Wilson, consultant engineer to both the Great Eastern and Great Western railways. He also worked as resident engineer on the Ipswich to Felixstowe line, and later Wroxham to County School branch and also the Great Western Railway branch from Bewdley to

Kidderminster. He also acted as resident engineer on the line from Cambridge to Mildenhall, Shenfield to Southend, and Wickford to Southminster and Maldon. In 1889 he was appointed district engineer of the GER Eastern Division.

The Great Eastern Railway Act 1882 (45 and 46 Vict. cap. clxvi) duly received the Royal Assent on 24th July, 1882 and by clause 43 authorized the company to construct:

Tramway No. 1: 3.90 chains or thereabouts in length in the Elm Road in the parish of Wisbech St Peter in the Isle of Ely in the County of Cambridge commencing by a junction with tramway No. 1 authorised by the GER Act 1881 and terminating near the place where the Company's Lynn and Wisbech Railway crossed the Elm Road on the level.

Tramway No. 2: 4 furlongs and 5.27 chains in length or thereabouts in length wholly in the parish of Wisbech St Peter in the Isle of Ely in the County of Cambridge commencing by a junction with Tramway No. 1 authorised by the 1882 Act and proceeding along Elm Road, Little South Street and Norfolk Street West and across the open space into which the last mentioned street, Church Street, Cemetery Street and Norfolk Street East lead and thence into and along Church Street and terminating at the south-eastern end of the Market Place of Wisbech.

Tramway No. 3: 1 furlong and 7.62 chains or thereabouts in length in the parish of Wisbech St Peter in the Isle of Ely in the County of Cambridge and commencing in Little South Street by a junction with Tramway No. 2 proceeding in a south-westerly direction into and along the Victoria Road and the Station Road leading to Wisbech GER station and terminating near the booking office.

Clause 44 required the tramway and passing place authorized by the Act to be laid and maintained in such manner as to be on a level with the existing road or surface of road as proposed to be altered. The gauge was to be 4 feet 8½ inches and except as declared in clause 45 was to consist of a single pair of rails. Clause 45 permitted a double pair of rails to form a crossing loop on:

Tramway No. 2 in the Elm Road between two points respectively about 15 yards and 59 yards north-westward of the south-east corner of the Black Horse Inn.

Tramway No. 2 in Little South Street between a point opposite the north-east corner of Ryan Street and a point 36 yards or thereabouts measured from opposite the said corner in a northerly direction.

Tramway No. 2 from a point opposite the north-west corner of the northern end of Norfolk Street West and across the open space aforesaid to a point in Church Street opposite the south-easternmost corner of St Peter's Churchyard.

Tramway No. 2 in the Market Place Wisbech between the termination of the tramway and a point about 25 yards measured in a southerly direction from the said termination.

Tramway No. 3 in the Station Road between two points respectively about 30 yards and 86 yards measured in a south-westerly direction from the north-western corner of the Engineers Tavern in Victoria Road.

The provisions of sections 41 to 48, 50, 51, 53 and 55 to 62 of the GER Act of 1881 also applied to the tramways in the 1882 Act. Clause 47 permitted the company to make alterations to crossings, curves, passing loops, sidings, loops and junctions subject to the consent of the local authority and provided that in the construction no rail was laid with less space than 9 feet 6 inches between the rail and the outside of the footpath on either side of the road. Clauses 48 and 49 granted the GER powers to purchase additional land not exceeding two acres for tramway works and power to use the tramways for passenger and goods traffic hauled by locomotive or other mechanical power or horse power. If 15 or more houses occupied by labouring classes were required to be compulsorily purchased, the company was required to erect notices of intent for a period of eight weeks until such time as judicial notice was confirmed, and before taking the property was to provide alternative accommodation.

The original proposal included a branch to Friday Bridge but that had been abandoned, as it was not considered remunerative and did not comply with standing orders. It was also proposed to extend the line from Upwell to Welney via Lakesend but the clause was withdrawn because of expected poor financial returns. At a meeting of Wisbech Town Council, W.S. Collins remarked that the extension was vital to the trade of Wisbech but in fact most freight traffic generated was sent direct by horse and waggon to the main line station or goods yard at Wisbech for conveyance to London and other markets, whilst commodities received were also conveyed by road.

In the meantime tenders were invited for construction of the Wisbech to Outwell Basin section of the tramway and on 6th June, 1882, D. McNee and Company was awarded the contract for the supply of track materials and preliminary ground work soon commenced. Approval was later given on 14th September, 1882 to Eastwood Swingler for supply of ironwork for the canal bridge at £14 5s. 0d. per ton. The same company also fixed the parapets at total cost of £101, this work being authorized on 16th January, 1883.

At the end of August 1882 John Wilson applied to the Wisbech Canal Company for a suspension on the navigation, as the railway engineer was experiencing difficulties obtaining a foundation for the replacement Newcommon bridge. It was agreed that the navigation could be closed on and after Monday 4th September for a period not exceeding eight days.

On 19th October, 1882 Edward Wilson sent a letter from his office at 9 Deans Yard, Westminster on behalf of the GER to the BoT enclosing plans of the new tramway. Detailed drawings were not, however, forwarded, as there were no points or crossings on public roads, only on private land. The BoT in acknowledging receipt requested that copies of the plans be sent to the Wisbech Town Council and local parish authorities. The plans were passed to Major General C.S. Hutchinson for his observations. On 23rd October the BoT sent a copy of their requirements for the tramway to Bishopsgate.

The closure of the Wisbech canal in September to enable the foundations of Newcommon bridge to be made was not as serious as expected, although in 1882 the downturn in trade on the waterway continued with only £157 tolls collected at Wisbech and £175 at Outwell. No dividends were paid that year.

Whilst infrastructure work was in hand at Wisbech and along the tramway, the GER Locomotive Committee, at their meeting on 16th January, 1883, authorized the construction of three 0-4-0 steam tramway locomotives to the designs of T.W. Worsdell for the new line. The engines were to be built at Stratford works.

The *Wisbech Advertiser* reported on 14th February, 1883 that progress on the new line was slow, 'it appears likely some time will elapse before the tramway is in operation'. At that date the track was laid from Wisbech station to Newcommon bridge and on a portion of the road between Newcommon bridge and Outwell. Most landowners on the route of the tramway were willing to sell land on reasonable terms as they realised it would ultimately increase the value of their property, but landowners at Elm about 1½ miles from Wisbech were claiming £590 for 2 roods, 15 perches of land and after an impasse, the case was taken to court. The *Wisbech Advertiser* announced that the Sheriff's Court was expected to convene at Wisbech in late February to determine the value of the portion of land taken for the line at Elm, and added 'It was desirable for the line to be completed for the coming summer traffic'.

The arbitration case for the disputed land was heard at the Rose and Crown Hotel, Wisbech on Thursday 22nd February, 1883 before the Under Sheriff, Mr Eaden of Cambridge. Mr Blofeld, instructed by E.H. Jackson of Wisbech, appeared for the claimants and Mr Simms Reeve for the GER. The matter in dispute related to land which the GER required for making a siding and other purposes for the Upwell tramway in the Parish of Elm. The land required was part of a field of 11 acres, 1 rood and 30 perches in area belonging to the estate of the late Thomas Newsham Neale, formerly of Emneth Hungate, and the Trustees, John Hanes and William Newsham. Both contended the severance of the plot of land in question would seriously depreciate the value of the remainder of the land, which would then be useless for building purposes and would not grow good crops as before. The 2 roods 15 perches of land comprised the whole of the frontage to the road to Elm, near Meadowgate Lane. At the hearing four witnesses for the claimant valued compensation at between £480 and £591 but J.B. Bird, a BoT Surveyor, appearing for the GER put the compensation at £160. Four other witnesses for the company valued the land at between £156 and £176. After hearing the lengthy evidence and addresses of counsel and the summing up of the Under Sheriff, the jury awarded the claimants £250 compensation consisting of £120 for the land, £30 for the compulsory sale and £100 damages for severance.

By the end of February 1883 tracklaying was completed for a distance of four miles, although much awaited consolidation and rails were also placed beyond Boyce's Bridge. The replacement Newcommon bridge, constructed of iron, was opened for road traffic by mid-April and incorporated the tramway rails across the span. The temporary wooden bridge was subsequently removed. In the same month a new tram locomotive and rolling stock arrived at Wisbech and these were immediately used on clearance tests in the station area and along the completed section of the tramway.

Progress on the new line improved throughout May and by the end of the month tracklaying was fully completed to Outwell Basin and a start was being made on the installation of sidings at the intermediate depots. Work had also started on the depot at Elm on the portion of land cleared by the arbitration settlement. The *Wisbech Advertiser* whilst noting that 'about four miles have been completed leaving 2½ miles to be laid', also commented that 'a station has been built on a piece of ground in Elm, which formed the subject of the recent arbitration case'.

By mid-June 1883 construction was completed as far as the canal basin at Outwell and the GER authorities were eager to arrange an early BoT inspection to enable the line to open to traffic before the end of the fruit and vegetable season. Several test runs were made on the newly-completed line by both light tram locomotives and tram engines hauling passenger coaches and goods vehicles. The trials culminated with the running of a train of loaded coal

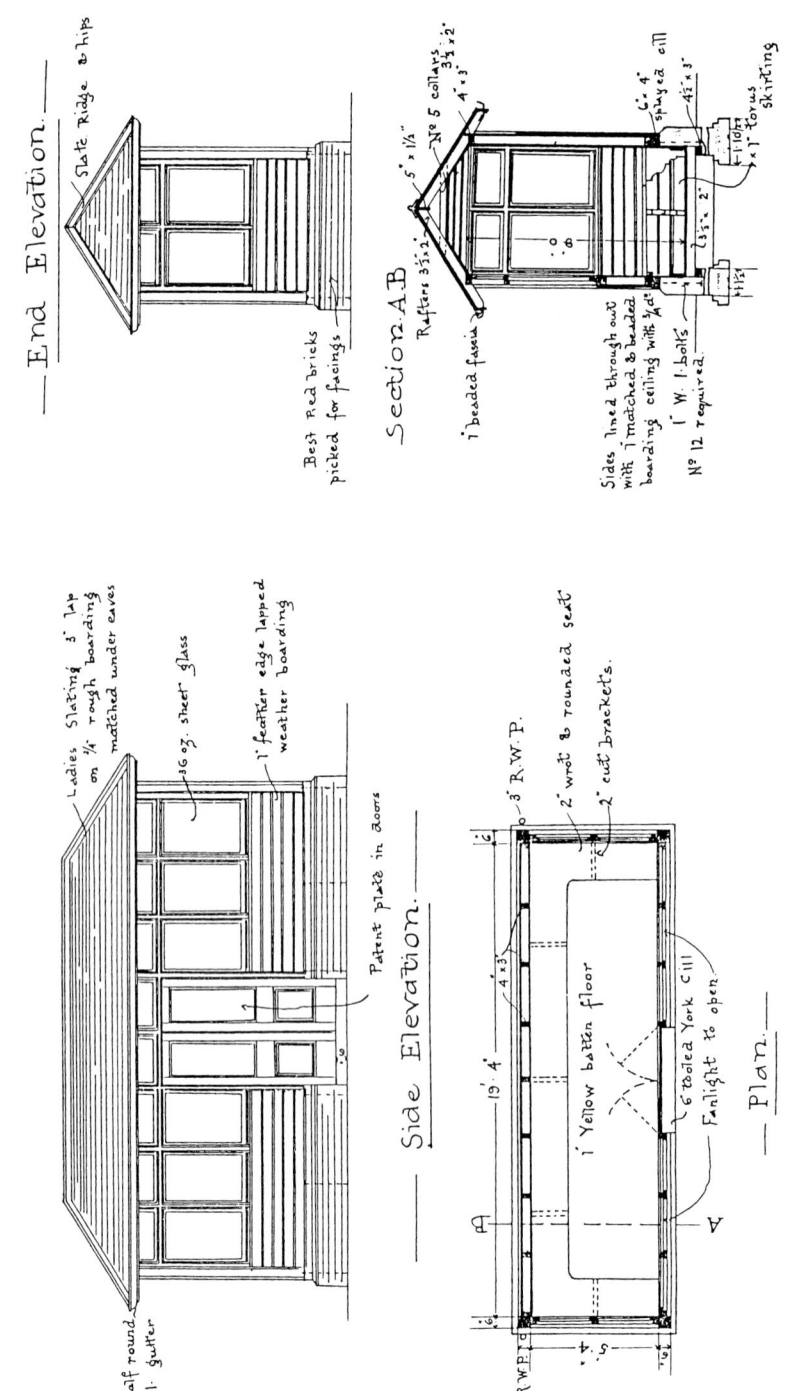

— End Elevation —

Slate Ridge & hips

Best Red bricks
picked for facings

— Section.AB —

Rafters 3½ × 2

5' × 1½"
Nº 5 collars
4' × 1 3'

6' 4"
splayed cill
3½" × 2'

4½ × 3'

7'10½"
× 1' torous
skirting

l beaded fascia

1 3½ × 2'

Sides lined through out
with 1 matched & beaded
boarding ceiling with ⅝ d"

1' W. 1 bolts
Nº 12 required.

— Side Elevation. —

Ladies Slating 3' lap
on ¼" rough boarding
matched under eaves

16 oz. sheet glass

1 feather edge lapped
weather boarding

Patent plate in doors

3' half round.
C. I. gutter

— Plan. —

19' 4'

4' × 3'

3' R.W.P.

2' wrot & rounded seat
2' cut brackets.

1' Yellow batten floor

6 tooled York Cill

Fanlight to open

A   A

3' RWP's

4'

10'

GER plan of waiting shelter at Elm Bridge.

wagons across the line to test fully the bridges and pointwork at the depots. In the same month a correspondent in the *Wisbech Advertiser* drew attention to the fact that the GER, during the construction of Newcommon bridge, had raised the surface of the railway and thereby become liable for the maintenance of the road across the structure. He alluded that if the surveyor were to inspect the approaches he would find the raised road would require widening so that vehicles could pass one another without fouling the railway line. There was danger that vehicles could overturn if they ran nearer to the side of the road.

On 26th June, 1883, the GER Secretary advised the BoT that the company intended to open for public traffic Tramways Nos. 1, 4 and 5 authorized by the GER Act of 1881and described in Section 24. The following day Major General C.S. Hutchinson was delegated to conduct the inspection. Edward Wilson wrote to H.G. Calcraft, Assistant Secretary to the BoT, on 29th June that he had sent to the GER the plans and also tracings of the brickwork and superstructure of the bridges in readiness for the inspection. Copies of the plans and tracings had also been sent to Wisbech Town Council, Wisbech Urban Authority, George Moore of Elm Council, John Newcome Wright and Moses Palmer of Emneth Parish Council and James Roseby Smith of Outwell Council, Norfolk.

Frederick M. Metcalfe JP of Inglethorpe Hall wrote to the BoT on 5th July, 1883:

> I understand the railway is shortly to be inspected. If you place yourself in the middle of the roadway as if driving towards Wisbech, from Emneth or Outwell it will be found that a train approaching and coming round the curve from Wisbech is quite hidden by the Duke of Wellington Inn and a quick hedge on the same side of the road and it appears to me that a danger of collision exists at that point. Whether this danger might be modified by the cutting down of the hedge, I am hardly able to judge.

The letter was acknowledged and passed to the inspecting officer for action.

Major General Hutchinson duly carried out the BoT inspection of the new line on Monday 9th July, 1883. The GER was represented by James Robertson, the traffic superintendent, Mr Sproul, district superintendent, John Wilson, the engineer; Harry Jones, assistant engineer; T.W. Worsdell, locomotive superintendent; Mr Gardner, goods manager; and Mr McNee, the contractor, who supplied the materials for the tramway. Others attending the inspection included the Mayor of Wisbech Mr Rust, the former Mayor Mr Pattrick, the Town Clerk F. Jackson, the Town Chamberlain Mr Pooley, Alderman Ford and Messrs T.D. Dearlove, E.R. Schofield, G.J. Moore, A.S. Andrews, A.J. Elworthy, H. Hudson, J. Gardiner and Moses Palmer. The party joined the special train formed of a tram locomotive and a composite carriage at Wisbech station.

Shortly before midday the special departed with the locomotive propelling the carriage watched by a large gathering of townsfolk assembled on the platform. The train proceeded at a funereal pace to allow Hutchinson to view the tramway infrastructure and at Elm Road crossing another group of spectators had gathered to watch the progress. Having negotiated Elm Road the train then swung to the left over Newcommon bridge where a halt was made to allow the inspector and party to alight. The locomotive ran back and forth over the structure with Hutchinson watching from the roadside and under the structure to test for deflections. The bridge was declared a 'fine piece of workmanship' with about 120,000 bricks supplied by Alfred S. Andrews of Wisbech, used in its construction, together with material recovered from the original structure. Departing from Newcommon bridge several horses were passed without incident most apparently ignoring the passing tram locomotive. News of the inspection special had spread and at intervals along the roadside people had gathered to watch its progress. At Elm Bridge siding and Emneth (Boyce's Bridge) siding the train was halted for Hutchinson to inspect the infrastructure and facilities and comment was passed by those on board of the growing crops in the lineside fields, which would benefit from the tramway. Within a short distance of the terminus the tramway left the main road to follow its own course over land formerly belonging to Mr Doubleday, thus cutting off a circuitous route alongside the road. On arrival at the temporary terminus at Outwell Basin a brief inspection was made of the works. The officials then led the way to a new station building which had been erected, and which was decorated for the occasion, where a recherché luncheon was provided on behalf of the GER by Mr Tidnam of the Rose and Crown Hotel, Wisbech.

The bill of fare comprised salmon, lamb, beef, chicken, duck, hams, tongues and cheese whilst the vegetables, green peas and new potatoes were served hot. Champagne and sherry was also served before the semi-official proceedings began with Robertson chairing the function. The mayor considered the tramway would play an important part in the welfare of the district especially for agriculturalists and farmers and thought there was justification for a connecting link to Wisbech Market Place. He then proposed 'Success to the Wisbech and Upwell Tramline'. Robertson, responding to the toast, thanked the mayor and explained to the gathering that:

> ... the tramline was entirely experimental; that it would be the medium of testing whether cheap communication could be made in this way by picking up passengers and goods in a district where there was no regular line of railway. If it proved a success it would be the precursor of other lines of a similar character in connection with the ordinary system.

He added that he was not in a position to comment on the possible extension to Wisbech town centre. F. Jackson, the Town Clerk, then proposed the toast to John Wilson, the Engineer, who responding reiterated that the line was an experiment and concluded by thanking all those on the local authorities who had provided assistance during the planning and construction of the tramway. At the conclusion of the speeches the party left the building to make way for the train crew and other railwaymen associated with the line to take the second sitting.

The return journey was marked by two incidents. Shortly after departing Outwell, two Midland Railway horse-drawn vans were passed travelling in the opposite direction, the first conveyance drawn by two horses passed without incident but the man in charge of the second lorry was so intent on looking at the locomotive and tramcar that he allowed his horse to blunder over a ditch and into a cottage garden. The other mishap occurred when the driver in charge of a horse-drawn waggon and riding on the vehicle had little control over the beasts and allowed them to plunge about as the tram locomotive approached. The man attempted to pull the horses up but only succeeded in further exciting the beasts and they were not stopped in their tracks until the entire harness and gear was broken. It was the opinion of those on the train that neither incident would have occurred if the men in charge had been controlling the horses' heads. The train duly arrived back at Wisbech station about 3.00 pm without further incident.

During the journey Hutchinson met with Frederick Metcalfe to see at first hand the problem at the Duke of Wellington Inn. In his report dated 10th July the inspector remarked, 'It is I believe, the first which has been constructed by a railway company as a feeder to their system and the experiment will therefore be an interesting one'. He noted the line submitted for inspection forming Tramways Nos. 1, 4 and 5 authorized by the GER Act of 1881 was a single line, of 4 feet 8½ inch gauge, with two passing places and a temporary terminus, constructed on private property at Outwell. The line commenced on a siding in Wisbech station and ran inside the railway fence for about 27 chains and thence along the side of a wide road from Wisbech to Outwell, and in many places along the side of the Wisbech canal. At a point about 3 miles 67 chains from its commencement the line entered private property and terminated at a point 4 miles 12 chains from its commencement.

The tramway was laid in accordance with the plans deposited with the BoT on 19th October, 1882, although Hutchinson noted that they had apparently not been approved. The mode of construction appeared well adapted to its purpose and allowed the passage of railway trucks. Macadam was used between and on the outside of the rails except at the crossing of important roads, where paving had been adopted. A new bridge of substantial character had been constructed where the railway crossed the canal. The inspector considered the line had been well laid and was in good order but required attention to several defects or shortcomings:

1. The bridge approaches at 2 miles 31 chains and 3 mile 42 chains should be paved.
2. The switch handles should be removed from the switches of the loops of the passing places and those leading to the goods sidings should be locked.
3   The approaches to the skew bridge over the canal should be flattened.
4   The hedge near the Duke of Wellington Inn should be cut down.
5   The engine pit at the temporary terminus should be covered over.
6   It is desirable that an arrival signal for the Tramway, interlocked with the siding points leading to the Tramway at Wisbech Station be provided.

Hutchinson observed the engines which were to work the line were much more powerful than ordinary tramway engines and weighed about 20 tons, and remarked that detailed particulars of the engines, which complied with BoT requirements, were yet to be supplied by the GER.

With regard to them it is desirable:

1. That some projecting steps and handles should be altered in form.
2. That a bell should be provided and communication with the car.
3. That the governor arrangements should be locked up so that the driver cannot tamper with them and the sensitiveness of the speed indicator should be increased.
4. The cars should be positioned with a rail to close the gangway on the side on which passengers should not be allowed to alight.
5. A complete stop should be made before crossing the road near the Duke of Wellington Inn.

The inspector noted the plans did not in all cases show the correct position of the tramway and required them to be returned to the Engineer for amendment. Hutchinson certified the line was fit for traffic, subject to the early rectification of the requirements, with a permitted speed limit of 8 mph. He added a rider that the various local authorities attending the inspection appeared satisfied with the arrangements.

On 17th July, 1883 the General Manager advised the GER Traffic Committee of the several points raised by the BoT inspector regarding the tramway and considered the requirements could be quickly resolved. Most of the work had been completed, but the contentious issue was the provision of signals at Wisbech to interlock with the tramway connection to the main line. As Wisbech station signalling was not interlocked the requirement raised the whole issue of interlocking at the junction. After due discussion the General Manager was instructed to advise the BoT that interlocking at the station would be completed within four months. The proposed work included the provision of a siding for the tramway, but one of the existing sidings to be used required extensive relaying as the sleepers were rotten. The Way and Works Committee authorized the expenditure of £240 for the proposed sidings on the same day, the cost including the required interlocking. On 28th July the GER Secretary advised the BoT that all requirements had been completed with the exception of the arrival signal and interlocking work at Wisbech. The Directors had already issued an order for the interlocking to be completed with a period of four months.

Henry G. Calcraft duly signed the BoT Regulations and Certificate on 10th August, 1883 and forwarded copies to the GER the same day. The following day a letter was received from Metcalfe expressing his satisfaction regarding clause 5 of the inspector's report (re the Duke of Wellington Inn).

On 13th August the GER Secretary advised the BoT that all regulations and bye-laws would be brought into use on the opening of the tramway. But on 17th August, 1883 at their quarterly meeting, Wisbech Town Council passed a resolution complaining that the 'gaps or space left in the rails or trams thereof for the reception of the flanges of the wheels of the locomotives and carriages' was too wide near Newcommon bridge, 'with consequent danger of ordinary carriage wheels catching in it'. The correspondence was passed to the GER management who initially chose to ignore the matter.

The *Cambridge Chronicle* on 18th August, 1883, reported, 'It is expected the Upwell Tramway, which was inspected several weeks ago by Major General Hutchinson will be opened in a short time. Wisbech Town Council has received a copy of the regulation and bye-laws from the BoT'. The remedial work had indeed been completed, aided by flat country and roadside nature of line, and the opening date of the tramway was fixed for 20th August, 1883.

Chapter Two

The Tramway is Opened

The tramway duly opened to traffic as far as Outwell Basin on Monday 20th August, 1883, with a service of six trains in each direction on weekdays only calling intermediately at Elm Bridge and Boyce's Bridge depots on weekdays only. The timetable also specifically stated 'tramcars will stop for the purpose of setting down and taking up passengers at any point along the line of route', and a timing of 45 minutes was allowed between Wisbech and Outwell. Reporting the opening the *Cambridge Chronicle* remarked: 'The line is almost as substantially built as a main line railway'. It also told its readers the company was permitted 'to use any rolling stock thereon except the engines, which must be of the tramway type specially built at Stratford'. The tramway proved popular and considerable numbers of people travelled especially during the evening when there was often only standing room available in the tramcars. The *Wisbech Telegraph* on 25th August, 1883 added: 'the novelty of the tram line has been a means of attracting a large amount of passenger traffic during the week and each evening the cars have been crowded'. It optimistically added, 'there will probably be alterations to the time table next month'.

The *Wisbech Advertiser* reported:

> Four large cars were brought into use during the day, and besides the conveyance of several trucks of coal and merchandise we are informed that 960 passengers paid their fares for a ride on the tramway car. That this means of locomotion will be highly popular there can be no doubt, and the low fares charged, viz 3*d.* first class and 2*d.* second [*sic*] class for the whole distance of 4¼ miles, brings it within the reach of all comers. The rates for goods also, are so moderate that a truck of coals may be forwarded from Wisbech to Elm Bridge at 2*d.* per ton, to Boyce's Bridge at 3*d.* per ton and to Outwell Basin at 4*d.* per ton.

The following day, 21st August, 1883, John Wilson, having conferred with Wisbech Council regarding the doubts over clearances on Newcommon bridge, held a site meeting with W.M. Rust, the Mayor, Alderman Stanley and the Borough Surveyor Mr Pooley, and conducted experiments with ordinary road vehicles proving that in the event of their wheels being trapped within the running rail and check rail, little or no difficulty would be encountered getting the wheel clear. Wilson explained that the BoT had sanctioned a space of 1¾ inches between the metal and the guardrail and at no point could Pooley find any excess of this limit. It was subsequently agreed that no further steps be taken. On the same day at Liverpool Street, the Way and Works Committee considered the question of the new locomotive shed at Wisbech and, after considering the comments of the locomotive superintendent, invited tenders from various contractors. On 4th September, 1883 the contract for new brick built engine shed was awarded to R. Girling after he tendered at £376 6*s.* 7*d.*

The *Wisbech Advertiser* continued to enthuse about the tramway and on 1st September, 1883 reported that it had been 'largely patronized since the opening and evening traffic had been immeasurably heavy'. The GER authorities were,

GREAT EASTERN RAILWAY.

WISBECH & OUTWELL TRAMWAY.

OCTOBER, 1883.

TRAMCARS WILL RUN AS UNDER:—

WEEK DAYS.

	a.m.	a.m.	a.m.	p.m.	p.m.	p.m.
WISBECH STATION	7 10	9 30	11 40	2 40	4 45	6 45
ELM BRIDGE	7 28	9 50	12 0	2 58	5 5	7 3
BOYCE'S BRIDGE	7 42	10 5	12 15	3 12	5 20	7 17
OUTWELL BASIN	7 50	10 15	12 25	3 20	5 30	7 25

	a.m.	a.m.	p.m.	p.m.	p.m.	p.m.
OUTWELL BASIN	8 0	10 40	1 35	3 40	5 50	7 45
BOYCE'S BRIDGE	8 8	10 48	1 45	3 50	5 58	7 53
ELM BRIDGE	8 22	11 2	2 0	4 5	6 12	8 7
WISBECH STATION	8 40	11 20	2 20	4 25	6 30	8 25

The Tram Cars will stop for the purpose of setting down or taking up Passengers at any point along the line of route.

FARES ANY DISTANCE:—

First Class.
3D.

Third Class.
2D.

Personal Luggage not exceeding 28 lbs. in weight will be allowed to be taken by each Adult Passenger free of charge if carried by hand.

MERCHANDISE TRAFFIC

Will be dealt with at the following Sidings or Depots:—

ELM BRIDGE, BOYCE'S BRIDGE, OUTWELL BASIN.

Very m... charges for hauliage will be made, particulars of these and other information can oe obtained from the Company's Inspectors at the Depots, from the Station Agent at Wisbech, the District Goods Manager at Cambridge, or the Goods Manager at Liverpool Street.

WILLIAM BIRT, General Manager.

GER Timetable 1883.

however, concerned with the blatant disregard for safety exhibited, not only by the travelling public but also by inhabitants living alongside the line. The Directors on a tour of inspection visited their new tramway on 6th September, 1883, and learned first hand of the batch of near accidents encountered since the railway opened to traffic. The party travelled by road from Wisbech to Outwell and then beyond, to look at the extension works in hand. John Wilson, the Engineer, was asked to prepare plans for fencing to be erected at strategic places to prevent the public crossing the tramway, except at authorized crossings, and also to prevent passengers from alighting from the tramcars between depots. Wisbech Town Council was still concerned at the danger of the wheels of road vehicles crossing Newcommon bridge falling between rail and check-rail, and the Mayor and Corporation accompanied the Directors to the bridge to affirm the complaints made by the Corporation on 17th August to the BoT. After surveying the bridge it was agreed that Wilson and the Corporation surveyor would again meet to consider the best course of action to alleviate the problem. As a parting gesture the GER Directors promised the provision of additional tramcars for the line. In the meantime the BoT were led to believe by the Engineer that the Town Council had approved of the construction of Newcommon bridge, including the gradients on the approaches to ease the problems of the tram locomotives crossing the structure. The *Wisbech Telegraph* reporting the visit also revealed, 'the Directors propose to put on additional tramcars', but did not elaborate.

Wilson and the Mayor and Borough Surveyor of Wisbech duly conducted further experiments at Newcommon bridge and it was found that nowhere did the width of the flange exceed the stipulated 1¾ inches maximum, and that the wheels of road vehicles could be easily released if trapped. On a positive note the local road surveyors welcomed the arrival of the tramway as granite chippings for road repairs could be delivered direct to the roadside at fraction of the previous cost; one surveyor estimated the tramway would benefit ratepayers by one penny in the pound.

In accordance with the promise made to the BoT inspector during the inspection of the tramway, on 18th September, 1883 a contract was placed with Saxby & Farmer Ltd for the provision of new signalling and the interlocking of points and signals at Wisbech station at a cost of £1,146. The award was made on the stipulation that installation would be completed within six weeks. A month later on 17th October the GER advised the BoT that its engineer and the Borough Surveyor of Wisbech had finally agreed to alterations at Newcommon bridge, including the easing of the severe gradients on each approach, the removal of a guard-rail and the setting back of an approach fence on the opposite side of the road. By 12th December, 1883 the GER Secretary was able to inform the BoT that the arrival signal for the tramway at Wisbech had been interlocked with the siding points and three days later Major General Hutchinson advised that there was no specific necessity for an inspection.

The extension of the line beyond Outwell to Upwell required slight alterations to the course of the Wisbech canal and the strengthening of the banks to support the weight of the railway. On 4th December, 1883, Head Wrightson was awarded the contract for the provision of the bridge over the River Nene

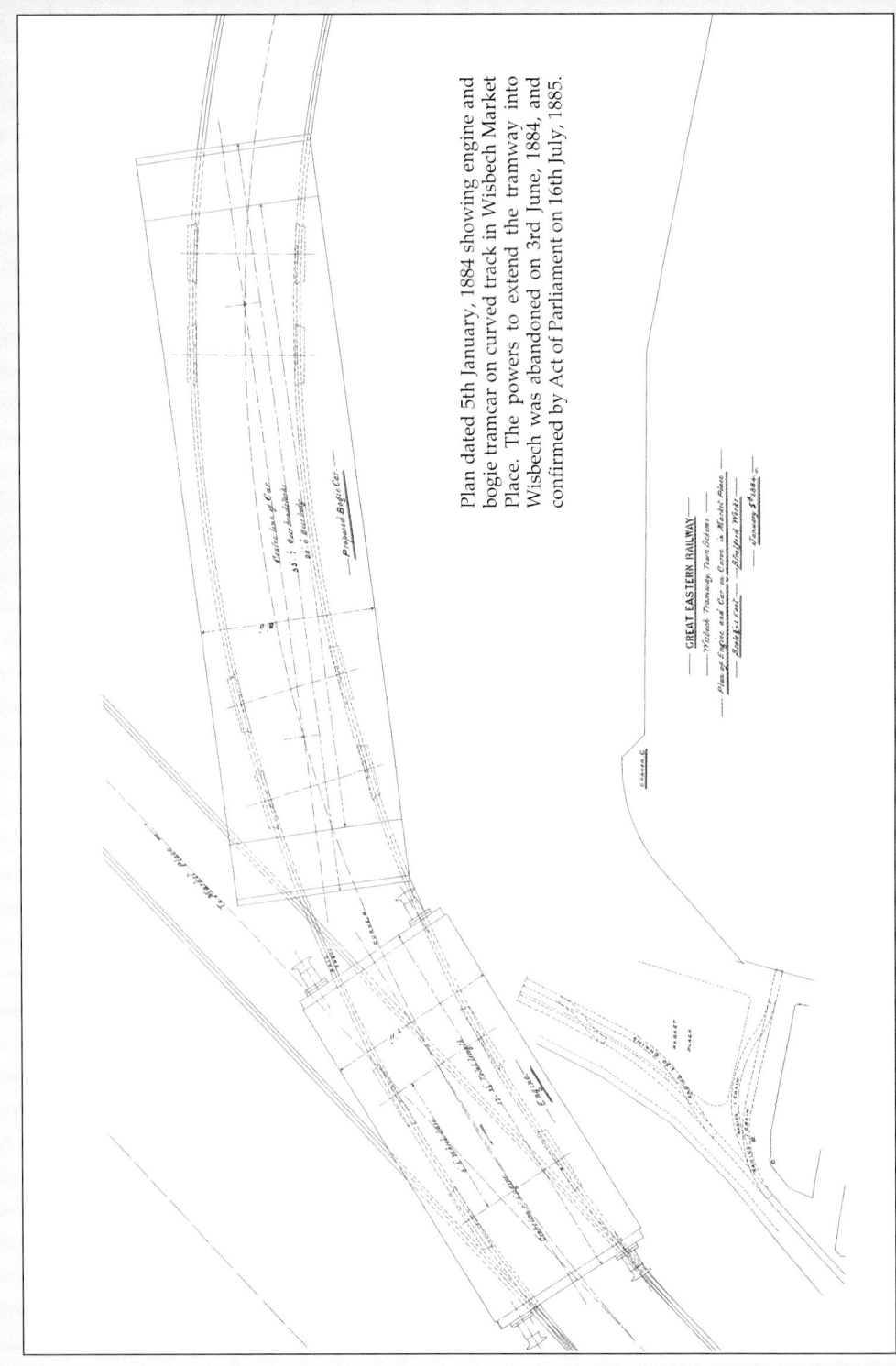

Plan dated 5th January, 1884 showing engine and bogie tramcar on curved track in Wisbech Market Place. The powers to extend the tramway into Wisbech was abandoned on 3rd June, 1884, and confirmed by Act of Parliament on 16th July, 1885.

(Old Course) at Outwell Village and the associated earthworks after they tendered at £545 3s. 4d., subject to completion by February 1884.

The new line suffered a troubled infancy, not the least when regular complaints were made regarding the poor condition of the passenger vehicles in which the public was required to travel. The General Manager was asked to investigate and on 1st April, 1884 reported that the four passenger vehicles operating on the tramway were old tramcars, which had previously worked on the Millwall line, and it was essential they were replaced. It was proposed to construct four new vehicles, two the same size as the existing tramcars, 20 feet in length over body to carry 22 persons at a cost of £230 each and two larger tramcars 28 feet in length over body to convey 34 passengers at a price of £350 each. It was also the intention to provide one small carriage, 12 feet in length, for the conveyance of passengers' luggage, market and general goods at a cost of £75. The GER Traffic Committee readily agreed to the capital expenditure of £1,235 for the four tramcars and one luggage van.

With the successful opening of the tramway all thoughts of the failed predecessor were forgotten and on 10th May, 1884 the Upwell and Wisbech Railway Abandonment Bill was read for the second time in the House of Lords.

By this time Wisbech Borough Council was also having second thoughts on the advisability of the extension of the tramway into the town for in May 1884 the Town Council solicitors wrote to the BoT:

We send you herewith a memorial against the proposed extension by the Great Eastern Railway of their tramline into Wisbech Town. If necessary even a larger number of signatories can be obtained as a great number of the public feel very strongly that it will be productive of great danger if it is carried out in its present unprotected form.

Needless to say the majority of the opposition to the scheme came from residents who lived in Norfolk Street or Church Terrace.

To the President and Members of the Board of Trade. The humble memorial of the undersigned Owners and Occupiers of the Borough of Wisbech Saint Peter, sheweth:

1. That the Great Eastern Railway company propose carrying out certain works - to wit a Tramline with carriages drawn and propelled by Steam from or between a certain point called Elm Road crossing to a certain point at or near the Market Place both in the Borough of Wisbech Saint Peter, a distance of about half a mile.

2. That it is proposed to carry such Tramline through and along Little South Street, Norfolk Street West and Church Terrace and by the Market Place in Wisbech Saint Peter aforesaid.

3. Such streets are exceedingly narrow, being in some parts only 16½ feet wide.

4. Your Petitioners are informed and verily believe it is not intended to fence or protect such Tramline in any way from the Public.

5. To drive from the Market Place to the Great Eastern Railway Station such Tramline would have to be crossed four or five times although the distance is hardly a quarter of a mile and there are also several very sharp and narrow corners and places where if a waggon or large cart was unloading you could not pass even in the present condition.

6   Should the proposed Tramline be carried out for the reasons before mentioned it will be so exceedingly dangerous for Horses, Carriages and Carts to proceed and

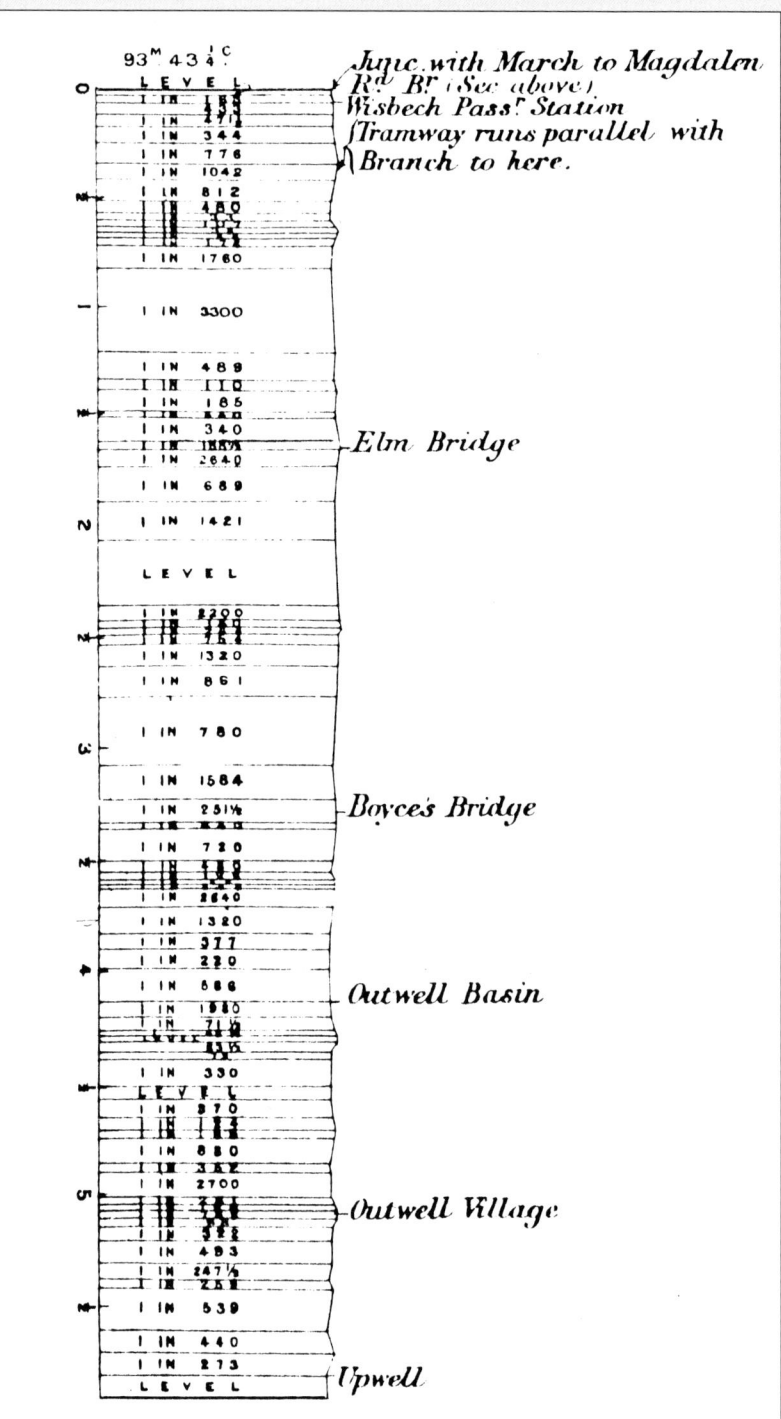

Gradient diagram.

use such streets for the General Public that they will become comparatively useless and the present traffic now carried on through such Streets will have to pass by a more securitious [sic] and longer route.

YOUR MEMORIALISTS therefore humbly pray that your sanction may be refused to the carrying out of such a Tramline so proposed, as for the reasons before given it will be dangerous to Life and Limb and the General Public.

The correspondence was heeded for on 3rd June, 1884 it was agreed to abandon the Upwell and Wisbech tram powers of extension into Wisbech, as the BoT was unable to certify tramways fit for traffic when worked by steam traction, owing to the narrowness of the streets. As an alternative the Wisbech Town Council wanted the GER to bring the existing passenger station nearer to the centre of the town, but the Board tersely advised that the question of the station accommodation would be considered at a future date.

Meanwhile the GER Secretary advised the BoT on 7th July, 1884 that Tramways Nos. 2 and 3 authorized by the 1881 Act were ready for inspection, and Major F.A. Marindin was delegated to cover the task. However, Major General Hutchinson conducted the inspection on Wednesday 3rd September, 1884. The inspector was driven by road from Wisbech to Outwell Basin where a special train formed of a tram locomotive and a new composite coach was waiting to depart. Hutchinson was accompanied by John Wilson, Mr Blaze representing the locomotive superintendent, Mr Adye representing the signal engineer, G.J. Moore, Surveyor of Roads for the Elm parish and Messrs J.R. Smith, A.J. Elworthy, James Webber, Samuel Robb and Lewis Holt representing the local authorities of Outwell and Upwell. *En route* the two new iron bridges and parts of the line were carefully examined before the train reached Upwell at 1.50 pm, from where the party retired to the Five Bells Inn for a luncheon provided for the GER by Mr Hurst. Hutchinson returned to London later in the afternoon, whilst the drivers, firemen, conductors and other tramway employees dined together at the Five Bells Inn, courtesy of the GER management.

Hutchinson had found the section of line offered for inspection comprising Tramways Nos. 2 and 3 enumerated in the 1881 GER Act were single with sidings. Tramway No. 2 commenced by an end-on junction with Tramway No. 1 in the parish of Emneth and passing through private ground for about 35 chains, crossed the Wisbech canal by a new iron bridge. It then ran alongside the side of the road skirting the canal for the remainder of its length, altogether 63½ chains. Tramway No. 3, an extension of Tramway No. 2, commenced in private grounds and crossed the Nene Old Course by a new iron bridge, shortly after which it passed alongside the road skirting the river for about 23 chains. It then entered private land in which it terminated, at its authorized terminus close to the High Road near Upwell, a total length of 69 chains.

The inspector found the construction adopted was precisely the same as employed on the sections inspected in July 1883 and the work was executed to the satisfaction of the surveyors of the parishes of Emneth, Outwell and Upwell, who were present at the inspection. Each of the canal bridges consisted of one large span measuring 38 feet and two smaller spans of 19 feet and 15 feet constructed of wrought-iron spans and cross-girders supported on screw piles.

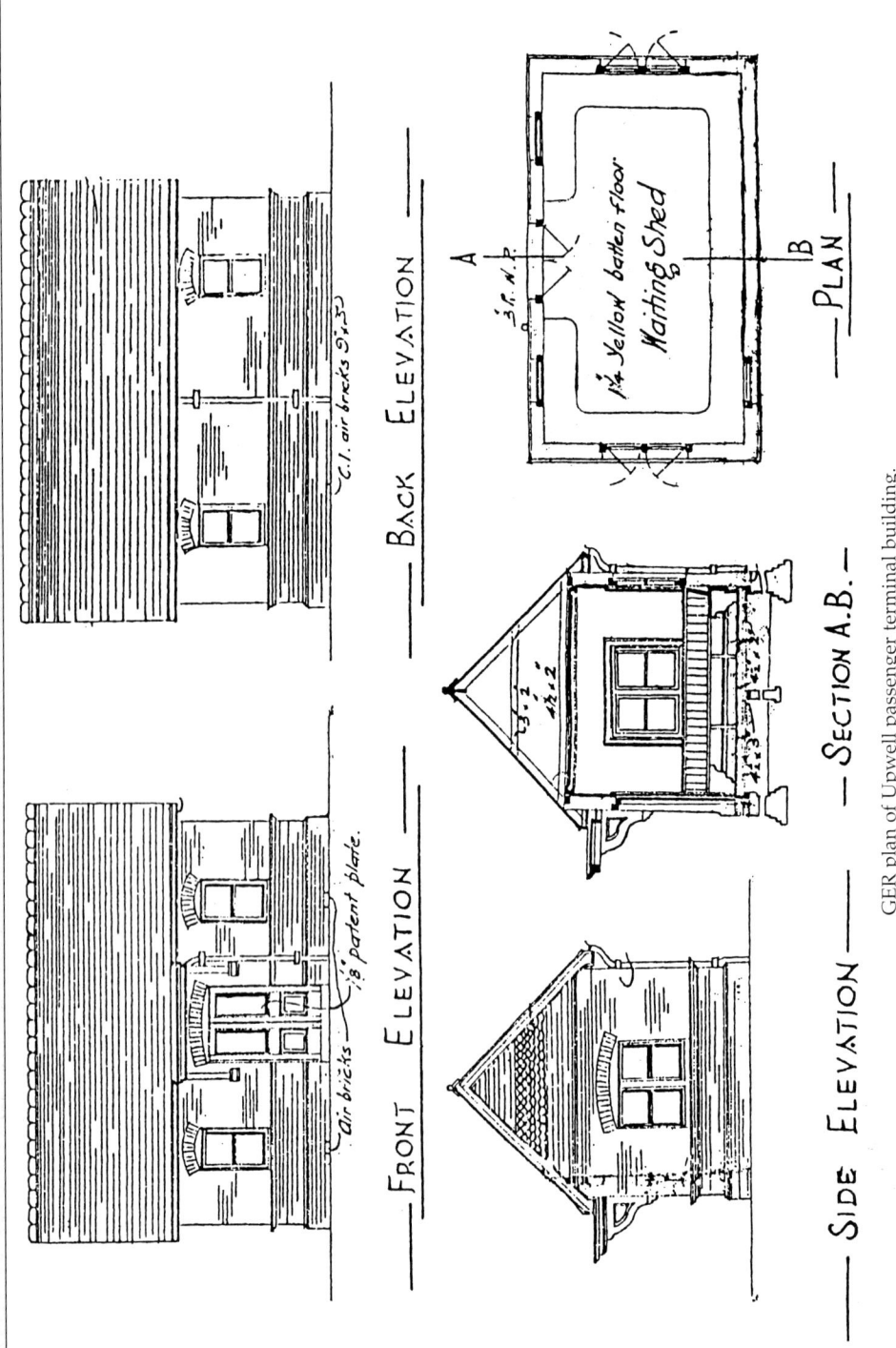

GER plan of Upwell passenger terminal building.

These had sufficient theoretical strength. There was also a smaller timber bridge over a ditch on Tramway No. 3.

Hutchinson noted the engines to be employed on the new section were the same as used on sections 1, 4 and 5 and had no further comments to make on the rolling stock. The inspector, however, noted several items, which required immediate attention:

1. Paving required on Tramway No. 1 where it crossed the road at 35 chains.
2. Gates to close across the Tramway at each of the three bridges.
3. The bridge over the ditch at 51 chains on Tramway No. 3 to be planked and provided with hand rails.
4. The ditch on the side of the road at the boundary of the parishes of Outwell and Upwell to be filled up.

The following rules were to be observed in the conduct of traffic. Complete stops were to be made:

1. Before crossing the canal bridge on Tramway No. 2.
2. Before crossing the road at 35 chains on Tramway No. 2.
3. Before crossing the road at 5 chains on Tramway No. 3.
4. Before crossing the road at 27 chains on Tramway No. 3.
5. Before crossing the road at 51 chains on Tramway No. 3.

In addition speed was not to exceed 4 mph at the narrow point of the road near 15 chains on Tramway No. 3.

Hutchinson duly authorized the use of the new section of tramway, subject to the early rectification of the requirements.

The section to Upwell opened to traffic on Monday 8th September, 1884 and several hundreds of passengers travelled on the first day. The GER introduced a new timetable together with revised fares to incorporate the depots on the extension, although there was no increase in the number of trains, which remained at six in each direction on weekdays only, taking a full hour on the journey. Third class accommodation was upgraded to second class from the same day. The *Wisbech Advertiser* reported:

> ... that there were a good many extra passengers on Monday and much interest was shown between Outwell Basin and Upwell in the working of the recently completed portion of the tramway. A large increase in traffic may be expected. One slight accident occurred, a cow which got on to metals having its leg broken. [The editorial enthused] In the arrangements of the Upwell Tramway the amount of traffic in goods and passengers, especially the former, has evidently been duly considered by the Company, and ample siding room is provided at the terminus, the yard at Upwell being more than two acres in extent. That the whole space will be required at no distant date, there is every reason to believe, for we have seen the yard at Outwell Basin (which is also of considerable extent) so crowded with railway trucks and farmers' waggons that there is barely sufficient accommodation for the speedy working of the traffic, and it is the opinion of those competent to judge that the railway authorities have underestimated the amount of business which will come to them now the line is complete.

The newspaper also urged for the line to be extended to Lakeside, Welney and Downham and other districts within a distance of three or four miles around

GREAT EASTERN RAILWAY

OPENING
OF THE
WISBECH & UPWELL
TRAMWAY
THROUGHOUT TO UPWELL

On MONDAY, 8th SEPTEMBER, 1884, the WISBECH a' ic
UPWELL TRAMWAY will be Open throughout to Upwell,
and Tram Cars will run as under:—WEEK DAYS.

	a.m.	a.m.	a.m.	p.m.	p.m.	p.m.
Wisbech Station	6 45	9 15	11 40	2 15	5 10	7 50
Elm Bridge	7 3	9 35	12 0	2 33	5 28	8 8
Boyce's Bridge	7 17	9 50	12 15	2 47	5 42	8 22
Outwell Basin	7 25	10 0	12 25	2 55	5 50	8 30
Outwell Village	7 35	10 10	12 35	3 5	6 0	8 40
Upwell	7 45	10 20	12 45	3 15	6 10	8 50

	a.m.	a.m.	p.m.	p.m.	p.m.	p.m.
Upwell	7 55	10 30	12 55	3 40	6 25	9 0
Outwell Village	8 5	10 40	1 5	3 50	6 35	9 10
Outwell Basin	8 15	10 50	1 15	4 0	6 45	9 20
Boyce's Bridge	8 23	10 58	1 25	4 10	6 53	9 28
Elm Bridge	8 37	11 12	1 40	4 25	7 7	9 42
Wisbech Station	8 55	11 30	2 0	4 45	7 25	10 0

The Tram Cars will stop for the purpose of setting down or
taking up Passengers at any point along the line of route.

FARES:—

	Wisbech 1st Class 2nd Class	Elm Bridge 1st Class 2nd Class	Boyce's Bridge 1st Class 2nd Class	Outwell Basin 1st Class 2nd Class	Outwell Village 1st Class 2nd Class
Elm Bridge	3d. 2d.				
Boyce's Bridge	3d. 2d.	3d. 2d.			
Outwell Basin	3d. 2d.	3d. 2d.	2d. 1d.		
Outwell Village	4d. 3d.	3d. 3d.	3d. 2d.	2d. 1d.	
Upwell	4d. 3d.	4d. 3d.	3d. 2d.	2d. 1d.	2d. 1d.

Personal Luggage not exceeding 28 lbs. in weight will be allowed to be taken by each Adult
Passenger free of charge if carried by hand.

MERCHANDISE TRAFFIC
Will be dealt with at the following Sidings or Depots —
ELM BRIDGE, BOYCE'S BRIDGE, OUTWELL
BASIN, OUTWELL BRIDGE, UPWELL

The moderate charges for haulage will be made, particulars of these and other information can be obtained from the Company
Inspectors at the Depots, from the Station Agent at Wisbech, the District Goods Manager at Cambridge, or the Goods k.
at Liv ol Street.

ndon, September, 1884.   WILLIAM BIRT, General Manager

GER timetable 8th September, 1884.

Wisbech without delay. The GER Directors, however, intimated that the company was unwilling to embark on further schemes until some experience had been gained of tramway operation, and its profitability was proven.

At 7.00 am on Friday 26th September, 1884 two horses in the charge of carter John Hunt were hauling a waggon of timber to Welney along Elm Road when a special goods train passing from Upwell to Wisbech frightened the animals. The waggon and horses were descending the slope from Newcommon bridge as the train approached the structure scaring the animals and causing the shaft horse, which was blind, to run into a ditch where it was speared by the shaft and killed. The Mayor of Wisbech took up the case of compensation for Hunt and wrote to the GER authorities stressing the death of the horse, valued at £30 to £35 was a great loss. James Robertson, the superintendent, replied in October saying he had enquired into the matter and was unable to admit liability on the part of the railway company for the accident to the horse. The mayor, on receipt of the reply, hoped as an alternative that the GER would subscribe a donation towards the purchase of a replacement animal but this was refused. In the meantime several local traders complained that the tramway was the cause of a downturn in business as the local populace took advantage to travel into Wisbech for their requirements instead of using the local village shops.

Because of the success of the tram locomotives and their reliability in service, on 7th October, 1884 the GER Locomotive Committee decided to provide Yarmouth tramways with engines similar to those in use on Wisbech and Upwell tramway and £1,300 was sanctioned for building at Stratford works. In the meantime one locomotive was temporarily transferred from Wisbech to Yarmouth for evaluation trials.

The *Wisbech Advertiser* on 8th October, 1884 stated:

The average number of passengers on the tramway is about 3,000 per week, but over 2,000 have been carried in one day, as, for instance last Wednesday, when visitors to Inglethorpe Hall Fete availed themselves of it. The weekly tonnage of goods is 600 tons and upwards, and is expected to increase considerably. Commercially there is every prospect of the experiment proving thoroughly successful, and it will probably solve the difficulty in the way of effectually opening up such productive agricultural districts without the excessive costs involved in the construction of a railway.

Wisbech Borough Council was preparing local bye-laws and regulations for the operation of the tramway within the borough boundary under the Tramways Act of 1870, and on 23rd October, 1884 the Town Clerk sent the following letter to the BoT seeking amendments to the regulations for the Tramway:

With reference to your letter of 11th September I am directed by the Councillors of the Borough as the local authority under the Tramways Act 1870 to send diagrams for consideration. The Council are desirous of making the additions set out in the rider A to the printed mode of the Bye-Laws if they have the power so to do, should the BoT deem this beyond the powers of the local authority.

[Rider A comes at the end of Article 2.] ... and whereas any car enters from the Great Eastern Railway on to Elm Road in this Borough the speed there shall not exceed 4 mph and the driver must sound the special bell at or about a distance of 50 yards from Elm Road and whenever approaching Newcommon Bridge at 50 yards, the driver should sound the special bell as a warning to persons in charge of animals or vehicles near the bridge.

The BoT do not think the proposal for the addition Rider A is beyond the scope of the Bye-Law but it is probably better that the first portion as to the speed be joined to No. 2 and the remainder as to the signal made into the new Bye-Laws to follow clause 6. In any case 50 yards from the point of danger is too remote for the use of the bell signal. As additional practice to those already made by the BoT as to the standard, it is desirous that General Hutchinson see them with the other papers.

By 30th October Hutchinson had replied that he had no objection to the proposals made.

The Bye-Laws and Regulations for the operation of Tramways within the Borough of Wisbech were finalized by the Mayor, Aldermen and Burgesses of the Borough on 21st November, 1884 and the Common seal affixed with the signature of Mayor Frederick Peating and the Town Clerk Francis Jackson:

1. For the purposes of these Bye-laws and Regulations the term 'car shall mean any Engine or Carriage using any Tramway laid down within the said Borough, and the term 'driver' and 'conductor' shall respectively mean the driver and conductor or other person having charge of an Engine or Car.

2. The driver of every car shall cause the same to be driven at a speed of not less than four miles an hour on the average, and not exceeding eight miles an hour; and whenever any car enters from the Great Eastern Railway on to the Elm Road in this Borough, the speed shall not exceed four miles an hour.

3. The driver of every car shall so drive the same that it shall not follow a preceding car at less distance than one hundred yards.

4. Subject to the requirements of Bye-law 3 and 5, the driver or conductor of a car shall stop for the purpose of setting down or taking up passengers, when required, by any passenger desiring to leave the car, or by any person desirous of travelling by the car, for who there is room, and to whose admission no valid objection can be made; Provided that nothing in this Bye-law shall require a car to be stopped on any gradient steeper than 1 in 25.

5. Except at a passing place or a terminus, no car shall be stopped at the intersection or junction of two or more streets or roads, nor within ten yards of a car on an adjoining line of rails.

6. The driver of a car on coming in sight of a vehicle standing or travelling on any part of the road so as not to leave sufficient space for the car to pass shall sound the bell or whistle as a warning to the person in charge of such vehicle, and that person shall with reasonable despatch, cause such vehicle to be removed so as not to obstruct the car.

7. Whenever any car shall be approaching the bridge called Newcommon Bridge and at or about the distance of fifty yards therefrom, in this Borough, the driver of such car shall sound his special bell or whistle as a warning to persons in charge of animals or vehicles in near proximity to the said bridge; and whenever any car shall be about to enter from the Great Eastern Railway on to the Elm Road in this Borough, the driver thereof shall sound his special bell at or about the distance of fifty yards from Elm Road aforesaid.

8. No person shall in any way willfully impede or interfere with the Traffic on the Tramways, nor shall any driver or conductor needlessly cause interruption to the ordinary road traffic.

9. Every driver, conductor or other person offending against any of these Bye-laws and Regulations shall be liable to a penalty not exceeding forty shillings for each offence, and not exceeding for any continuing offence, ten shillings for every day during which the offence continues.

On 20th December, 1884 the Wisbech Town Clerk forwarded a letter to the BoT enclosing copies of the Bye-Laws (made by the Council under section 46 of the Tramways Act 1870) on 21st November sealed and signed asking for the approval of the BoT. Copies were included in the *London Gazette* for 20th December and the *Wisbech Advertiser* for 26th November and 3rd December, 1884. The BoT acknowledged receipt of the documents on Christmas Eve stating that, subject to no objection being received, on expiration of the prescribed period of two months one copy of the Bye-Laws would be returned duly certified. The document was returned under the signature of Henry G. Calcraft, an Assistant Secretary to the BoT, on 24th February, 1885.

A minor incident in December 1884 showed that not all road users were aware of the dangers of conflicting movements between flesh and steel. A horse and cart owned by Mr Judd, a beerhouse keeper, were standing by the flour mill at Upwell when the man in charge pulled the horse round just as a train was approaching. Unfortunately as it wheeled round the animal fell across the rails and was dragged under the cowcatcher and protecting guard on the front of the locomotive sustaining injuries. Witnesses claimed the train could have stopped before hitting the animal and blamed the accident on the tram engine driver, a claim that was vehemently denied.

The tramway settled down to a relatively peaceful existence but not everyone was satisfied for the BoT received the following letter dated 24th April, 1885 from the Rector of Outwell the Reverend John E. Briscoe:

As Rector and the largest ratepayer in this parish, I beg respectfully to bring before the Board of Trade –

1. The most dangerous practice of the steam tram shunting across the highway at the foot of a very narrow bridge situated between our schools across which, in addition to a very heavy traffic, over 100 children have to cross four times every day.
2. The great inconvenience and great nuisance of their leaving their trucks of coals to be unloaded on our highway - with the horses standing nearly halfway across the roadway, while the dust and noise is a nuisance which ought not to be allowed. I have called the attention of the officials to these evils but their reply is, while admitting the facts, they have no room in their yard. But I submit that ample accommodation for the correction of all these evils may be obtained by their purchasing more land adjoining their land and with the aid of a 'turntable' and other appliances their business may be conducted on their own premises and I trust the Board of Trade will at once issue an order for the correction of these evils.

The BoT passed the complaint to the GER and on 16th May, 1885 William Birt the General Manager replied:

The letter from the Reverend Briscoe contains two complaints; (1) that of shunting across the highway at the entrance to the Goods Yard at Outwell Village; (2) that of unloading trucks of coal in the goods siding on the Wisbech side of the bridge leading to the Goods Yard at Outwell Village.

I am instructed by my Directors to state that this gentleman preferred the same complaint to our Goods Manager who went full into them, and gave instructions with regard to the first that in no case was shunting to be performed into and out of Outwell Village goods yard across the highway unless the guard or inspector was stationed at the crossing; which arrangement has been carried out. With regard to the second complaint I am instructed to state that the goods siding on the Wisbech side of the bridge is used for the standing of trucks of coal and the public carts stand alongside it whilst the coals are being unloaded; this is found to be of great convenience to the neighbourhood and as far as my Directors are aware no one else has complained. It appears that the road vehicles standing against the trucks do not stand more than two feet on the public highway, and that really the inconvenience, if any, is very slight indeed.

I am also instructed to state that if the Board of Trade should consider further enquiries necessary, my Directors would be quite prepared to facilitate it; but they believe that the existing arrangements are considered reasonable, convenient and a great advantage, by the residents of the district generally.

The contents were passed on to the Reverend Briscoe, who within 10 days had vehemently responded stressing again he was 'the largest ratepayer':

I submit the Directors of the Great Eastern Railway admit the evils I complain of but try to minimize them by false excuses. They admit that I have shewed my good faith and goodwill by first bringing these matters before them when they sent the Goods Manager who strongly deprecated my bringing these things before the Board of Trade knowing well that they ought not to be allowed. Permit me to make the following of their excuses.

1. There is no inspector here but only a porter who has his hands full in attending to the loading of trucks and who locks up and leaves the premises at 6 and two trams pass after that hour and if the guard has instructions to attend to the crossing it is simply impossible for him to look out as he has also to turn the points and do the coupling. I have had to wait at this dangerous bridge where many accidents have happened even before there was the obstruction of the Tram, for the Tram to pass or for the carts to come over the bridge and I repeat, *does this give them power thus to obstruct our highway?*

2. I deny that the place where the trucks are left for unloading coals, timber etc. is a 'siding' at all inasmuch as it is not enclosed with rails as all their sidings are; nor is it true that the carts stand *alongside* the trucks but waggons and carts *back to the trucks* it being much easier to put coals etc. in this way than to lift them over the side of the waggons or carts and I have frequently seen the horses standing nearly halfway across the road while the rails on which the Trams run are very much on the road at this point to enable them to get over the bridge and they thus save the expense of making the bridge longer. The 'convenience' thus boasted of only relates to one small coal yard opened since the Tram trucks have been allowed to unload there and the absurdity of this excuse is seen from the fact that the population of Outwell Isle where the evil exists is only 399 while that of Outwell, Norfolk *just over the river* where their yard is situated and where the trucks ought to be unloaded is more than double, being 894. I *very much* wish the Board of Trade would send someone to see what people will say to further their own interests.

The truth is, the whole of the evils exist to save them a little expense in acquiring a little more land and such plant as I begged them to secure before they removed here and they told me it would be of no avail but which they *have not dared to tell the Board of Trade*.

But it is not merely the nuisance caused by the loading of coals etc. for this parish alone, but as their charge is less for bringing trucks to Outwell than to Upwell a good deal of carting from the 'siding' takes place all of which goes past this house so that as the largest ratepayer I have a right to complain.

Nor is it true that others have not complained of the nuisances as may be clearly read between the lines where the writer says 'as far as my Directors are aware no one else has complained'. To which reply how easy to stop the complaints of some by a sop such as a Champagne Luncheon etc. and if he also goes about the parish so much as the Rector or who having repeatedly seen these evils and having heard others complain of them, is it not clearly his duty to bring them before the Board of Trade which I trust will use its authority at once to put a stop to these evils and compel these people to do their business on their own premises, and not to endanger the lives of their most Gracious Majesties humble servants or to be a nuisance on the Queen's highway.

The continual complaining by the Rector found the GER almost in daily contact with the BoT on how to placate the clergyman. It was subsequently agreed that Major General Hutchinson would visit Outwell and the re-inspection took place on 3rd May, 1885. The intrepid rector was about to travel to London but agreed to meet Hutchinson, who was also approached by a deputation of the principal inhabitants of the village emphatically advising that they did not support the Rector's case. After hearing from railway officials and other parties, the inspector thought the only train likely to affect the schoolchildren was the 3.55 pm up mixed working from Upwell. He suggested the train depart at the earlier time of 3.44 pm when shunting would stop before the children left the school. He noted a second set of points connecting the siding from Outwell Yard with the main line, a short distance south-west of the bridge, were not authorized on the deposited plans. The GER officers attending the inspection advised Hutchinson that the points had been installed after consultation with the local authority when the line was first inspected. The points were used only about once a day.

On the question of the second complaint Hutchinson noted the unloading of wagons took place on an authorized siding at a point 60 chains from the commencement of line No. 2. When carts were backed against trucks the horses' heads projected some distance into the actual road, though still leaving sufficient room for traffic to pass. The inspector failed to see the problem, whilst the deputation from Outwell found no fault with the railway company. Hutchinson concluded no further action was necessary provided shunting was not carried out when children were leaving school. On 9th July, 1885 the GER issued local instructions 'forbidding the shunting of trams over the road at Outwell when children are going to or leaving school'.

Having quelled the problems at Outwell the line again settled down to a mundane existence until Section 29 of the GER (General Powers) Act 1885 (48 and 49 Vict. cap. xciii, of 16th July, 1885), formally gave powers of abandonment of the three tramways to Wisbech town centre authorized by section 43 of the GER Act of 1882.

As the traffic interchanged between the main line and the tramway at Wisbech continued to increase so the lack of siding space became an embarrassment to the railway company. Shunting was taking an excessive time and the outsorting of wagons and forming of trains resulted in considerable delay to services. To obviate the shortcoming, the provision of additional sidings on the tramway was authorized on 15th August, 1885 at a cost of £365 and confirmed on 1st September, 1885.

Early in 1886 the goods manager complained of the lack of facilities to handle cattle traffic at Upwell. The number of animals conveyed by rail was increasing and staff had difficulty loading and unloading beasts from the cattle wagons. On 2nd February, 1886 the Way & Works Committee readily agreed the expenditure of £65 on a new cattle pen and cattle dock at the terminus, charging the work to the goods manager's account. After several complaints from Wisbech Town Council regarding the poor condition of Wisbech station, the Directors agreed to meet the Mayor and other officials on 3rd November, 1885 where a petition for a new station was presented. The Directors promised to give the matter their attention but little was done in the succeeding months until on 16th February, 1886 the Traffic Committee were presented with a letter from Jackson the Town Clerk:

> I am desired by the Council of this Borough again to request the favourable attention of the Directors of the Great Eastern Railway Company to the Memorials presented to them by the Mayor of Wisbech at the interview he had with them on 3rd November last, praying that a suitable Station might be erected at Wisbech in lieu of the present very inadequate one.
>
> The Council feel that the necessity for this improvement of the Wisbech Station is very pressing and they trust the Directors will give immediate instructions for carrying out the requisite work.

The Committee were evidently swayed by the arguments for they instructed the Engineer to prepare a plan for the new station, with estimates of cost and resolved to send representatives on a site visit to Wisbech to meet members of the Council.

On 4th March, 1886 the Reverend Briscoe again complained to the BoT, declaring the evils and nuisances of unloading coal had 'intensified to a tenfold degree'. He registered 'an immense coal traffic' not only for local consumption but also for onward transport along the canal in fen lighters. He reiterated 'they have made the middle of this village into a coal depot and that in the most objectionable manner possible'. The promise of the curtailment of shunting when children were leaving school was a 'miserable deception and delusion' for the tram often did not leave until after four in the afternoon, with shunting still going on even in the dark winter evenings. To add insult to injury the Reverend was being asked for a second rate of 10*d*. in the pound and was not amused. The following day the BoT declared their continuing interest in the matter and suggested that subject to regulations covering the tramway it might be possible to prohibit the practice of shunting.

To this latest tirade the GER replied, on 26th March, that the shunting was performed by a single train only, which had mistakenly been adhering to the old timing. The timetable was to be amended in April to obviate movement of stock at school going home times and evening shunting. Matters were, however, reaching impasse at Outwell for Churchwarden Anthony Horne had raised another petition signed by 150 persons of all classes including landowners, teachers, farmers, shop owners and labourers *against* the Rector's complaints. Horne was also embroiled with other charity trusts in libel action against the Reverend Briscoe.

On the evening of Friday 6th August, 1886, 65-year-old widower Frederick Clarke, nicknamed Grocer, a former cattle and pig dealer of Wisbech but latterly a recluse, suffered fatal injuries when he was hit by a train near the Prince of Wales public house at Emneth. The mangled body once removed from under the locomotive was stored in a nearby outhouse until the conclusion of the enquiry, held on the evening of the following day at Scrafield's public house at Elm, and conducted by the deputy coroner for the Isle of Ely. John Wilson, locomotive superintendent from Lynn, station master Bowker of Wisbech and traffic inspector Watson of Lynn represented the GER. In evidence it was established the deceased had left a public house in Outwell after drinking, with the intention of catching the train to Wisbech. John Hardman, the tram driver, advised the deputy coroner that the train had departed from Upwell at 9.10 pm and had an uneventful journey until it was 200 yards on the basin side of Boyce's Bridge between Mr Newling's farm and the neighbouring farm in the ownership of Mr William Grieves. The train was travelling at 8 mph when fireman Dunbabbin called to say there was an object close to the line. Despite Hardman shutting off steam and reversing the engine, the cowcatcher struck the object a glancing blow before stopping within 25 yards. The driver took his lamp and ran back to discover the deceased, whilst at the same time the conductor arrived with his lamp to provide additional illumination. Both agreed Clarke was dead as a result of the injuries sustained and fireman Dunbabbin was sent to summon help as the two men removed the body from under the engine. When cross-examined driver Hardman explained the body was caught under the guard, which was fitted to within a height of 4 inches above rail level all round the engine. He also explained it was too late to sound the whistle or ring the bell on the locomotive to warn Clarke of the approaching train. The statutory red and white lights were carried on the front of the engine in fixed positions, the red on the right-hand side. Because of the slight curvature of the line the beam of the light would shine away from the object on the track. To final questioning on the braking distance, the driver estimated the train would take 40 yards to stop from a speed of 8 mph, taking into consideration the weight of the tram locomotive and the tail load of the train. William Dunbabbin, the firemen corroborated the driver's evidence and added that he only saw the body in the reflection from the ashpan as the engine passed the site of the incident. On being recalled driver Hardman advised that when the train had arrived at Wisbech he had closely inspected the locomotive and found traces of blood on the cowcatcher and side apron. At the conclusion of the hearing the deputy coroner recorded a verdict of accidental death.

Following complaints from the travelling public concerned at waiting in the open for the tram especially in adverse weather, the GER Way & Works Committee on 19th October, 1886 authorized the provision of a waiting shed at Upwell at a cost of £110. The new building incorporated a room for the foreman-in-charge and was completed the following year.

The opening of the tramway was not proving as disastrous as expected for the Wisbech Canal Company; in 1886 tolls collected included £80 at Wisbech and £237 at Outwell, the latter due to transhipment of coal from the railway for onward transit.

The Great Eastern Railway (General Powers) Act 1887 (50 and 51 Vict. cap. clxi), which received the Royal Assent on 8th August, 1887, included powers to acquire land and construct the new station at Wisbech. Later on 18th October, 1887 authority was given for waiting shelter at Outwell at a cost of £60 after local inhabitants had objected to waiting for the train in the open and exposed to the elements, especially in inclement weather. The following day as the 7.50 am train from Wisbech to Upwell was running about one mile from Wisbech, a female passenger, Mary Oglesby, alighted whilst the train was in motion and fell on the public road bruising her shoulder. A male passenger Edward Scott, who descended from the carriage to assist, also fell and his right leg was run over by the following vehicle the, luggage van. At the subsequent inquiry the woman stated that when she got on the step of the carriage her little boy told her to wait until the train stopped, an instruction she apparently ignored.

On 6th December, 1887 the Directors approved of the final plans of works for the new Wisbech station costing £10,362, without land purchase. Preliminary work had actually commenced on site as early as Thursday 5th August, 1886 when GER surveyors began the task of measuring the tract of land chosen. The contract for the construction of the new Wisbech station was subsequently awarded to Harold Arnold and Son of Doncaster on 17th March, 1888 at a cost of £4,367. The award was made subject to the up side being completed by 31st July, 1888 and the down side by 31st December, 1888. Land for the new station was purchased on 1st April at a cost of £494 and a further plot was obtained on 1st May at a cost of £300.The GER Engineer was responsible for the demolition of the existing station buildings in time to allow Arnold to commence construction work. The contract for the resignalling and interlocking of points and signals at the new station was later awarded to Saxby & Farmer Ltd of Kilburn.

Another accident occurred on the tramway on 18th September, 1888 when a Mr Gill alighted from the train before it had been brought to a halt with the result he fell into the road and suffered bruises to his leg and back. It was pointed out the injured man was lucky to escape so lightly when others not so fortunate had fallen under the wheels of the train with fatal consequencies. The accident was due to 'own want of caution'.

Progress on the new Wisbech station was somewhat retarded by the failure of the contractor to find a suitable sub-contractor for the provision of a footbridge to connect the platforms. Arnold had written to Jonathan Wilson on 25th September:

> We have submitted the drawings to several firms of iron founders but cannot find one who would accept our schedule for this class of work. Therefore our price for the cast columns would be 10s. 0d. per cwt, handrails 12s. 6d. per cwt, riveted girders, stringers and risers 16s. 0d. per cwt and holes ½d. each. All the other work we are quite willing to take at scheduled prices.

Wilson was evidently satisfied with the revised prices for he replied to Arnold on 4th October, 1888 to put the work 'in hand at once'. Whilst Arnold continued to search for a contractor for the station footbridge, the GER awarded a contract to A. Handyside on 19th March, 1889 for the provision of a footbridge beside Victoria Road level crossing after the firm tendered at £350.

Serious congestion within the yard at Outwell depot brought many complaints from local traders who encountered delays in the loading and dispatch of their produce. Problems were experienced in shunting operations and the timetable was often disrupted as the locomotive spent unnecessary time extracting fully loaded wagons from behind empty vehicles. Matters came to a head and on 2nd April, 1889 authority was given to purchase an additional plot of land for expansion of the yard and provision of an additional siding at a cost of £30, with pressure for the siding to be completed before the fruit harvesting season.

On Thursday 16th May, 1889 the GER Directors on one of the regular tours of inspection of their system visited amongst other places Wisbech to see at first hand the new station and its facilities, which were 'inspected and approved'. Whilst at the station they had the opportunity to review the latest earnings from the Upwell tramway and enquired of the station master future traffic trends. Following the inspection, the GER Secretary on 19th June, 1889 advised the BoT of the new station and signalling works being carried out at Wisbech and requested an early inspection.

Major General C.S. Hutchinson duly inspected the new facilities at Wisbech on 16th October, 1889. He found the station was built nearly on the site of the old one and the work had involved large alterations in the general layout of sidings. The new station was provided with up and down side platforms with a dock [sic] at the back of the up platform for the Upwell tramway trains. The booking office and waiting rooms contained ample accommodation and Hutchinson observed the GER had provided two footbridges, one for the public at an occupational crossing, next the public level crossing at the up end of the station, over which, the inspector noted, was a great deal of traffic, and the other connecting the station platforms. The points and signals were operated from three signal boxes: Wisbech Goods Junction with a 25-lever frame, all levers working; Wisbech Station with a 32-lever frame, with 21 working and 11 spare levers, and a ground frame at Wisbech North with a 12-lever frame, all levers working.

At the conclusion of the inspection Hutchinson required the GER to carry out some remedial work: at Wisbech Goods Junction signal box levers Nos. 10 and 24 and 8 and 24 required interlocking; lever No. 9 was to precede lever No. 24; lever No. 8 was to be freed when No. 23 signal was pulled off for No. 1 siding. At Wisbech Station signal box the lettering 'or 11 and 12' was to be added to the label on No. 10 lever, and 'or 16 and 17' to that on No. 15 lever. Levers Nos. 20 and 22 were to be freed if levers Nos. 3 and 22 were interlocked. Hutchinson also required mutual control between the signal at Wisbech Harbour Branch Junction and Wisbech Station down starting signal. At Wisbech North ground frame Nos. 3 and 9 points required the provision of locking bars. During the inspection a visit was made to Wisbech Harbour Branch Junction where the level crossing gates required interlocking with the signals. Subject to early completion of the remedial work, Hutchinson sanctioned the use of the new works but warned a re-inspection would be made at an early date. The remedial work was completed as a matter of urgency and Major General Hutchinson carried out the re-inspection of the works at Wisbech station on 7th February, 1890 when he found that the remedial tasks enumerated in his report of 16th October had been completed. He also visited the new signal box at Wisbech

Outwell Village depot is dwarfed by St Clement's church. In the yard are a Girling, Peterborough 5-plank open wagon and another wagon with a sheeted load. No space is wasted in this 1887 view for an allotment is located between the main single line and the back siding.
Lilian Ream Gallery

A down passenger train has just swung across Elm Road and stopped to pick up passengers at the first stopping point. Elm Road main line crossing No. 3 gates are across the road to help regulate the traffic. Note the tall signals on the main line, which were later replaced by signals on shorter posts. The rear vehicle on the train is 4-wheel van No. 9, later transferred to the Downham to Stoke Ferry branch and then the Elsenham & Thaxted Light Railway.
Author's Collection

Harbour Branch Junction, containing a 16-lever frame with 13 working and 3 spare levers. This had been provided with facilities for block signalling. The interlocking was correct and the inspector sanctioned use of the new works.

On Wednesday 1st October, 1890, 73-year-old cattle dealer Henry Brown, who lived with his son near Newcommon Bridge, was run over by a train and killed instantly. He was driving some pigs along the road beside the tramway accompanied by his grandson when one of the pigs strayed on to the line. Brown gave chase but being deaf failed to hear the approaching 11.40 am Wisbech to Upwell train and was struck by the locomotive as he stepped on to the line, with fatal results. The body was extracted from under the engine by the train crew and laid beside the line covered with sacks until Police Sergeant Roughton and Doctor Mason arrived to certify death, after which a stretcher was obtained and the body taken to the Royal Standard Inn at Elm to await the inquest.

The inquest was duly held the following Friday 3rd October in the Royal Standard Inn, Newcommon Bridge, chaired by the local coroner W. Welchman, with station master Bowker of Wisbech and John Wilson, the Lynn district locomotive superintendent representing the GER. Giving evidence driver James Palmer stated the train was formed of the tram engine hauling two passenger cars and eight wagons loaded with fruit baskets. After leaving the main line station the train stopped at Elm Bridge Depot and departed five minutes late as wagons had to be collected from the goods yard. Palmer confirmed that he noticed the deceased near Mr Kingston's hedge and then saw the pig run from the middle of the road on to the line. He opened the cylinder cocks to frighten the pig and slowed the train to about 2½ to 3 mph. The pig ran off but Brown stepped on to the line immediately in front of the engine. Steam was immediately shut off and the brake applied but the cowcatcher caught the man's leg and dragged him along. To cross-examination Palmer confirmed the engine was only equipped with a hand brake. Asked if a vacuum brake would have stopped the train in a shorter distance, the driver stated that if the engine had been equipped with the Westinghouse brake, he could have halted the train immediately and averted the accident, as Brown was some 15 yards away when he first noticed him on the track. The coroner recorded a verdict of accidental death whilst pointing out 'the accident to Brown was the result of a want and care on his own part and not neglect on the part of the GER company servants'. The foreman of the jury recommended the GER adopt the vacuum brake on the tramway stock. Bowker being a non-technical man replied that he thought the company was about to adopt the vacuum brake on the line but was contradicted by Wilson; the latter informed the gathering the necessity for a continuous brake had been realized for some time and, to ensure standardization, the Westinghouse air brake would be provided on locomotives and coaching stock, although no time scale for completion was proffered.

The BoT was concerned with the recommendation of the jury and on 16th October, 1890 enquired as to what action the GER was to take to fit the Westinghouse brake to locomotives, passenger carriages and brake van on the Upwell tramway. The correspondence also pointed out that the certificate granted on 10th August, 1883 for the operation of the tramway for a period of seven years had now expired.

As a result of the fatal accident to Brown and the earlier accidents on the line, it became all the more imperative to equip the tramway rolling stock with continuous brakes. On 21st October, 1890 the locomotive superintendent was duly instructed to equip all tramway locomotives and passenger train vehicles with the Westinghouse brake as a matter of urgency. The order was passed on 24th October with completion within six months and the next day the GER General Manager announced that engines and passenger train vehicles on the tramway were to be equipped with the Westinghouse brake and screw couplings between the engines and the coaches. The GER Secretary reported to the BoT on the same day that his Directors had given orders for the fitting of the continuous brake but questioned the date for the renewal of the certificate. The start of the regulations governing the tramway was 6th September, 1884 and therefore the licence did not expire until the end of 1891. The BoT was terse in its response: 'The licence had expired on 10th August and Major General Hutchinson was to inspect the tramway!'

Hutchinson inspected the tramway for the renewal of its licence to operate steam power on 26th November, 1890. He noted the condition of the rails and sleepers were substantial but the top ballast in many cases had been allowed to fall considerably below the level of the tops of the rails. He considered it was 'not a matter of importance' where roads were wide and vehicular traffic could easily pass the train but where the roads were narrow it was 'very necessary' that ballast be kept to the top of the rail. The GER Civil Engineer agreed to rectify the lack of ballast as a matter of urgency. The Major General remarked that the rolling stock was the same character as on previous visits and that the engines were fitted with 'a species of life protection and whistle'. The engines had screw couplings and were shortly to be fitted with the Westinghouse brake as were the coaches and brake van. In other respects the engines appeared to comply with BoT regulations, with the exception that it was necessary to make the speed indicator more legible for the driver to read. In his report Hutchinson noted that representatives of all local authorities attended the inspection with the exception of Norfolk County Council. He recommended that the BoT accept a licence could be issued subject to work on the ballast and the provision of the brakes being completed as soon as possible. On 29th November the licence was renewed for a period of seven years with expiry on 10th August, 1897, with the proviso that application for re-inspection of the 1884 section of the tramway be made six weeks or more before the period expired.

The sheer number of movements on the tramway was causing problems, especially during the fruit season as freight loads increased and extra pathing was required for the additional trains. To ease the problem the crossing loop at Boyce's Bridge depot was extended to allow longer trains to pass one another. The work costing £55 was authorized on 3rd February, 1891, and the longer loop was available in time for the summer season traffic. Rather belatedly and after much disagreement over prices, on the same date Arrol Brothers of Glasgow belatedly received the authority to provide the footbridge at Wisbech station at contract price - a structure, which had been completed two years earlier in 1889.

The Directors instructed the Secretary on 6th March, 1891 to write to the BoT advising that the Directors were 'sorry that due to exceptional difficulties that have arisen the fitting of passenger rolling stock with the Westinghouse brake would not be completed by 24th April', and requested an extension of time to 30th June, 1891. This was due to the difficulty in equipping the tram engines, which were of a 'peculiar construction'. The correspondence was passed to Major General Hutchinson, who on 10th March agreed to the extension of time.

By 4th July, 1891 the BoT was advised that all locomotives and passenger carrying vehicles on that tramway had been fitted with the Westinghouse brake, whilst on the 10th of the month application was made to the BoT for a re-inspection of the two sections of the tramway where the licence expired on 6th September, 1891. The papers were passed to Major General Hutchinson who decreed there was no need for a further inspection and the licence was duly granted.

The facilities at Upwell were also further improved in 1891 when the provision of toilets was sanctioned on 29th September at a cost of £110. Whilst the work was in progress it was decided to provide a separate office for the foreman-in-charge, located away from the passenger waiting shed, and construction was authorized on 2nd February, 1892 at a cost of £48.

On the evening of Saturday 24th September, 1892, 15-year-old Letitia Mary Hall from Walsoken travelled by the 7.55 pm train from Wisbech to visit her aunt at Outwell. She rode in the second class section of a composite tramcar and during the journey entered into conversation with a fellow passenger Elizabeth Turner, stating she was unacquainted with the tramcar and asked how she would know when the train reached Outwell. Turner advised that she would notice the lights of the waiting room in the window. As usual the train stopped near the sluice on the approach to Outwell before crossing the bridge into the station yard to allow passengers to alight. After waiting for the usual time at the sluice the train moved off over the bridge, at which time the 15-year-old rose from her seat to move along the tramcar. Elizabeth Turner advised her not to go through the second class section of the car because of the noisy altercation of drunks in that compartment. Letitia Hall duly took the advice and went through the first class section to the end balcony, which was occupied by a Mr Webber and a colleague who were sitting on the end railing. Both men noticed the girl open the end door and then continued their conversation, which was interrupted by a dull thud. On turning they found the teenager had disappeared from the end platform and realizing she might have fallen Webber rang the bell for the train to stop. Unfortunately the train continued into Outwell station yard before halting. Webber's fears were confirmed for Letitia Hall had attempted to leave the moving train and fallen under the following vehicle in the formation, the luggage van, which passed over her head causing instant death. The body was removed and taken to the nearby Crown Hotel to await the inquest.

The inquest was held on Monday 26th September starting at 5.15 pm and chaired by W. Welchman, after initial problems were experienced composing a jury of equal numbers from both the Isle of Ely and Norfolk sides of the village. After hearing the evidence of Elizabeth Turner who said that five or six girls were riding in the compartment next to the engine during the journey, Mr Webber, the coroner called James Edgeley, the conductor of the train to account for the events of the journey. Edgeley stated the train was formed of an engine, a second class coach, a composite coach and a luggage van. He had received no complaints of disturbances and considered only one man was slightly the worse for drink. The deceased had not asked to be put off at any particular place when he checked the tickets and he had first heard of the accident at Outwell Village station yard. Edgeley then advised the coroner he had taken his lamp and walked back along the train and found the body. After removal of the torso, the train continued to Upwell, where he closely examined the vehicles and found traces of blood on the luggage van. The conductor concluded his evidence stating he was not normally employed on the Upwell line and as he was a relief guard based at March had previously only travelled in the afternoon and not at night. Driver James Palmer then told the inquest that on hearing the bell he had not stopped the train on the bridge as he was afraid passengers might alight in the darkness and fall into the sluice. At the conclusion of the hearing the foreman of the jury announced a verdict of accidental death and was of the opinion a light mounted on the side of the tram coaches would be advantageous to passenger joining and leaving the train, especially at night.

The incident resulted in harsh criticism against the railway company for failing to ensure the safety of passengers travelling on the tramway. Whilst some were vehement in their comments, other were constructive. J. Gill having read the account of the accident wrote to the *Wisbech Observer*, which published his comments on 5th October, 1892:

> I cannot help but readily assume the accident occurred through her trying to alight whilst the train was in motion. If I remember, the platforms at each end of the carriage terminate within six inches of the width of the carriage and have on the edge a chequered metal plate, which is invariably in the shade when the train is artificially lighted and this is likely to deceive. It appears to me the girl fell from the platform after going there to be better able to see and be at hand when arriving at her destination - than deliberately attempting to descend three feet by steps only six inches wide from a carriage in motion, particularly when it is dark. [Gill observed,] it was possible for accidents to occur as the gates at the ends of the vehicles were more often open than closed [and questioned whose duty it was to close these gates before the train set off in motion. He ventured to suggest that] if the vehicles were always illuminated during the hours of darkness, both inside and outside the carriage on the steps, and the gates were closed and the train adequately attended, then serious accidents would be avoided.

Almost unnoticed 'Whybrow's Boat', the ferry which latterly had sailed every Saturday from The Royal Inn at Wisbech conveying passengers and goods along the canal to Outwell and Upwell, was withdrawn in 1892 having survived almost a decade in opposition to the faster tramway service at the same 2*d.* fare. It was reported 'few mourned its passing'.

On 5th September, 1893 the question of the limited accommodation in Wisbech engine shed was raised, as additional locomotives were required for the tramway. It was estimated that a new structure to house the increased allocation of tram engines would cost £640, but this was considered prohibitive and the proposal for a completely new structure was put in abeyance.

The various recommendations and suggestions for safety improvements on the tramway went unheeded for yet another accident occurred on Saturday 10th November, 1893. Arthur Charles Arnold of Walsoken joined the 8.00 pm train from Wisbech to Upwell but as the train approached Elm Bridge depot he left his seat and walked to the end platform of the coach. Thinking the train was not stopping, he lifted the gate latch and stood on the side steps waiting to jump off. Unfortunately as he leapt off into the darkness he held on to the side rail and then fell under the wheels of the following coach, which severed his legs. Arnold was taken to Wisbech Hospital but died of his injuries the following day. W. Welchman, the Coroner for the Isle of Ely, held the inquest at the hospital on Tuesday 13th November. A youth, John Hutchinson, who was riding in the same car, told the coroner that he had heard the deceased cry out as he jumped from the train. Guard Josiah Rollison stated that when the train stopped at Elm Bridge depot he had gone back and found the deceased lying across the line. The coroner recorded a verdict of accidental death and absolved the GER from all blame.

In the spring of 1894 the locomotive superintendent resurrected the necessity for the increased accommodation for locomotives at Wisbech. After detailed discussion the Way and Works Committee recommended additions to the existing shed at a much cheaper cost. The locomotive superintendent agreed to this course of action and tenders were duly invited. The contract was subsequently awarded to S. Hipwell of Wisbech on 5th June, 1894 at a cost of £295. Later in the same year on 2nd October a sleeper boundary fence for the depot was sanctioned at a cost of £33.

The financial returns for the year ending 30th June, 1894 showed that £33,618 had been expended on construction of the tramway, £4,800 on construction of the five 0-4-0 tram locomotives, £2,485 on nine coaching vehicles and £1,016 on Parliamentary expenses, making a capital total of £41,919. Gross receipts for the year ending 30th June were:

	£
Passengers	1,042
Goods, animals and coal	1,457
Parcels and mail	42
Total	2,541

As the working expenses for the same period amounted to £2,137, the net receipts were a meagre £404, barely 1 per cent of the capital expenditure.

Receipts for the half-year ending 31st December, 1894 were disappointing for earnings totalling £1,287 compared unfavourably with the £1,315 earned during the similar period in 1893. Despite the poor returns the reputation of the Wisbech & Upwell Tramway spread far and wide, for in May 1895 Mr Buckwell of Brighton, lecturing to the Rye Traders Association in Sussex, advocated similar possible schemes in the South of England, citing the Cambridgeshire line as an ideal example, as it had carried 100,000 passengers and earned £15,000 on goods traffic up to 1894.

Although the Whitsun Bank Holiday Monday was dull and overcast, over 1,250 tickets were issued from Wisbech to Upwell during the day with smaller totals to intermediate destinations. Then on the evening of Monday 29th July, 1895 a young man named Drew, employed as an engine cleaner on the Great Northern Railway, sustained serious leg injuries when returning with his friends by train from Upwell to Wisbech. The group was riding on the end platform of one of the tramcars when for reasons unknown Drew climbed over the railings to gain access to the next car and fell between the moving vehicles.

A down passenger train departs from Outwell Village depot and across Church Terrace level crossing. The timber passenger waiting shelter authorized in October 1887 at a cost of £60 is to the extreme left. The yard sidings are full of vans awaiting loading on inner and middle roads whilst the yard entrance is to the right of the boundary fence.

Author's Collection

The train was immediately halted and the injured man removed from under the wheels of the coach. He was conveyed to North Cambridgeshire Hospital on the back of Mr Yates waggon, which was commandeered for the emergency. Both legs were crushed and on arrival at hospital one immediately amputated.

From 1st January, 1893 second class accommodation had been downgraded to third class on the tramway but this had little effect on receipts which for the half-year ending 31st December, 1895 totalled £1,454, compared with £1,288 earned during the same period of 1894, an increase of £166. For the six months ending 30th June, 1896 the receipts were £1,177 compared with £1,109 for the similar period in 1895. The GER management, wary that the tramway was but a feeder to the main line, with little prospect of making a profit, was nonetheless satisfied with the modest gains made and hopes for the future were encouraging.

'G15' class 0-4-0 tram locomotive No. 128 hauling a down passenger train from Wisbech to Upwell alongside Elm Road and parallel to the Wisbech canal. The leading vehicle is passenger brake van No. 16 followed by third class 4-wheel tram No. 6 and a bogie tram.

Author's Collection

Chapter Three

Halcyon Years

The weather was hardly encouraging on Saturday 25th January, 1897 when a snowstorm swept across the fens blocking both roads and railways around Wisbech. The tramway services were suspended until the following Monday as permanent way staff were fully occupied clearing the lines to March and Magdalen Road as first priority.

Despite the precautions taken by the GER and the many warnings issued, from the opening day of services children living in the vicinity of the tramway had often used the railway as a playground by running across the line in front of moving trains or by clambering on the steps or buffers of coaches or wagons to ride for a short distance before jumping off. Footplate staff, conductors and guards working the services constantly remonstrated with the youngsters and regularly complained to management, but to no avail. The dangerous practice inevitably resulted in a tragic death on 27th March, 1897. On that fateful day 7-year-old Harold Atkins tried to mount the steps of the rear coach of a moving train near the Methodist Chapel at Elm but slipped and fell under the wheels of two wagons coupled behind the coach and received fatal injuries. The occupants of the train were unaware of the accident but Atkins' companions watched with horror as he died and fetched a doctor who pronounced the boy dead. W. Welchman again conducted the necessary inquest on Monday 28th March in the Methodist School Room at Elm, where it was established the lad had previously lived with his stepfather, James Woodbine, a GER platelayer, but latterly lived with his mother. Giving evidence William Blake stated he was one of the conductors travelling on the 3.55 pm train from Upwell to Wisbech, which was formed of the engine, brake van, passenger coaches and two wagons. The train departed from Elm Bridge depot and ran at about 5 mph before stopping at Elm Corner. He had not seen the boy jump on to the train as he was travelling on the road side of one of the coaches and knew nothing of the incident until the train arrived at Elm Corner on the return trip. He reiterated, 'the railway was frequently troubled by children running alongside and jumping on moving trains', although he did not know if the company officials were fully aware of the situation. The coroner recorded a verdict of accidental death and asked the GER to take urgent steps to stop the practice of children riding on the outside steps and buffers of trains.

As the expiry date for the renewal of licence 7th August, 1897, was again approaching the GER made application for an examination of the line on 10th July, 1897. The correspondence was passed to Major Sir Francis Marindin who carried out the inspection for the renewal of the licence on 21st July. During the inspection the Major was accompanied by the GER Engineer and superintendent of the line and was met by representatives of the local road authorities, F.W. Moore, Surveyor to the Isle of Ely County Council, Messrs Hislop and Jackson from Norfolk County Council and representatives of the parish council of Outwell Village. After travelling by special train between Wisbech and Upwell and return, the inspector expressed satisfaction with the line. In his report of 23rd July, 1897 Major Marindin noted the tramway 7 miles 64 chains in length had not altered in form since the previous inspection made by Major General Hutchinson. The permanent way was found 'in very good order' and all parties professed themselves 'quite satisfied with the manner in which the Tramway was maintained and worked'. The rolling stock was 'in good condition'. The siding at Outwell was, however, still a problem to be resolved. The Council had asked for the siding alongside the road at Outwell Sluice not to be used for unloading coal traffic, which in their opinion should be carried out in Outwell Village station yard. There was also danger from the scotch block on the siding and they requested it to be replaced by a lightweight scotch. The scotch block was essentially put in to keep wagons clear of the footpath. It was also desirous for a shelter to be erected at both Outwell and Upwell with a lamp by the level crossing at Small Lode. Despite these minor matters the BoT granted a licence for steam power for a further period of seven years dating from 8th August, 1897 and also advised Wisbech Town Council and Upwell Parish Council of the renewal. The GER General Manager reported the satisfactory conclusion of the matter to the Traffic Committee on 5th October.

In the meantime further complaints had been made of the nuisance caused by dust blowing across adjoining property when coal was unloaded from wagons at Outwell Sluice siding. The Council in a letter to the BoT:

... objected to the danger and obstruction that is caused to the ordinary traffic by the unloading of coals at the siding alongside the main road. It frequently happens that there are several carts and wagons unloading at one time, a tram comes along and all have to move, blocking the road and thereby causing obstruction, danger and delay.

The GER was duly advised and replied on 10th August that the use made of the siding alongside the main road was very limited. There had been no objections from the inhabitants who lived in the cottages opposite the siding and on questioning they had no desire to make one. In the same letter the GER Secretary confirmed a smaller patented block had replaced the existing scotch block. Upwell Parish Council requested the provision of a passenger shelter at Outwell Basin and a lamp on Small Lode level crossing. The GER authorities replied on 9th September, 1897 that it was the council's prerogative to stop the coal dust blowing by advising fuel merchants to dampen down the loads in dry weather before offloading. The request for the shelter was to be considered but the lamp was the responsibility of the council. However, the Outwell Isle Parish Council was dissatisfied with the GER response and on 18th September, 1897 persisted in its complaint, saying that when coal was being unloaded from wagons it was being carried out on one wagon at a time and when a train came along the work had to stop to allow the train to pass. After detailing the points of the complaint they were content to leave the final decision to the occupants of the cottages opposite the siding. On 4th October the GER authorities finally agreed to stop the unloading of wagons at Outwell Sluice siding and on 1st November issued an instruction, effective from 4th November, that a trial would be made of transferring the loading and unloading to the main Outwell Village depot yard and the closure of Outwell Sluice siding. The traders of Outwell were highly displeased and at a meeting in the Infant School Room Outwell Isle, the Parish Council unanimously passed a resolution that the closing of the siding 'should be rescinded and that the GER be allowed to reopen the Outwell Sluice siding for coal merchant traffic only'. A memorial signed by 49 traders was sent to the GER General Manager.

UPWELL, OUTWELL AND WISBECH TRAM LINES

Sir,

We, the undersigned ratepayers and inhabitants of the parish of OUTWELL, while deprecating the action of the Parish Councils, which has resulted in the closing of what may be termed OUTWELL Sluice Siding respectfully desire that you will at your earliest opportunity reopen the above named siding for the purpose it was used heretofore.

It is a matter of very great inconvenience to certain trading firms and private individuals to have to haul and cart goods from the OUTWELL BASIN SIDING, which might just as readily be unloaded at the SLUICE SIDING.

It is a subject of monetary importance to us as inhabitants, as we shall have to pay the cost of the increased cartage etc. and furthermore the Councils did not represent the general wishes of the parish in this matter, nor yet those of the General Parish Meeting.

Probably the Great Eastern Company, while granting the request of the petitioners, could also provide some means of lessening or completely doing away with the alleged grievance.

William Birt, the GER General Manager advised the BoT on 1st November that the siding would be closing on and from 4th November, but from local information gleaned in the village all parties would be happy if the loop at Outwell Sluice was slewed so that carts would not block the main running line and so let trains pass without hindrance. Later he wrote, 'As was expected considerable complaints resulted from the order'. The matter was further discussed locally and agreement to the slewing of the siding was made by Outwell Isle Council on 11th November. By 15th December the work was completed but the siding remained closed to traffic, much to the chagrin of local traders.

The Light Railways Act of 1896 had been promoted to alleviate the distress of the agricultural depression by allowing inexpensive railways to be constructed in rural areas, with the proviso that those so constructed would be freed from the obligation to build to the high standards laid down by the BoT for main lines. Section 5 of the Act stated that where the Board of Agriculture certified that the provision of the light railway would benefit agriculture, the Treasury might agree to aid the building of the line out of public money. Another significant feature was that application for an order could be made by the county, borough or district through which the railway would pass, or by any company or individual to the Light Railway Commissioners. This resulted in a spate of proposals, most of which were unsuccessful, but the GER Board showed a passing interest.

The GER Chairman and some of the Directors made a tour of inspection on Thursday 2nd, Friday 3rd and Saturday 4th June, 1898 visiting such outposts as Brightlingsea, Hadleigh and Hunstanton. On 4th June they visited the Upwell tramway and were driven by road through the district south of Outwell and Upwell to Manea and Welney to inspect the area with the possibility of purchasing small pockets of land for coal depots and the extension of the tramway. The General Manager advised against any extension as the district was too sparse and was not ready to accommodate the railway. On the way the party halted at Outwell, where the goods manager requested authority to purchase of a small portion of land for a coal depot. The plans were not, however, finalized and the matter was placed in abeyance. Following pressure from local coal merchants and traders, on 9th June the local council wrote to the BoT asking again for the closing of the Sluice siding to be rescinded but on 14th June a reply was sent saying the decision for reopening was entirely within the hands of the GER authorities. After consultation, the GER replied to the BoT that the siding was to be reopened on and from 24th June.

The tramway receipts for the half year ending 30th June, 1898 totalled £1,233, compared with £1,972 earned during the same period in 1897. The Directors immediately requested the local officers to investigate the £739 deficit and report on how receipts could be improved.

The 9.43 am Wisbech to Upwell train was travelling sedately along Elm Road on Monday 1st August, 1898, when the locomotive became derailed at a point opposite Ward's Brewery. The driver immediately shut off steam and applied the brakes bringing the train to an abrupt halt. On investigating he discovered the two leading wheels were off the line. After consulting with the conductor-guard and ensuring no passengers were injured, the driver with the assistance of the fireman wedged the screw jack (carried on the engine as standard equipment in the event of a derailment) under the locomotive and gradually raised the machine above rail level. An hour elapsed before the engine was re-railed and without further delay set off with its train to Upwell.

As a result of the earlier visits to the tramway and ventures into the fens, the GER Directors at a meeting on 5th October, 1898, with Lord Claud J. Hamilton as Chairman, discussed the possibility of a new railway for freight traffic from Manea to Tipps End. This had replaced an earlier proposal for a line from Stonea. The building of a goods line from Three Horse Shoes, on the March to Peterborough line, to the small fenland town of Benwick had earlier been authorized by the Great Eastern Railway (General Powers) Act, 58 Vict. cap. xxvi, of 30th May, 1895 and the first section to Burnt House had opened for traffic on 1st September, 1897. Authority had been sanctioned provided the 4½ mile branch, with sidings approximately every half mile, was operated with main line locomotives and not tram locomotives, as it involved no roadside running. The second section from Burnt House Drove to Benwick was opened to traffic on 2nd August, 1898, and although the success of the venture was yet to be realized it was considered a further fenland line from Manea on the Ely to March line to Tipps End, five miles south-east of the tramway terminus at Upwell, might further open up the fenland market and increase receipts. The proposed line was to be worked by ordinary locomotives and it was agreed to include the scheme in the submissions for the 1899 session of Parliament.

During 1898 a total of 114,307 passengers were conveyed on the Upwell tramway and as a goods line it had carried cattle, root crops, vegetables, hay fruit, straw and corn as well as coal, which encouraged some members of the Board to seek to open the new line as quickly as possible.

Scott Damant, a member of the GER General Manager's staff writing on the Wisbech & Upwell Tramway in the February 1899 edition of the *Railway Magazine*, sounded a note of caution to would be promoters of light railways and tramways implying that it was still considered an experiment:

And now a word of caution to those interested in light railway undertakings. The Wisbech and Upwell Tramway pays the Great Eastern Railway Company not so much directly as indirectly. This is because the great bulk of the goods traffic does not commence or terminate at Wisbech, it is carried over the main line of the railway to or from that place. Were the tramway a separate undertaking solely dependent on its own earnings, with a manager, secretary, and clerical staff drawing salaries, and board of directors receiving fees, if asked whether it would then pay or not, the writer could only piously exclaim with the erstwhile Doctor Byrom, 'God bless us all, that quite another thing'!

Wiser counsels thus prevailed and initially the Manea to Tipps End scheme was held in abeyance. After further investigation on 2nd October, 1901 the GER Board agreed to abandon the proposed goods line, although it was not officially aborted until 1902.

From the opening of the Upwell tramway an inspector had been employed at the terminus to supervise the loading and unloading of wagons. Complaints had regularly been received that the member of staff was forced to live away from the station and rent property locally. This was considered unsatisfactory and the matter was placed before the goods manager who supported the case for residential railway-owned accommodation at the isolated terminal. The Directors finally agreed on 1st May, 1900 to sanction provision of the inspector's cottage at Upwell at an estimated cost of £220. Even then there was indecision, for on 19th October authority was given for an iron building to be provided and a contract was duly awarded to Humphries at a cost of £260. The provision of such a building was unpopular and by 15th January, 1901 the contract was withdrawn when it was decreed the building was to be of brick and tile not iron. A full six months elapsed before the contract for the erection of the brick cottage was awarded on 16th July, 1901 to W. Sutton at a cost of £255. The building was finally completed over a year later on 7th October, 1902, at an increased cost of £291. In the meantime gas prices at Upwell were reduced by 2s. 9d. per 1,000 cubic feet on 19th November, 1901. Whilst work was progressing on the cottage a contract for repairs and painting of the station and yard buildings at Upwell was awarded to Elsworthy & Company on 15th April, 1902 at a cost of £85.

A fatal accident occurred on Boxing Day 26th December, 1901, when 81-years-old Henry Upcroft, a roadman in the employ of Wisbech Rural District Council, attempted to join the 1.13pm train at Upwell. Just as the train started away the deceased tried to jump on the rear steps of the second coach but slipped and fell on the rail stunning himself. Unable to pick himself up, the wheels of the third coach in the formation ran over his body with fatal results. There were several passengers on the train including Dr C.H. Garman, a house surgeon at the North Cambridgeshire Hospital, who pronounced the man dead. The body was removed from under the train and deposited in the railway waiting room until the enquiry was concluded. The inquest was duly conducted by T.M. Reed, the Coroner of the Downham Division, the following Monday 30th December, 1901 in the clubroom of the Five Bells Hotel. George Ablitt, the Wisbech station master, represented the GER. Giving evidence William Collett, the conductor on the train, said he saw the man fall but could not attract the driver's attention to stop the train immediately. Michael O'Shea, the inspector in charge at Upwell tram station stated he gave the 'right away' to the

A busy time at Elm Road stopping point as passengers leave the Upwell to Wisbech train to make their way to the town centre. The train hauled by a 'G15' class 0-4-0 tram locomotive is formed of the entire passenger tramway stock, two bogie tramcars, six 4-wheel tramcars and 4-wheel brake van No. 16. The absence of road traffic is very evident.   *Cambridge Collection*

GER 'G15' class 0-4-0 tram locomotive No. 132 hauling the 11.45 am Wisbech to Upwell mixed train overtakes competitive transport near Inglethorpe Hall on 27th July, 1912.

LCGB/Ken Nunn Collection

conductor and turned to return to his office when he heard shouts from passengers on the train. He glanced round and saw the deceased hanging from the steps of the car before losing his grip and falling under the vehicle. He emphasized he was powerless to do anything to prevent the accident. The coroner recorded a verdict of accidental death.

On 2nd February, 1904 James Watson wrote to the BoT as he had been greatly agitated by the GER's decision to make improvements on the tramway. Whilst he had no qualms with the powers for fixing the stopping places or the better carriage accommodation he was concerned that a new and more powerful tram locomotive capable of hauling trains at an increased speed of 12 mph, instead of the stipulated 8 mph, was about to be introduced.

> On the line the present speed is very dangerous; a great many bad accidents have occurred, many people have been killed and injured and cattle and horses too. The damage to houses and other property is bad from the vibration and a great annoyance to occupiers of houses by the side of the line, also from the vibration caused by passing trams, especially at night.

The BoT considered the epistle but as no application had been made for an increase in speed, replied to assure Watson that there were no increased dangers.

Watson had certainly gained prior knowledge of the new motive power for the expiry of the seven year licence for steam operation of the tramway occurred in July 1904 and on the 2nd of the month James Gooday, the GER General Manager, wrote to the BoT requesting the necessary inspection and for an increase in speed limit from 8 mph to 12 mph, as complaints had been made that the tram service was too slow: 'a great waste of time as it now takes one hour to travel the six miles from terminus to terminus'. The company had also introduced a more powerful type of tram locomotive with 0-6-0 wheel arrangement but none were as yet operating on the Upwell tramway.

Colonel P.G. Von Donop conducted the re-inspection on 18th July, 1904, travelling by special train departing Wisbech at 11.40 am. As well as the usual railway officers, representatives of the Isle of Ely County Council, Norfolk County Council, Upwell and Outwell Rural District Councils attended and 'all supported the argument for increased speed'. The inspector found the tramway in a fair order and the locomotives and rolling stock appeared in good condition and fully compliant with the BoT Regulations. The Colonel could see no reason why the speed limit could not be raised to 12 mph as the line was mostly laid at the side of the road, well away from houses and clear of vehicular traffic. He, however, stipulated that the 8 mph speed limit should continue to apply at:

Elm Road Crossing
When crossing Newcommon bridge
Between Elm Brewery Siding and Elm Goods depot
When crossing the road adjacent to Outwell Post Office

A stop was also to be made before crossing the road at Outwell Village Goods depot, whilst speed through facing points was to be restricted to 4 mph. It was also agreed bye-law 5 was to be expunged and regulation iv was to alter the speed to 14 mph. Von Donop duly reported his findings on 23rd July but three

Chip baskets of fruit are loaded in to GER van No. 1836 at Wisbech goods depot by A. Baker, a grower from Emneth in the early years of the 20th century. During the soft fruit season similar scenes were enacted at depots on the tramway and goods yards at the main line stations radiating from Wisbech. *Author's Collection*

'G15' class 0-4-0 tram locomotive No. 131 hauls an up train from Upwell to Wisbech past the entrance to Inglethorpe Hall Estate. *Author's Collection*

days later James Watson was again complaining of the speed and resultant vibration. Despite the continuing doubts by local residents of the 12 mph speed limit, the GER advised the BoT on 2nd August, 1904 that a clause would be included in the next Bill being presented to Parliament.

The new year found James Watson again complaining but his epistle of 2nd March fell on deaf ears and the 12 mph speed limit was authorized by clause 20 of the GER (General Powers) Act of 1905. Sections 55 to 60 of the 1881 Act were also repealed by clause 20 of the new statute. On 9th November the GER requested the BoT to revise the Bye-law to incorporate the 12 mph speed limit and by 9th December, 1905 the draft regulation replacing the regulations dated 6th September, 1884, was circulated.

The Town Clerk of Wisbech wrote to the GER in January 1906 complaining of the 'excessive smoke' emitted from the tram engines, which constituted 'a great danger to the public'. On 19th of the month the Isle of Ely County Council wanted all the locations in clause 3 of the regulation where 8 mph was permitted to be reduced to 4 mph. Norfolk County Council added their voice to the growing list of speed restrictions by demanding a 4 mph speed limit at Outwell Post Office. The GER ignored the correspondence but in March 1906 there was further complaint from the Wisbech Town Clerk, 'notwithstanding the observations, the emission of steam and smoke from the tram engines still continues'. Ultimately the GER General Manager replied:

> Further to your letter the local authority must be under some misapprehension as I am informed that there is no smoke emitted by the engines. What probably is referred to, is the exhaust steam which of course during the cold weather is visible. The exhaust steam however is passed into a condenser when horses are passed and the company's servants are instructed to use every care in order to avoid any cause of complaint in this matter.

Soon after midnight Christmas Day 1906 (a Tuesday) a blizzard swept across north Norfolk and parts of Cambridgeshire and continued well into 26th December. The snow varied between 6 and 14 inches in depth with drifting in the high winds causing considerable delays to services on the Wymondham to Wells branch, the Lynn to Dereham line and between Wroxham and County School, whilst the Wisbech and Upwell tramway service was severely disorganized. Only three return services ran to Upwell on the Wednesday and the following day because of the condition of the track, all passenger trains operated with two engines on each trip. It was not possible to work goods traffic or mixed trains and urgent perishable items were conveyed in covered vans attached to the passenger services. Conditions had improved sufficiently for normal services to resume on the Friday.

The popularity of the tramway, especially during the summer months, resulted in overcrowding on some services. The GER management was reluctant to provide additional stock for the line, as the existing passenger fleet was adequate for most times of the year. In March 1907, however, plans were prepared with the possibility of providing seats on the roof of the two bogie tramcars. Stairs were to be provided at the end of the vehicle leading to a central gangway with two rows of seats on either side with reversible backs, so that they could be adjusted to the direction of travel. The scheme provided 40 additional seats. The strengthening of the roof and provision of railing around the sides of the roof were considered too costly as the seats could only be used in fine weather and the scheme was subsequently abandoned.

On 9th December, 1910 excessive rainfall resulted in the tramway flooding at Outwell village. Then on Thursday 12th December three-quarters of an inch of rail fell on Wisbech and the surrounding fens bringing the total to 3.26 inches for the first half of the month. Services on the tramway were seriously delayed as the track was waterlogged in several places and many sleepers were displaced from the underlying ballast. Working in atrocious conditions the permanent way gangs attempted to rectify faults quickly but the mission was nigh impossible and delays persisted for the next few days before the track bed was consolidated. Earnings on the tramway for 1910 were, however, encouraging with receipts of £4,819 against expenditure of £4,332, leaving a healthy profit of £487 for the year, 122,092 passengers had travelled and 14,549 tons of freight conveyed.

As the 1.11 pm train from Upwell to Wisbech was about to pass over the crossing by Outwell Post Office on Friday 8th September, 1911, a man riding a motor cycle attempted to pass in front of the engine and was knocked from his vehicle sustaining a fractured thigh and bruising. Witnesses agreed the train was travelling very slowly with the driver ringing the locomotive bell continuously. After the impact the train was brought to a stand within 15 feet. On 6th October, 1911 Southwell and Dennis, Solicitors advised the BoT that 'their client riding a bicycle had been run over by a speeding tram locomotive' and sought damages. The GER advised the BoT that on investigation they found the victim riding the motorcycle 'attempted to overtake a tram, which was going very slowly and stopped in only 5 yards with its engine bell ringing all the time'. He said he neither 'saw nor heard it' and duly lost any claim to compensation.

For the year 1912 the tramway carried 113,953 passengers and made an operating profit of £855, although the GER always considered the line as a feeder system for the main line rather than a self-contained and financing branch line.

On 17th November, 1913 Walter H. Hyde, the GER General Manager wrote to the BoT seeking official permission to introduce the larger and more powerful 0-6-0 tram engines on the Upwell tramway. Representatives of the class had been working on the Ipswich and Yarmouth dock lines since 1903. 'In order to deal expeditiously with traffic at certain times of the year, especially the fruit season, the Company Locomotive Superintendent considers it desirable that 6-coupled tram engines be used instead of 4 coupled engines. These locomotives were to be fitted with the Westinghouse brake with brake blocks on four of the six wheels and 'braking would be ample'. The BoT had no objections to the proposals provided the regulations authorized in 1905 were adhered to and No. 139 was the first to be sued on the tramway.

The tram stations had been included in the regular repairs and painting programme for infrastructure, the contract for the buildings at Upwell being awarded to Rands on 6th June, 1912 at a cost of £40, whilst on 23rd April, 1914 repairs and painting at Outwell Basin tram depot were authorized at a cost of £65 10s. 0d.

On 25th April, 1914 a horse-drawn trap owned by Frank Scott was approaching Boyce's Bridge when the horse became restive and backed the trap into the path of an approaching train. The tram locomotive driver was unable to brake the train in time to prevent a collision and in the ensuing melee one of the cart's wheels was torn off and Mrs Scott was thrown under the wheels of the last two wagons on the train. The unfortunate woman sustained serious injuries, which necessitated both legs being amputated.

In the spring of 1914 revised cartage arrangements were introduced at Wisbech, as traffic handled had increased by 31 per cent between 1912 and 1913, and this had a knock-on effect on the Upwell tramway when it became necessary to provide additional accommodation for fruit loading at Upwell. The alterations were sanctioned at a meeting of the Traffic Committee on 7th May when authority was given for the road in the yard to be extended to provide additional loading room at a cost of £145.

On 2nd July, 1914 Emneth Parish Council wrote requesting the provision of a danger signal at Chapel Lane, Emneth, the public having no warning of an approaching train as two large buildings flanked the road near the tramway. The GER had refused to consider the proposal four months earlier and the Council duly wrote to the BoT seeking their authority. On 19th August, 1914 the BoT supported the GER case and refused to sanction the provision of the signal considering it would set a precedent.

The outbreak of World War I on 4th August, 1914 found the GER, with other British railway companies under Government control. Train services continued to run to pre-war timetables and initially there was little disruption to the day-to-day operation of the tramway. Rather belatedly, the GER management agreed to provide a cottage for the goods foreman at Outwell, similar to the building at Upwell, and a contract was duly awarded to Elsworthy on 1st October, 1914 at a cost of £269 18s. 0d.

The Wisbech canal continued to run down over the years as traffic dwindled and more and more produce was conveyed on the tramway. Repairs to the ailing waterway could not be financed from receipts and the outlook was bleak. In 1914 canal tolls totalled a mere £35 from Wisbech and £21 from Outwell, the latter mostly onward transit of commodities brought by rail, and soon afterwards the canal was abandoned.

After the commencement of hostilities, the GER set up a War Relief Fund with collections being made at stations throughout the system. Collections from the tramway were incorporated with the takings at Wisbech and typical receipts were: three months ending 31st March, 1917 £3 7s. 9d., three months ending 30th September, 1917 £4 14s. 3d., £4 9s. 2d. for the next quarter and £4 5s. 6d. for the first quarter 1918.

The revenue earned by the Wisbech & Upwell Tramway for the year ending 31st December, 1914 makes interesting reading for it shows a considerable increase in both passenger and goods receipts, and extra passenger journeys compared with 1910:

	£	s.	d.
Passengers	1,337	7	10
Mails	16	0	0
Parcels, up to 2 cwt	37	10	6
Other merchandise by passenger train	55	8	3
Merchandise	3,923	4	4
Live stock	51	8	0
Coal and coke	343	4	6
Other minerals	329	18	10
Rents	31	12	1
Total	*6,125*	*14*	*4*

'G15' class 0-4-0 tram locomotive No 127 is in charge of the 10.25 am Wisbech to Upwell goods train near Elm Road brewery on 27th July, 1913. The train is formed of a GER covered van and a selection of GER and Midland Railway open wagons with a GER 20 ton goods brake van at the rear of the formation. The locomotive was withdrawn from traffic in December of the same year.
LCGB/Ken Nunn Collection

Brewery siding loop in 1911. The brewery was badly damaged by fire in the early hours of Wednesday 24th May, 1911, when the proprietor Percy Philips, his wife and their seven children escaped unhurt from the conflagration. The flames were extinguished by 6.00 am with firemen pumping water from the adjacent canal but not before spirits stored in the building had enhanced the inferno. *Author's Collection*

The number of passengers travelling in the same 12 month period showed a slight reduction compared with 1910 and was

First class	3,547*
Third class	114,340*
Total	*117,887**

* Return tickets counted as two single journeys.

By 1915 the public were warned that delays or cancellations could be caused by enemy action, however goods traffic flourished as increased produce was dispatched from local farms and fen estates to London and other towns and cities to make up for the loss of imported foods. Several local railwaymen answered the call to arms and some working on the tramway joined the colours. The war did not stop the GER from making improvements and by The Great Eastern Railway Act (5 and 6 Geo. 5 cap. xvi) which received the Royal Assent on 9th June, 1915, the company was authorized to acquire additional land on the south-east boundary of Outwell Village depot for the purpose of providing improved facilities for traders loading and unloading wagons.

As the years progressed so the strain of the war was taxing the resources of the railways and, in December 1916, the Railway Executive Committee issued an ultimatum to the effect they would only carry on if drastic reductions were made to the ordinary services, as locomotive power was short through lack of coal supplies. The Lloyd George Coalition Government thus agreed to the reduction of passenger services from 1st January, 1917, but despite this edict the tramway services were unaffected as extra freight trains were operated, some conveying a coach for passenger use. British farmers and growers were urged to increase yet further the production of vegetables and fruit to offset the deficit of imports caused by enemy action against shipping. Growers and breeders of Cambridgeshire, Norfolk and the Isle of Ely, like their counterparts all over the country rallied to the call and as a result a considerable number of additional freight trains were operated on the Upwell tramway. As the war years progressed, hay traffic also increased as fodder and bedding was required by the many military establishments in East Anglia. The tramway was not so strategically placed as many other East Anglian branches and few military personnel were carried. For the occasional military exercises conducted in the area most men were conveyed by motor lorry, whilst special trains conveyed the horses.

After the cessation of hostilities on Armistice Day (11th November, 1918) flags were displayed at some of the tram depots and gradually the affairs of the tramway returned to as normal as they could after the war to end all wars. The conflict had affected Wisbech and every hamlet and village served by the line, for many men had not returned from the conflict. Early in 1919 Essex County Council sought the advice of the GER on the future development of light railways and were invited to inspect the Wisbech and Upwell tramway. The *Essex Weekly News* of 21st February, 1919 set out the sub-committee's recommendation for nine schemes and the report was subsequently sent to the Ministry of Reconstruction, Department of Agriculture and Essex Members of Parliament.

The junction of the Wisbech canal (*left*), Well creek (*centre*) and the River Nene Old Course (*right*) with Outwell Village depot goods yard dominated by the tower of St Clement's church. Wagons in the yard include a Great Northern Railway open and an Austin & Company private owner open. In its heyday a considerable tonnage of coal was offloaded into fenland lighters for conveyance to isolated locations via fenland waterways.   *Author's Collection*

A down train from Wisbech to Upwell hauled by 'G15' class 0-4-0 tram locomotive No. 126 departing from Outwell Village depot and about to cross Church Terrace level crossing No. 12 with Isle Bridge over the River Nene (Old Course) in the foreground. The depot foreman is on the crossing to stop road traffic. The parish church of St Clement's overlooks the scene.

Author's Collection

In April 1919, the *Great Eastern Railway Magazine* extolled the virtues of the line and reported: 'The tramway carried over 2,700 passengers on a recent Saturday. On one trip the six miles journey was done in the scheduled 39 minutes including twelve stops *en route*, with all cars and three loaded cattle trucks. Not bad for a small four coupled tram engine'. However, the seeds of competition against the railway came to fruition in 1919 when the Eastern Counties Road Car Co. Ltd was formed and took over certain routes operated by Thomas Tilling. Five routes were initially operated with 12 double-deck petrol electric buses and in 1920 and 1921 services commenced in Wisbech, and by the end of that year the company owned 40 vehicles. On Thursday 20th May, 1920 the company introduced a bus service between Wisbech and Three Holes following the same route as the tramway and very quickly rail travellers found the competitive bus overtaking their train as it meandered along at its obligatory maximum speed of 12 mph. Certainly the support for the railway had been dented by a damaging but short-lived railway strike, which lasted from 26th September to 8th October, 1919 when all services were suspended and the new bus services added to the management's problems. Then in 1921 the miners' strike affected coal supplies although services were not curtailed but this industrial action and the later General Strike of 1926 began the serious decline in railway services. Farmers and growers realized that with improving roads, goods could be conveyed by lorry, using, in some cases, vehicles purchased second-hand from the army permitting short-haul journeys at a far quicker speed than the tramway and at cheaper rates than charged by the GER. The door-to-door services were more convenient than the double-handling caused by loading and unloading into and out of railway wagons. The primitive commercial vehicles of the day were not, however, capable of continuous long hauls and the middle and long distance traffic remained safely in the lands of the railway company. In the meantime the competing Eastern Counties bus service was extended to Welney from 9th June, 1921 and given route numbers 21 and 21A but the entire service was abruptly discontinued on 29th June, 1922 leaving the railway as the sole public operator.

To emphasize the importance of the tramway, in the spring of 1922 members of Elm Parish Council, Isle of Ely County Council, Emneth Parish Council and Wisbech and District Fruit Growers Association gathered together and jointly petitioned the GER of the need for improvements in facilities at Elm Bridge depot. The Traffic Committee discussed the matter on 16th June, 1922 and learned the accommodation at that depot was insufficient to cope with the growth of traffic. Congestion was created especially in the vegetable and fruit loading season when wagons were standing across the main running lines whilst being loaded. The practice was considered dangerous for staff and train operations and the engineer provided plans for a new siding and loop line at a cost of £1,490. Annual maintenance was estimated at £15 5s. 0d. The tonnage of produce loaded at the siding had been increasing steadily from 2,431 tons in 1913 to 3,521 tons in 1919, 3,216 tons in 1920 and 2,038 tons in 1921. The reduced loadings in 1920 and 1921 had been influenced by the poor weather. Authority was duly given for the work to be carried out and the task was completed by the early summer. Results for June to October 1922 were encouraging when Wisbech dispatched 15,609 tons of fruit by goods and passenger train, with the majority coming from depots on the tramway. Thus the GER, prior to amalgamation with other companies to form the

After the turn of the century the fencing separating the passenger terminal from the goods yard at Upwell was removed. The former ground level platform soon became littered with fruit baskets as 'G15' class 0-4-0 tram locomotive No. 125 waits to depart for Wisbech. Her train is formed of a 4-wheel tram, bogie tram, then 4-wheel passenger brake No. 16 and two horseboxes. Another tram locomotive is standing on the run-round loop headshunt probably taking water from the adjacent water column. Another hazard for an intending passengers was the horse droppings in the foreground.   *Author's Collection*

A passenger train from Wisbech has just arrived at Upwell and 'G15' class 0-4-0 tram locomotive No. 134 is waiting to run-round its train formed of a passenger brake van and three passenger tramcars. Beyond the passenger terminal can be seen the roof of the coal storage ground used by local fuel merchants. The passenger building bears an ornate porch over the main entrance.
                                                                                          Author's Collection

Compared with earlier views of Upwell, the vegetation has been allowed to grow and the track and platform have an unkempt appearance. An unidentified 'G15' class 0-4-0 tram locomotive and her train await hopefully for passengers before departing for Wisbech.
Author's Collection

London & North Eastern Railway (LNER) (*see next chapter*), was encouraging the continuing use of the roadside tramway before handing over to the new management. Their cause was not helped in October 1922 when Charles Robb of Outwell reintroduced the competitive bus service between Wisbech and Three Holes using buses purchased from the London General Omnibus Company. Trying times were ahead, especially for the tramway passenger traffic, and questions were asked as to whether it would survive under the new regime.

A down mixed train hauled by 'G15' class 0-4-0 tram locomotive No. 0125 is halted at Elm Road stopping point. Behind the locomotive are two of the GER sundry vans, later converted to Fruit Traffic Office Vans by the LNER and no doubt used for the same purpose by the GER. The three rear vehicles forming the passenger accommodation are passenger brake van No 16, a bogie tram and a four-wheel tram. A road sweeper has taken position by the train in this posed photograph in place of the guard. *Author's Collection*

	Passengers	Passenger receipts £	Parcels receipts £	Season Ticket receipts £	Total £
1923					
Wisbech	98,007	15,479	7,856	604	23,939
Elm Depot	15,446	108	1,914		2,022
Boyce's Depot	7,561	96	286		382
Outwell Basin*	6,974	122	567		689
Outwell Village*			367		367
Upwell	24,656	517	2,247		2,764
Total for branch	54,637	843	5,381		6,224
1924					
Wisbech	102,459	15,149	7,377	870	23,396
Elm Depot	14,233	94	1,501		1,595
Boyce's Depot	6,573	83	123		206
Outwell Basin*	7282	126	768		894
Outwell Village*			222		222
Upwell	20,105	418	4,090		4,508
Total for branch	48,193	721	6,704		7,425
1925					
Wisbech	106,772	15,350	7,609	808	23,767
Elm Depot	15,154	105	1,488		1,593
Boyce's Depot	7,248	91	345		436
Outwell Basin*	7,792	136	665		801
Outwell Village*			1,081		1,081
Upwell	23,469	481	4,107		4,588
Total for branch	53,663	813	7,686		8,499
1926					
Wisbech	87,873	12,821	7,120	687	20,628
Elm Depot	11,663	80	1,465		1,545
Boyce's Depot	9,544	102	33		135
Outwell Basin*	7,896	114	923		1,037
Outwell Village*			194		194
Upwell	24,442	427	3,624		4,051
Total for branch	53,545	723	6,239		6,962
1927					
Wisbech	92,506	12,936	6,146	638	19,720
Elm Depot	11,902	78	1,209		1,287
Boyce's Depot	11,009	115	49		164
Outwell Basin*	8,173	120	681		801
Outwell Village*			168		168
Upwell	26,641	435	2,947		3,382
Total for branch	57,725	748	5,054		5,802

* Outwell Basin and Outwell Village passenger totals and passenger receipts combined.

Chapter Four

Grouping and Decline

In accordance with the 1921 Railways Act, from 1st January, 1923 the GER was amalgamated with the Great Northern, Great Central, North Eastern, North British and several smaller railway companies to form the London & North Eastern Railway. Industrial action soon affected affairs when a seven day railway strike from 24th January, 1924 brought a further decline in traffic. The new regime had made few initial alterations to the Tramway but for some time fruit growers had complained about delays incurred in the dispatch of their traffic. The area of cultivation had increased considerably and there was serious inadequacy of accommodation in the goods yards, which retarded loading and working of trains on the line. The chief goods manager, reporting to the Traffic Committee on 19th February, 1925, proposed the provision of two additional sidings at Wisbech with access for carts accommodating 58 wagons and another siding for the stowage of 45 wagons costing an estimated £1,967. An additional siding with road access to accommodate 40 wagons was also proposed at Outwell Basin costing £1,935 whilst at Upwell two, later amended to four additional sidings, one with road access, accommodating 68 wagons were required costing £3,550. The expenditure was duly authorized, together with expenditure for sidings at Emneth and Smeeth Road on the Wisbech to Magdalen Road line.

The centenary of the opening of the Stockton & Darlington Railway was celebrated by the LNER in July 1925 by a cavalcade of railway locomotives from various railway companies. Probably one of the strangest in the procession was the Wisbech and Upwell 'Y6 'class 0-4-0 tram locomotive No. 7133, which as exhibit 35 and in spotless livery, trundled past the viewing galleries and enclosures minus cowcatchers and side aprons. The *Northern Echo* newspaper reported, 'A roar of laughter greeted the appearance of what appeared to be a cross between a railway engine and a guard's van'.

The tramway services were again affected by the General Strike in early May 1926. Union members withdrew their labour in support of the miners and subsequently train services could not be guaranteed and on several days rail services around Wisbech were suspended. Fortunately within a week or so regular railwaymen returned to work but the impact of the continuing miners strike meant coal stocks to the railway companies were low. The LNER authorities decided on the only course of action available and reduced train services to conserve coal supplies. From 31st May, 1926, when the revised timetable was introduced, the Upwell tramway service was reduced by two trains in each direction for a short period of time. Further inroads into the tramway passenger services came in March 1927 when an independent operator, Mr Washington of Littleport, provided further bus competition introducing a Monday to Saturday service between Wisbech and Three Holes, running on roads alongside the railway and providing an almost door-to-door and speedier service for patrons. Despite the competition the tramway passenger numbers fluctuated little, save for 1926 when the General Strike brought a reduction.

'Y6' class 0-4-0 tram locomotive No. 7133 waits in the back platform at Wisbech in the 1920s with a mixed train for Upwell. The first two vehicles in the formation are ex-Great Northern Railway and ex-North Eastern Railway horseboxes followed by a goods brake van and two 4-wheel tramcars. *Author's Collection*

LNER warning notice posted above the doorway inside tramcar.

L. N. E. R.

PASSENGERS ARE NOT ALLOWED TO TRAVEL ON THE OUTSIDE PLATFORM OF THE CAR, AND ARE CAUTIONED NOT TO ATTEMPT TO ALIGHT FROM THE CAR WHILE IN MOTION.

Curiously enough over the five years the number of passengers travelling and receipts were almost constant. In 1923 an average of 1,051 passengers were booking tickets at the tram depots or on the tram each week, compared with 1,032 in 1925 and 1,110 in 1927. The average weekly passenger receipts in the same period were £16 4s. 0d. in 1923, increasing to £16 12s. 6d. in 1925 and reducing to £14 7s. 6d. in the final year of operation. The cost of operating the line in 1925 was £10,229. The steady increase in competitive bus services on improving roads was a continuing cause for concern to the management. Buses were improving in design with the comfort of passengers paramount and compared to the spartan luxury offered to rail travellers riding in the increasingly ageing tramcars, there was no comparison. The bus companies offered better journey times between Wisbech and Upwell than by rail and it was obvious to the authorities at Liverpool Street and Marylebone that the situation would not improve, even in the long term. The only course of action was to operate the tramway exclusively for freight traffic and withdraw the passenger services.

Early in December 1927 the LNER authorities duly announced that the passenger services between Wisbech and Upwell would be withdrawn on and from Monday 2nd January, 1928 but as the line was closed on Sundays the last trains ran on Saturday 31st December, 1927. The *Wisbech Advertiser* of 4th January, 1928 reported the passing of the passenger service:

> Among the obituary notices of the beginning of the new year is that of one which, though honoured for past services does not seem to warrant the wearing of crepe or even the bestowal of a wreath. The passing of the passenger train from the Wisbech to Upwell seems to have called for little protest and the only points which have been raised are those of public rights and the carriage of flowers to catch the train to the market. The former seems to have inspired little enthusiasm and the latter, no doubt, will be dealt with by the proper organisation so that a growing industry in more sense than one may not be handicapped.

Amongst those travelling on the last train was Councillor Charles T. White, who as a three-month-old babe in arms travelled on the first train in 1883. The inaugural journey was slightly delayed as it stalled on the tight curve at Newcommon bridge but passengers' annoyance was humoured when his father William White claimed the stoppage was caused by the extra weight of his son! The *Wisbech Advertiser* concluded:

> So passes the tram, sometimes it is said the full appreciation of the service remembered is not attained until sometime after the decease of the person or instrument and it will be interesting to note how much this departure will affect the public in future and whether the memory will occasion any thoughtful regrets or only an appreciation of the way it served its day and generation.

Outwell Bus Services announced that from 4th January, 1928 return tickets would be available on Wednesdays and Fridays, except for Bank and Public Holidays between Wisbech and the intermediate villages. From the following day additional buses would operate on Thursdays and Fridays, departing Wisbech at 2.45 and 5.30 pm and from Three Holes at 1.15 and 4.30 pm, all journeys being operated via Emneth.

On the last day of passenger train operation, 31st December, 1927, a Wisbech to Upwell passenger train hauled by a 'Y6' class 0-4-0 tram locomotive negotiates the awkward gradients and curves over Newcommon bridge in wintry weather.   *Author's Collection*

On the final day of passenger train operation 31st December, 1927 'Y6' class 0-4-0 tram locomotive No. 7133 passes the snow-clad Boyce's Bridge depot with a down freight train. In the formation are Coote and Warren and Clay Cross private owner coal wagons.
                                                                    Author's Collection

In July 1928 Peterborough Electric Traction Company introduced a daily bus service, Route 60, between Wisbech and Three Holes, which within days was extended to Welney and three months later the company purchased outright the business of Robb of Outwell. The Peterborough company control had been passed to the joint ownership of Tilling and the BAT companies in May 1928 and the LNER and London Midland & Scottish Railway purchased a financial interest in the undertaking in December 1929. The undertaking was later absorbed into the Eastern Counties Omnibus Company on 14th July, 1931 and during the lifetime of the Upwell tramway they operated their service 360 between Wisbech, Welney and Ely.

Parcel receipts for the year 1928 were slightly down on the previous years as some traffic was now conveyed by road:

	£
Wisbech	6,370
Elm Depot	1,191
Boyce's Depot	66
Outwell Basin	716
Outwell Village	210
Upwell	2,788
Total for branch	*4,971*

After the withdrawal of passenger services the tramway coaching stock was placed into store until further use was found for six of the vehicles, which were transferred to the Kelvedon & Tollesbury Light Railway in Essex in September and December 1928, and January 1929. The LNER authorities also arranged for Wisbech station to be repaired and repainted. Estimated at £400, the contract was awarded on 21st March, 1929 to N.S. Long who tendered at £322 16s. 0d. The redundant timber carriage shed beside the engine shed at Wisbech was also demolished but the rails remained *in situ* as a locomotive siding.

A scheme, which indirectly affected the Upwell tramway, was the proposal made on 26th June, 1930 for the replacement of Wisbech Harbour Junction signal box by a ground frame. The Divisional General Manager (Southern Area) explained to the Traffic Committee that the ground frame would be used to control the gates of the adjacent level crossing, which were at that time controlled by the signalman. The scheme involved the appointment of one resident and one non-resident crossing keeper to take charge of the crossing. Nearby was a cottage owned by the LNER occupied by one of the signalmen whose wife attended to the crossing over the Upwell tramway, located 20 yards from Harbour Junction signal box. For this duty the lady received 2s. 6d. per week whilst the cottage was rent free. The new resident crossing keeper would occupy the gate cottage rent free in consideration of the service to be performed by his wife in attending to the crossing over the tramway for which she would receive the weekly payment of 2s. 6d. The cost of the scheme was estimated at £291 less £10 for recovered materials. The current annual cost of wages of the three signalmen, including night duty was £417 whilst uniform, insurance and holiday pay amounted to £27. The maintenance and repairs to the signal box was £67. Against this total cost of £511, the proposed annual wages for the

Wisbech engine shed in December 1927 showing 'Y6' class 0-4-0 locomotives Nos. 07126 and 07125 waiting their next turn of duty outside the newer building dating from 1893. Note the tramcar on middle stabling road to the right. *The late H.C. Casserley*

'Y6' class 0-4-0 tram locomotive No. 07125 stands at Wisbech on 25th June, 1929 prior to working the 12.40 pm empty van train for fruit traffic from Wisbech to Upwell. The leading vehicle is 62085 a former GER six-wheel brake third vehicle acting as a fruit traffic office van.

The late H.C. Casserley

'Y6' class 0-4-0 tram locomotive No. 7134 trundles along the up main line on the approach to Wisbech station on 25th June, 1929. The Upwell tramline is to the right, with the starting signal for the tramway in the foreground.   *The late H.C. Casserley*

'Y6' class 0-4-0 tram locomotive No. 07125 standing at Upwell with the 12.40 pm fruit empties from Wisbech on 25th June, 1929. The second vehicle in the train is the six-wheel brake third, LNER No. 62085.   *The late H.C. Casserley*

On 6th July, 1932 as local fruitgrower Robert Allen was returning from Outwell Basin after delivering a consignment of strawberries the animal pulling the cart shied and backed the vehicle into the 3.30 pm train from Upwell as it passed Horn's Corner. The cart was smashed and the unfortunate Allen killed.   *Lilian Ream Gallery*

On Thursday 20th April, 1933 driver Kenneth Johnson, accompanied by Henry Hulme, was taking a lorry loaded with cattle towards Wisbech when the steering failed. The vehicle swerved off the road and guided by the rails of the adjacent tramway travelled a distance of 28 yards before somersaulting into the canal. Unfortunately Hulme was killed but the driver and cattle survived the impact.   *Liliam Ream Gallery*

resident and non-resident crossing keepers' was £237, with uniforms, insurance and holiday pay totalling £17. The annual maintenance cost of the ground frame was £34 bringing the total to £288 and realising a net saving of £223 per annum. The outlay of £291 was readily agreed but the scheme was later deferred and ultimately withdrawn. Wisbech Harbour Junction signal box survived and was finally abolished when the Wisbech to Magdalen Road line closed on and from 9th September, 1968.

Early in 1931 the Isle of Ely County Council approached the railway authorities regarding the danger to traffic on Newcommon bridge. The Council recommended widening the bridge, which carried the Upwell Tramway and a public road over the Wisbech canal. The LNER authorities replied: 'The bridge was quite sufficient for their purposes' but 'if the council wished to carry out the work at their own expense the Company would have no objections provided the plans and specifications were approved by railway engineers'. The Council subsequently decided to replace the bridge with an embankment with a four feet diameter culvert for the passage of the water in the canal which by this time was disused. The works required the slewing of the Wisbech & Upwell Tramway to a new position clear of the road. The LNER was responsible for the maintenance of the railway but with the construction of the embankment the obligation would cease. The Council duly asked the LNER to contribute towards the legal costs of £50 and this was agreed on 4th June, 1931, together with a sum of £50 to reposition the rails and £22 for resurfacing of the road previously occupied by the tramway. The full agreement was signed and sealed on 9th July and work was completed in 1932, abolishing the awkward gradients previously encountered on the approach to the bridge.

Two incidents then occurred involving the tramway over which the railway company had no control. Local fruit grower Robert Allen (age 65) was taking his horse-drawn cart home near Horn's Corner after delivering a consignment of strawberries to Outwell Basin on Wednesday 6th July, 1932 as the 3.30 pm tram from Upwell to Wisbech was approaching. Unfortunately for Allen the animal shied as the train neared, before rearing up and backing the cart into the path of the tram locomotive with tragic consequencies for the fruit grower. Then on Thursday 20th April, 1933 motor driver Kenneth Johnson and his mate Henry Hulme were taking a lorry loaded with five cattle along the main road near Collett's Bridge when the vehicle's steering failed. The lorry veered towards the tramway and guided by the rails travelled 28 yards towards Wisbech before overturning and somersaulting into the Wisbech canal. Johnson and the five animals managed to escape but unfortunately Hulme was killed in the accident.

During the mid-1930s the LNER authorities were seeking ways of reducing costs, including permanent way maintenance. After investigating the March to Magdalen Road line and the Upwell tramway, the Divisional General Manager (Southern Area) reported to the Works Committee that the Coldham to Wisbech double line and the Tramway equated to 13½ route miles, whilst the single line mileage including sidings was 29. It was thought road transport would prove a more economical way of conveying men to site than a rail motor with lineside equipment. The cost of a 30 cwt road motor with a garage and a bicycle was estimated at £244 gross or £243 net, whilst the number of men in the gang could be reduced from 15 to 13 giving a net saving of £109 per annum. The new arrangement was duly authorized on 30th January, 1936 and introduced later in the same year.

After years of neglect the depots on the Upwell tramway received some needy repairs and painting in 1937. The work, which included sites on the Wisbech Harbour branch estimated at £155, was awarded to J. Arundell & Company on 22nd July after they tendered at the reduced price of £119 12s. 2d. by using the spray paint method.

Just prior to the outbreak of World War II from 3rd September, 1939, the LNER with other major railway companies came under the control of the Railway Executive Committee. Once hostilities were confirmed staff utilized shielded hand lamps to attend to train and shunting duties during the hours of darkness as a precaution against air raids. In order to hinder possible enemy invasion station nameboards were removed and stored in lock-up buildings. The agricultural nature of the freight at all branch depots was of the utmost importance in the war years as vital provisions of home grown food, vegetables, grain, fruit and sugar beet were dispatched and conveyed to markets. In addition to the outward flow of commodities, the war bought an influx of tinned fruit and dried milk for distribution to the Ministry of Food storage depots in the area. As a precaution against attacks by enemy invasion, several bridges on the line were protected by anti-tank barricades ('dragon's teeth') including Newcommon bridge.

A fatal accident occurred during the hostilities on 22nd June, 1943 at Upwell when 43-year-old goods porter W.A. Crouch sustained severe chest injuries whilst sheeting a wagon and died almost instantly. At the subsequent BoT enquiry, conducted by inspecting officer J. Birch, it was established the accident was not witnessed although Crouch had been seen on the wagon a few moments earlier. From the evidence given there was little doubt that the deceased was crushed between the buffers of two wagons. The wagon on which Crouch was working was in the rear of 24 vans when it was drawn out of the siding and was then the first of 16 to be loose shunted, mostly one at a time, on to the main line ready to form an up departure. When the vehicle came to rest against a brake van, which had been secured 200 yards from the points, foreman Wilson Peacock decided it was necessary to provide a tarpaulin sheet on the wagon. Crouch assisted Peacock with the work and was still on the vehicle when the foreman descended the ladder in use in order to go to the toilet located on the same side and a short distance beyond the brake van. A few minutes later as Peacock returned he saw Crouch stagger away from the buffers but on the opposite side of the wagon to that, which the ladder was mounted. Birch had no reason to doubt the foreman's statement that there was no prior opportunity for sheeting the wagon in question, but thought there was risk in the actions taken by both Peacock and Crouch in climbing on to the wagon before it and other wagons in the line had been properly secured. The deceased would then have been exposed to less danger whilst passing through the gap between the buffers instead of being trapped by the closing up of the buffers from a vehicle being loose shunted. The inspecting officer found no blame on the part of the guard of the train being formed, as he was not aware of Peacock's intentions to sheet the wagon and concluded the blame rested entirely with Crouch. Although he had only been working for the LNER for a month prior to the accident, Crouch had worked at Upwell during previous fruit harvesting seasons and was fully aware of the local procedures and should not have taken unnecessary risks, which unfortunately led to his death.

In 1941 two of the 'Y6' class 0-4-0 tram engines Nos. 7133 and 7134, were loaned to work wagons of sugar beet on the Wissington Light Railway which branched off the neighbouring Downham to Stoke Ferry branch at Abbey and West Dereham station, but as they were prone to derailment they were replaced by two of the 'J70' class 0-6-0 tram locomotives in 1943. The pair worked on the fens until 1944 before returning to their native haunts. One of the 0-4-0 locomotives No. 7134 found further employment in 1943 with the United States Army Transportation Corps at Burton-on-Trent and later with the Royal Army Ordnance Corps at Derby before returning to Wisbech in 1944. During the latter years of the war, Italian Prisoners of War based at the nearby Friday Bridge camp were conveyed by tram to work in the fields.

After the war the railways resumed peacetime activities with run-down and life-expired rolling stock and equipment, and stations and depots in need of maintenance. Questions were raised in Parliament regarding the deteriorating service provided by the LNER and the poor condition of the rolling stock. The Wisbech & Upwell Tramway was no exception and frequently the company was unable to provide wagons to local traders. More seriously the branch freight train was sometimes cancelled because Wisbech shed was unable to provide a tram locomotive for one of the diagrams. Severe weather early in 1947 with heavy snowfalls caused further delays to services and on more than one occasion a freight train had to be dug out of a drift as snow blew off the fields across the roads and rails of the tramway. During the spring and summer availability of rolling stock improved, and it was hoped the impending Nationalisation of the railways would provide fresh impetus in the drive to increase freight traffic and receipts on the tramway.

'J70' class 0-6-0 tram locomotive No. 7130 raises the echoes and blackens the surrounding countryside on 2nd July, 1946 as she passes Shepherd's Cottage with a lengthy train of vans during the height of the fruit picking season.   *A.F. Cook*

'J70' class 0-6-0 tram locomotive No. 68217 runs light engine alongside the River Nene (Old Course) between Goodman's Corner and Outwell Village depot on 25th August, 1950.
The late H.C. Casserley

'J70' class 0-6-0 tram locomotive No 68217 departs from Outwell Village depot with the 12.45 pm Wisbech to Upwell train formed of empty covered vans for fruit traffic on 25th August, 1950. The tramway is wedged between the road and the River Nene Old Course just visible to the left.
The late H.C. Casserley

Chapter Five

Nationalisation and Closure

The Nationalisation of the railways from 1st January, 1948 brought little change to the Upwell tramway and the line initially retained its GE/LNER atmosphere. The tram engines soon lost their NE or LNER identity in lieu of 'BRITISH RAILWAYS' on the side tanks, whilst wagons soon appeared in the BR corporate colours of grey for unfitted stock and bauxite for fitted vehicles. The easing of petrol rationing allowed road transport to make further inroads into the freight traffic, as the local haulage contractors soon attracted trade with their door-to-door service obviating the loading and unloading of wagons in the local goods depots. Livestock traffic also declined rapidly as cattle, horses and occasionally sheep for local markets almost wholly transferred to road transport. From 27th September, 1948 the former GER station at Wisbech was re-titled Wisbech East to differentiate it from the former Midland & Great Northern Railway (M&GN) station, which became Wisbech North.

The quaintness of the tram locomotives and the peculiarity of roadside running soon attracted railway enthusiasts to sample a journey on the tramway and on Wednesday 7th June, 1950 Cambridge University Railway Club availed themselves of a trip, the first of several; members travelling in two brake vans added to the formation of a normal service train for the occasion. In the same month Wisbech Harbour was renamed to Wisbech Harbour East, whilst the former M&GN Harbour branch was renamed Wisbech Harbour North. BR was at that time seriously investigating the replacement of steam shunting locomotives with diesel shunting locomotives to reduce the costs of yard shunting and short trip working. At the end of 1951 the Railway Executive, Eastern Region considered the ageing tram locomotives working the Upwell tramway and at other locations in East Anglia were priority for substitution by the modern diesels. The Railway Executive subsequently placed an initial order with the Drewry Car Company Limited for thirteen 204 bhp diesel-mechanical shunting locomotives and the first four, Nos. 11100 to 11103 inclusive, were delivered as tram engines being equipped with side valances, cowcatchers and a governor which put the final drive out of mesh at speeds over 12 mph. Initially No. 11102 was allocated to work on the Upwell tramway and the first Wisbech to Upwell diesel-hauled train ran on Wednesday 4th June, 1952 conveying members of the Cambridge University Railway Club on the 12.55 pm return working from Upwell; an additional guard's van being provided for railway club members.

The declared intention was to operate the diesel locomotives on the tramway in the fruit season and, if necessary, disperse the class to other work during the winter and spring when the 'J70' class 0-6-0 tram engines would work the services. It was proposed to change over to full diesel locomotive operation from 4th July, 1952. Teething troubles deferred the official changeover to August 1952, by which time No. 11101 had joined her sister at Wisbech from her previous allocation of Yarmouth. Because of frequent diesel failures 'J70' class

'J70' class 0-6-0 tram locomotives Nos. 68217 and 68225 stand in the sunshine outside Wisbech shed on 25th August, 1950. The well-filled coal stage is to the left and the sand bins to the right. Alongside the shed is stabled a Gresley corridor coach. Note the locomotive inspection pits in the shed roads; when the newer shed was demolished on the introduction of diesel traction, the corresponding inspection pit was filled in.   *The late H.C. Casserley*

'J70' class 0-6-0 tram locomotive No. 68217 standing at Small Lode level crossing with the 12.45 pm Wisbech to Upwell freight train on 25th August, 1950. In the right hand side of the cab is the youthful R.M. Casserley son of the late H.C. Casserley, whilst driver Albert South is standing by the locomotive.   *The late H.C. Casserley*

'J70' class 0-6-0 tram locomotive No. 68217 hauls the 12.45 pm train to Upwell through Wisbech East station on 25th August, 1950. The train formed mostly of empty vans for up road traffic is being routed through the up platform instead of the back platform in order to gain access to the tramway. *The late H.C. Casserley*

'J70' class 0-6-0 tram locomotive No. 68217 sets off along Elm High Road with the 1.50 pm Wisbech to Upwell goods train formed of engine and brake van on Tuesday 28th August, 1951. In the cab are fireman Arthur Banyard, driver Albert South and guard Tim Downes. The train has just come off the former Newcommon bridge curve with Brown's Newcommon Bridge Stores in the left background - a family business established in the 1830s. *LCGB/Ken Nunn Collection*

'J70' class 0-6-0 tram locomotive No. 68217 negotiates Ramnoth Road crossing No. 2 and over the site of the former Newcommon bridge with the 11.50 am Upwell to Wisbech goods train on 28th August, 1951.   *LCGB/Ken Nunn Collection*

There is no traffic to collect from Boyce's Bridge depot as 'J70' class 0-6-0 tram locomotive No. 68225 takes the main single line *en route* from Upwell to Wisbech. The loop siding is parallel to the main single line, whilst the depot office is to the centre. Covered vans are stabled in the back siding.   *Stations UK*

'J70' class 0-6-0 tram locomotive No. 68225 heads past Outwell Basin depot with an Upwell to Wisbech train. In the centre is the goods yard entrance gate from the main Wisbech to Downham road and the depot office alongside. To the left is the former passenger waiting room, ex-GER first class family saloon No. 5 built in 1864 and withdrawn in 1897, long converted to a parcels store at this depot. *Stations UK*

'J70' class 0-6-0 tram locomotive No. 68225, with lion and wheel emblem on the side tanks, at Elm Bridge depot with a short train *en route* from Upwell to Wisbech comprising two open wagons, a covered van and a former Great Central Railway goods brake van. *Author's Collection*

The Railway Club brake van special train hauled by Drewry 204 hp 0-6-0 diesel-mechanical locomotive No. 11101 *en route* from Upwell to Wisbech crossing Elm Road at the Duke of Wellington open crossing No. 3 at 1 mile 28 chains from Wisbech on 9th July, 1955.

The late B.D.J. Walsh

The Railway Club brake van special train hauled by Drewry 204 hp 0-6-0 diesel-mechanical locomotive No. 11101 stands in the up main line platform at Wisbech after arrival from Upwell on 9th July, 1955.

The late B.D.J. Walsh

0-6-0 No. 68222 was retained for use on the tramway and was last used in March 1953 when, with driver Charlie Rand at the controls, she deputised for the ailing diesel locomotive. Diesel locomotives Nos. 11101 and 11102 became members of BR class '2/13', later class '04' and were subsequently renumbered D2201 in December 1961 and D2202 in January 1958 respectively, and allocated to March depot for repairs and maintenance.

On Friday 3rd September, 1954 a lorry bound for Outwell came into collision with the 11.50 am Upwell to Wisbech train near the Duke of Wellington road crossing. Needless to say the lorry suffered considerable damage finishing up on its left-hand side alongside the railway. By 1954 most of the permanent way of the tramway had been relaid, a process started in 1947 and continued piecemeal, with second-hand rails removed from the main line.

The withdrawal of the steam tram locomotives did not deter railway enthusiasts from the uniqueness of the roadside line in East Anglia, for on 9th July, 1955 members of the Railway Club travelled across the tramway with diesel locomotive No. 11101 hauling three goods brake vans. In the following year on 9th September, 1956 the Railway Correspondence & Travel Society 'Fensman No. 2' Railtour visited the Upwell tramway. The participants having departed Kings Cross for Peterborough then travelled to Whittlesea for a visit to the Three Horse Shoes to Benwick goods branch, where they were hauled in open wagons by 'J17' class 0-6-0 tender locomotive No. 65562. After returning to Whittlesea the 310 participants rejoined their main line train hauled by 'B1' class 4-6-0 No. 61391 of New England shed for the short run to Wisbech before transferring again to open wagons for the trip to Upwell. The 15 open wagons and two brake vans provided for passengers on the tramway were hauled by diesel locomotive No. 11102, with the engine carrying a suitable headboard, but unfortunately most of the journey was made in torrential driving rain.

By the late 1950s road transport continued to attract greater tonnages of goods traffic in rural Cambridgeshire, Norfolk and the Isle of Ely and BR marketing officials found it increasingly difficult to persuade farmers and growers to increase their use of the tramway facilities. Many conveyed small consignments of produce direct by road or conveyed it to Wisbech East goods yard for onward transit, thereby saving precious time on perishable produce getting to market. The situation had deteriorated to such an extent that in 1961 British Railways proposed to close the tramway, but such was the opposition from local fruit growers that the decision was deferred. Closure was to come by stealth over a protracted period of time.

Rationalisation of sorts took place at Wisbech station when footbridge No. 2320 at the west end adjacent to Victoria Road level crossing was removed by steam breakdown crane on Sunday 19th February, 1961. With little traffic Boyce's Bridge and Outwell Village depots were closed completely on and from 5th November, 1962, but from 1st March, 1963 the latter reopened as a private siding for one coal merchant. Outwell Basin also closed on 5th November, 1962 but then reopened each year during the summer months from February until September following complaints from farmers and growers and after the Transport Users' Consultative Committee made representations for a daily goods train.

Drewry 204 hp 0-6-0 diesel locomotive No. 11102 stands on the main single line beside the Wisbech to Littleport/Ely A1101 road at Boyce's Bridge depot with the afternoon down train on 27th March, 1957 prior to shunting into the back siding to collect wagons. The depot foreman was responsible for working the points and the guard for shunting movements.   *W. Naughton*

Traffic is brought to a stand as Drewry 204 hp 0-6-0 diesel-mechanical locomotive No. D2202 hauls her train across Elm Road *en route* from Wisbech to Upwell. The crossing was No. 1 on the Upwell tramway and was located 0 miles 31 chains from Wisbech Tramway Junction.

The late Dr I.C. Allen

On Sunday 19th February, 1961 footbridge No. 2320 adjacent to Victoria Road level crossing at Wisbech was removed with the assistance of a steam breakdown crane. Here the span is raised off the stanchions - the footsteps each side having already been removed.

Lilian Ream Exhibition Gallery

In the high sunshine of a summer's day, Drewry 204 hp 0-6-0 diesel-mechanical shunting locomotive No. D2202 ambles beside the Wisbech to Littleport/Ely road towards Outwell Sluice siding with a Wisbech to Upwell freight working. *The late Dr I.C. Allen*

Drewry 204 hp 0-6-0 diesel-mechanical locomotive No. D2202 shunting vans from her train, the 1.30 pm Wisbech to Upwell at Elm Bridge depot on 18th August, 1964. The covered vans have been shunted on to the inner loop line ready for loading and collecting by the up service. *Ken Paye*

After the fire of 24th May, 1911 damaged the brewery and former mill in Elm High Road part of the mill was rebuilt as a private residence and the tramway loop siding lifted. Drewry 204 hp BR class '04' 0-6-0 diesel-mechanical locomotive No. D2202 passes the house with the 1.30 pm Wisbech to Upwell freight train on 18th August, 1964. *Ken Paye*

In 1963 the infamous Beeching Report was published, and whilst referring specifically to passenger traffic, the map included with the report also showed freight tonnages and receipts. The surviving depots on the tramway provided poor statistics of 0 to 5,000 tons per annum with Upwell showing 5,000 to 25,000 tons per annum; the entire line carried less than 5,000 tons per week. It was evident the tramway could only survive with an injection of additional traffic but this was not forthcoming. Road traffic was going from strength to strength and continuing ailing receipts forced British Railways, Eastern Region authorities to effect economies throughout East Anglia. Many freight services were withdrawn on and from 13th July, 1964, including the neighbouring goods line from Three Horse Shoes to Benwick.

The *Wisbech Advertiser* in September 1964 proclaimed the 'Beeching Bombshell' was imminent when the closure of Elm Bridge depot was announced, together with Wisbech North Goods and Wisbech St Mary on the former M & GN line. Investigations continued to eliminate unremunerative freight sidings and, after a short reprieve, Outwell Basin depot closed completely on and from 5th October, 1964. Facilities for handling passenger and goods rated 'smalls' traffic was also withdrawn from Elm Bridge depot and Upwell from the same day leaving the tramway open for truck-load traffic only from Elm Bridge and Upwell, the 'smalls' traffic being handled by motor lorries based at Wisbech. Elm Bridge depot subsequently closed completely on and from 28th December, 1964, leaving just Outwell Village open for coal traffic and Upwell for wagon load traffic.

By now BR was accelerating the withdrawal programmme for unremunerative services and from 28th December, 1964 freight services were withdrawn from the former M&GN Wisbech North. A few days later on 4th January, 1965 freight services were withdrawn from the Wisbech Harbour North branch.

By 1965 the tramway traffic had dwindled to one or two wagons a day from Upwell with little or no coal traffic for Outwell Village. The tram was already in its death throes as growers and traders deserted rail for road transport and the *Wisbech Advertiser* correctly commented, 'Most growers have long regarded the closure as inevitable'.

The closure of the tramway took effect on and from Monday 23rd May, 1966 but, because there were no booked services on Saturday and Sunday, the last train ran on Friday 20th May, 1966. The final service was hauled by Drewry 204 hp diesel mechanical shunting locomotive No. D2201 in charge of driver Albert South, with fireman Derek Norman as secondman. The locomotive made a leisurely run to Upwell with its attendant ex-Southern Railway goods brake van, manned by guard Tim Downes, to collect three 16 ton all-steel mineral wagons. The return journey which departed Upwell at 3.30 pm was watched by many local people and several railway enthusiasts who turned out to bid farewell to the line. F. Goodey of Basin Farm, Outwell later provided an obituary in the *Wisbech Advertiser*: 'The passenger days were a bit before my time, but I did have a ride on the tram. We used to take our fruit to the tram, and it always frightened the life out of the horses. Its closure will make no difference to me. We send our goods by road, but we used to like the old tram, especially the steam one'. Many other users would have said 'Amen to that'. Soon after the withdrawal of services from the tramway BR was seeking to

Parking of cars for some residents living alongside the tramway was a hazardous business requiring exact positioning to prevent damage to road vehicles or cause delays to trains. Drewry 204 hp 0-6-0 diesel-mechanical locomotive BR class '04' No. D2202 negotiates one such hazard on Elm High Road with the 1.30 pm Wisbech to Upwell freight train on 18th August, 1964.
Ken Paye

Drewry 204 hp BR class '04' 0-6-0 diesel-mechanical shunting locomotive No. D2202 soon after departing from Elm Bridge depot with the 1.30 pm Wisbech to Upwell freight train on 18th August, 1964.   *Ken Paye*

BR class '04' 0-6-0 diesel-mechanical shunting locomotive No. D2202 crosses Outwell Bridge No. 2337 and enters Outwell Village depot with the 1.30 pm Wisbech to Upwell freight train on 18th August, 1964. The locomotive is crossing the former Wharf or Water siding which at one time bisected the main single line. Note the defensive gun placement dating from World War II in the background.   *Ken Paye*

Drewry 204 hp 0-6-0 diesel shunting locomotive No. D2202 trundles along Elm High Road soon after passing the Duke of Wellington crossing with the 3.30 pm Upwell to Wisbech freight train on 18th August, 1964. A narrow pavement separates the road from the railway and the van driver has parked sensibly clear of the track alongside the kerb.   *Ken Paye*

Drewry 204 hp 0-6-0 diesel-mechanical locomotive No. D2202 trundles alongside the River Nene (Old Course) and approaching Goodman's Corner with the 1.30 pm Wisbech to Upwell freight train on 18th August, 1964. The river and railway parted company at Goodman's Corner, which was the penultimate intermediate stopping point for passenger trains. In the background is the tower of St Clement's church at Outwell. *Ken Paye*

A sad occasion as Drewry 204 hp 0-6-0 diesel locomotive No. D2201 works the final train from Upwell to Wisbech near Dial House on Friday 20th May, 1966 formed of three 16 ton all-steel mineral wagons and a former Southern Railway goods brake van. *Lilian Ream Gallery*

make further economies and freight services were withdrawn from Wisbech Harbour East branch on and from 12th September, 1966.

After closure of the tramway the track remained in position for over three years gradually disappearing under a carpet of weeds and undergrowth, whilst some of the depot buildings became unofficial bus shelters. The official closure date of the tramway was 24th July, 1967 and the appointed contractor, J. Watling & Sons Ltd of Leverington Common, commenced lifting of the permanent way on 27th October, 1969. By 12th November the track was lifted from Elm Road crossing Wisbech to Elm Tramway crossing. The delay in placing the contract appeared to have been due to protracted legal battles over the ownership of land used by the tramway and although the disputes had been settled the full decision had not been made public. The condition of the contract was that the bed of the track was filled with earth and levelled for seeding. The *Wisbech Advertiser* reported that the County Council owned only the metalled surface of any road, whilst the soil beneath belonged to the owners of the property on either side of the road. It then appeared the bed of the railway might become the property of house owners. The work was expected to take 10 to 16 weeks for full completion and by February 1970 little remained of the tramway. In the meantime in accordance with the 'Network for Development' plan of 1967, which advocated the closure of the remaining passenger lines to Wisbech, the East station, together with other stations on the line, were reduced to the status of unstaffed halts on and from 5th June, 1967. In just over a year the threat of closure became reality when Wisbech East station closed following the withdrawal of the March to Kings Lynn passenger service on 9th September, 1968. Demolition commenced on Wednesday 5th May, 1971, the buildings having been vandalized in the period after closure. On the tramway the buildings at Elm Bridge survived in ever decaying condition until demolished by local council workers on 15th November, 1978.

The Wisbech canal gradually silted up and became a dumping ground for old rubbish; it was later filled in and between Wisbech and Outwell, much of it has been used to provide a base for the realigning of the former meandering road to Downham Market. Where the tramway ran alongside the road, wide verges remain in the front of houses and tangible traces are few. By April 1974 Upwell depot site was cleared to make way for the new Townley Close housing estate and the Upwell Heath Community Centre, although the foreman's cottage still stands at the corner of the development. The trackbed is used as a farm track between Small Lode and Goodman's Crossing, whilst at Outwell Village further housing development called 'The Tramways' had engulfed the former depot yard. Standing almost hidden by modern buildings but facing the village street and under the shadow of St Clement's Church is the brick-built depot office, now protected by a preservation order. Part of the trackbed between Horn's Corner and Outwell Basin is a farm access track but the site of the depot is buried under a roundabout and bypass road. The sharp curves of the road at Boyce's Bridge and Elm are extant but there are no signs of the former railway. The wide tree-lined section of Elm Road runs parallel to the filled-in canal and parallel Wisbech bypass road; a hump in the road being the only evidence of the former level crossing on the main line. A road junction has replaced the site of the infamous Newcommon bridge. The tramway is not forgotten as a tram locomotive is commemorated on the village sign and road signs at Upwell and Outwell.

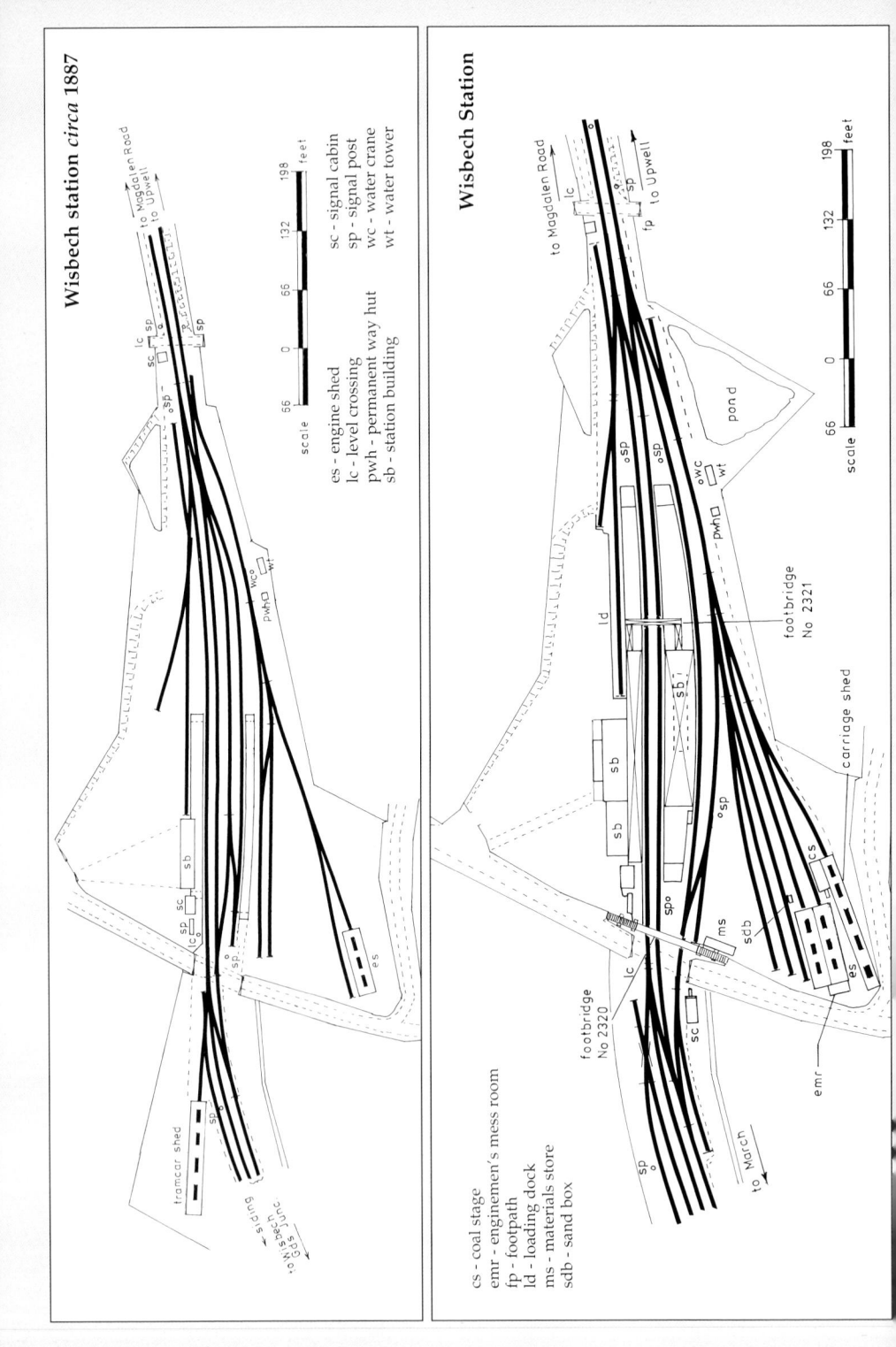

Wisbech station *circa* 1887

scale

```
66        0        66      132      198
|---------|--------|--------|--------|
                                    feet
```

es - engine shed
lc - level crossing
pwh - permanent way hut
sb - station building

sc - signal cabin
sp - signal post
wc - water crane
wt - water tower

Wisbech Station

footbridge No 2321

footbridge No 2320

carriage shed

to Magdalen Road
to Upwell
to March

cs - coal stage
emr - enginemen's mess room
fp - footpath
ld - loading dock
ms - materials store
sdb - sand box

scale

```
66        0        66      132      198
|---------|--------|--------|--------|
                                    feet
```

Chapter Six

The Tramway Route Described

Before embarking on this chapter, the reader must be made aware that compared with other GER lines, where mileages and distances were fairly uniform between civil and signalling engineering documents, and working timetable information, no such uniformity existed for the Wisbech & Upwell Tramway. The author has consulted over 60 such documents issued by the GER, LNER and BR, operating, civil engineering and signalling departments and some gross errors are evident. The problem appears to stem from the fact that few mileage posts were erected beside the tramway and the zero point taken for surveys varied between the points at Wisbech Goods Junction, the points leading from the up main line west of Wisbech station, close to Wisbech Station signal box known as Tramway Junction, and the centre of Wisbech station platform. There were even four different variations in bridge mileages and five for level crossing mileages! In this description of the route the zero point has been taken as the points by Wisbech Station signal box (Tramway Junction), as used by the GER and BR and by process of elimination and allowing for minor discrepancies of a quarter chain, a fairly accurate record has been achieved. Some details will therefore differ from previously published works.

The ECR opened a new station on the site of the former East Anglian Railway station in 1855. It was single storey of timber construction with tile roof, with the main buildings 90 ft in length, on the 220 ft-long down side platform and with the original Wisbech Station signal box located at the west end of the platform adjacent to the Victoria Road level crossing. At first there was no up side platform but a temporary timber structure was provided before the advent of the tramway. In these early years horse-drawn buses from the White Hart, White Lion and Rose and Crown Hotels met every train travelling between March and Watlington, renamed Magdalen Road from 1st June, 1875. In May 1888 the GER commenced the construction of a new station with ornate brick buildings again on the down platform. Demolition commenced on 27th August and the new structure built by Harold Arnold and Son of Doncaster was opened on Monday 3rd December. The timber up side platform was then replaced by a new island platform with the outer or south face for the Wisbech & Upwell Tramway trains in the spring of 1889.

The tramway was laid to standard gauge with the junction with the March to Magdalen Road line at 93 miles 43¼ chains from Liverpool Street via Cambridge, Ely and March and 4¾ chains west of Wisbech station; the mileage for the Upwell tramway commencing at 0 or zero from this junction. Curiously the mileage for the Wisbech to Magdalen Road line was originally from Liverpool Street but was then amended and commenced at zero at the mid-point in Wisbech station. The tramline climbed at 1 in 163 from the junction points past Wisbech Station signal box at 93 miles 44 chains and over Victoria Road level crossing at 93 miles 44½ chains and under footbridge No. 2320 at 93

The only known photograph of the exterior of the Wisbech station opened by the Eastern Counties Railway in 1855 replacing the temporary structure opened by the East Anglian Railway on 1st February, 1848. The single-storey timber station buildings are to the left and the tall signal box on the right. The sign on the gatepost advises 'This Way to the Tramcars'.

Wisbech and Fenland Museum

The ornate frontage to Wisbech East station in March 1966 showing the building erected by the GER in 1888.

R. Powell

Right: Wisbech station from the east with the Upwell tramway single line in the centre and the Magdalen Road single line to the right. In the left background is the locomotive water tank serving the water column beside the tramway loop road. Beyond that is the engine shed and associated sidings. The starting signal at the end of the back road of the island platform is cleared to denote a train is scheduled to pass on to the tramway. The up main line is served by the inner face of the island platform and the down road by the down platform with its main station buildings. Footbridge No. 2321 connecting the platforms spans the main lines. Sidings at the back of the down platform serve the horse loading dock and end loading dock, whilst a headshunt siding is to the extreme right.

NRM/Windwood Collection

Wisbech East station 93 miles 48 chains from Liverpool Street via Cambridge and Ely facing March on 25th August, 1950. The Upwell tramway line is to the left and is elevated to allow for the low 1 ft 2 in. high platform. The other face of the island platform served the up line to March whilst the main station buildings are on the down platform. Station footbridge No. 2321 connects the platforms whilst beyond the station is Victoria Road footbridge No. 2320 at 93 miles 45 chains adjacent to Victoria Road level crossing.   *The late H.C. Casserley*

The west end of Wisbech East station; the down platform to the left is host to the main station buildings fronted by an ornate canopy. The up main line and the Upwell tramway run each side of the island platform. Wisbech Station signal box up starting signal and Wisbech Goods Junction signal box distant signal share the same post at the end of the up platform.

Author's Collection

Facing west from the up side of the island platform at Wisbech East in May 1959 showing the ornate canopy provided over the island platform and down side platform. In the background is Victoria Road footbridge No. 2320 spanning the line adjacent to Victoria Road level crossing. Note the bookstall on the down platform.

R. Powell

miles 45 chains to the west end of the 350 ft outer face of Wisbech station up island platform, which was of low height 1 ft 2 in. against the normal height of 3 ft to facilitate the use of the tramcars with their side steps. Located at 93 miles 48 chains, the station also had the inner face of the island platform 390 ft-long serving the up main line and the 400 ft-long down platform, which was host to the 140 ft main station buildings, including booking hall, booking and parcels office, station master's office, waiting rooms and staff accommodation. The building and a section of the platform were protected by an ornate 210 ft awning, which provided passengers with protection in inclement weather. The island platform also had waiting rooms, a parcels storage and staff accommodation, with an ornate awning 165 ft in length over both platforms. Through the station the main lines and the tramline fell at 1 in 433, where the speed limit for all trains was restricted to 20 mph because of the sharp curve. The platforms were connected by footbridge No. 2321 at 93 miles 49½ chains. Wisbech station was originally titled Wisbeach but from 4th May, 1877 the 'a' was dropped. Further renaming to Wisbech East by British Railways from 27th September, 1948 was made to differentiate the former GER station from the former M&GN station which was re-designated Wisbech North from the same date.

South-west of the station the 90 ft-long single road engine shed, provided in 1883 for the stabling, maintenance and repair of the tram locomotives was originally served by the 420 ft-long shed road with an additional road 180 ft in length to the north of the building. Two sidings 310 ft south and 350 ft north with a crossover between the two were located between the station and the shed for the stabling of tramway stock. In 1894 a second shed, 85 ft in length, was built alongside and attached to the north of the original and the pair could accommodate six of the tram engines. Entry to the two sheds was by the 370 ft No. 1 road serving the original building and the 320 ft No. 2 road serving the new shed, with access from trailing points in the run-round loop road. Locomotive inspection pits were provided on each of the shed roads and alongside No. 1 road and backing on to the carriage shed was the locomotive coal stage where engines were hand coaled by the cleaner or shedman and more often than not the crews of the tram locomotives. To the north side of the engine shed were three stabling sidings, the south 330 ft, middle 240 ft and north 220 ft in length respectively for rolling stock used on the tramway, but on occasions main line passenger stock or wagons were also stored awaiting their next utilization. Between No. 2 shed road and the south siding was a sand box containing sand for replenishing the tram engines. The 140 ft-long timber single road shed for tramcars, served by the 350 ft-long tram road, was located alongside and to the south of the locomotive shed but this was removed after the withdrawal of the passenger services, the track remaining *in situ* as another locomotive siding. This carriage shed had replaced an earlier structure 80 ft in length located on a 150 ft siding to the immediate west of Victoria Road level crossing and served by trailing points from the down main line. With the arrival of diesel traction in 1952 new locomotive stabling and maintenance facilities were required, and originally proposals were made for a new shed to be provided. A far cheaper alternative was achieved when the north side shed

Wisbech East station on 4th June, 1952 from Victoria Road footbridge showing the island platform with the low face provided for the Upwell tramway passenger traffic. The truncated west end is planted with shrubs and flowers and the ornate garden bordering the run-round loop headshunt is evidence of the pride exhibited by the keen gardeners on the railway staff. A tram locomotive has just arrived from Upwell and is waiting the road to depart with the wagons to Wisbech goods yard.   *B. Nathan*

View from the station footbridge at Wisbech East in March 1966 showing the down and up main lines in the foreground and the connection from the tramway sidings to the Upwell tramway on the right. The single lines to Emneth and Upwell run parallel to each other in the distance.   *R. Powell*

A rather poor photograph of Wisbech shed *circa* 1910 showing the tramcar shed to the left of the building, which was later demolished. It was evident the tramcars could not have been kept in pristine condition with the coal stage located alongside and sulphurous smoke wafting across the yard. *Author's Collection*

Wisbech tramway yard with the back platform to the right occupied by tramway passenger stock forming a train to Upwell. Alongside the platform road is the loop road with connections leading to the carriage shed on the left Nos. 1 and 2 shed roads serving the engine shed and the three sidings used for stabling rolling stock. Railway allotments occupy the land between the siding connection and the boundary fence. *British Railways*

Wisbech yard after the demolition of No. 2 shed and the conversion of No. 1 shed for the servicing of the diesel-mechanical shunting locomotives. Rationalisation has taken place and the stabling siding to the south of the shed has been removed. A rake of covered vans occupy the former No. 2 shed road, whilst other vehicles are stabled on Nos. 2 and 3 sidings. *Author*

Locomotive water supplies at Wisbech shed came from a tank mounted on timber trestles standing 43 ft in height, located by the siding outlet points. This served a water column beside the run-round loop. *J. Stafford Baker*

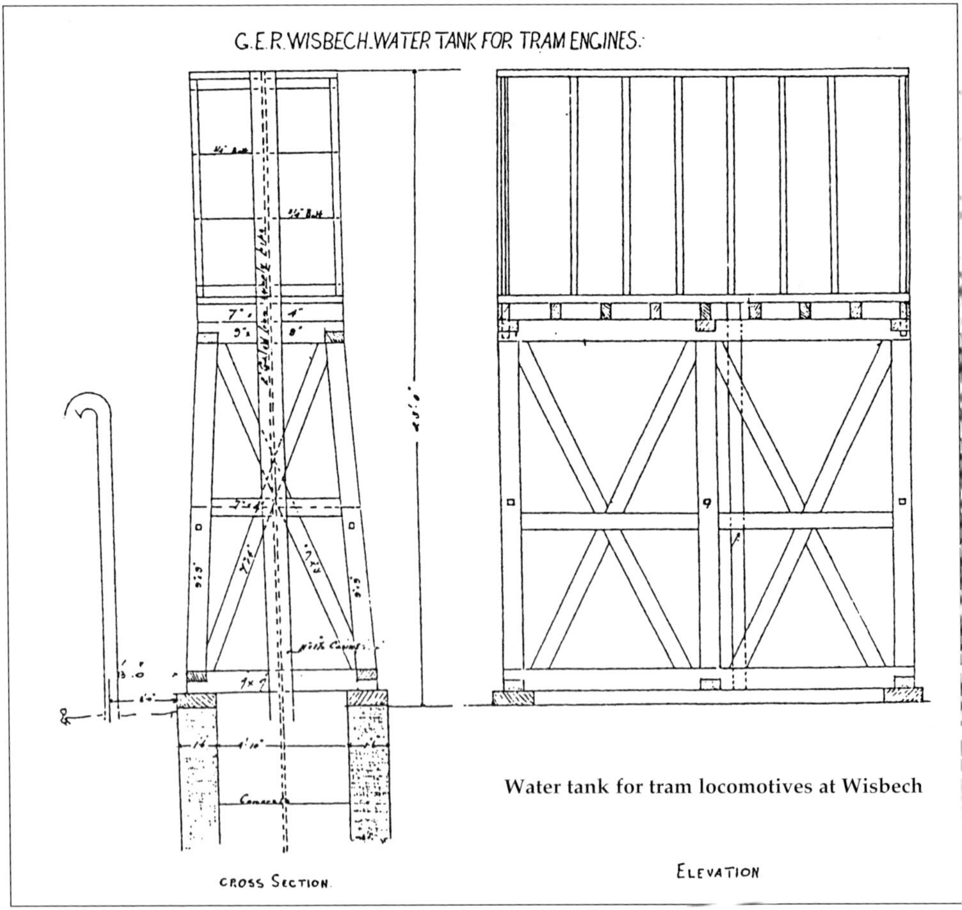

G.E.R. WISBECH. WATER TANK FOR TRAM ENGINES.

Water tank for tram locomotives at Wisbech

CROSS SECTION.

ELEVATION.

occupying No. 2 road was demolished and the original shed was cosmetically restored and re-roofed, the inspection pit on No. 1 road being retained but the other was filled in. On the south side of the engine shed line and opposite the east end of the station platforms was a water tower mounted on timber trestles standing 43 ft in height. This fed a water column located alongside the tramway loop avoiding line. The tank was supplied by Wisbech Water Works Company, with the charge in 1883 of 1s. 0d. per thousand gallons.

Points and signals at the station were controlled from Wisbech Station signal box, originally located to the east of Victoria Road level crossing and at the west end of the down main line platform. In 1888 this was replaced by a new Station signal box located to the west of the level crossing and on the south side of the tram loop line. This contained a 32-lever Saxby and Farmer frame. Before the construction of the new Wisbech station a small signal box, Wisbech North, was located on the down side of the main single line, east of the station, adjacent to an occupational crossing and previously Prospect Place public crossing. This box contained a 12-lever frame.

Although the passenger tram service arrived at and departed from the up back platform, goods traffic from and to the tramway was taken by the tram locomotive to Wisbech goods yard, which occupied the site of the original ECR station on the line from March, and which latterly had siding capacity for 427 wagons. Wisbech Goods Junction signal box controlled access from and to the goods yard to the up and down main lines and was located 14 chains west of the Tramway Junction at the end of a sharp 10 chains radius curve. Goods traffic was taken through the station and then via the down main line to the Goods Junction before being propelled back into any of the several sidings in the yard. Down services for the tramway were propelled out of the yard by the tram locomotive to the down main line and then hauled over to the up main line, before diverging on to the tramway via the facing points by Wisbech Station signal box or by the points at the east end of the up side island platform.

Leaving Wisbech station and passing the down starting signal, the tramway ran parallel to the main line to Magdalen Road following a gradual left-hand curve for a distance of 27½ chains, initially falling at 1 in 433/471 over Prospect Place main line footpath crossing No. 1 at 0 miles 7½ chains (main line mileage) or 0 miles 13 chains (tramway mileage) and Milner Road footpath crossing No. 2 at 0 miles 16½ or 0 miles 22 chains respectively. It then rose at 1 in 344/776 and veered sharply to the south on a 1 in 1042 falling gradient past a stop signal, controlled by the signalman in Wisbech Harbour Junction signal box, and a small ornate crossing cottage to emerge through a gate which could be closed against rail traffic on to Elm Road, the main Wisbech to Downham Market/Littleport road, later A1101. This was immediately crossed just south of Elm Road main level crossing No. 3 at 0 miles 25 chains from Wisbech on the main line. It was the duty of the signalman from the nearby Wisbech Harbour Junction signal box located at 0 miles 26 chains, to stop road traffic and flag the tram service across the road, which was tramway level crossing No. 1 at 0 miles 31 chains. On most occasions the signalman achieved traffic control by closing the north side barrier of the main line crossing gates across the road but this did not happen on every working. This point alongside the canal on Elm Road was

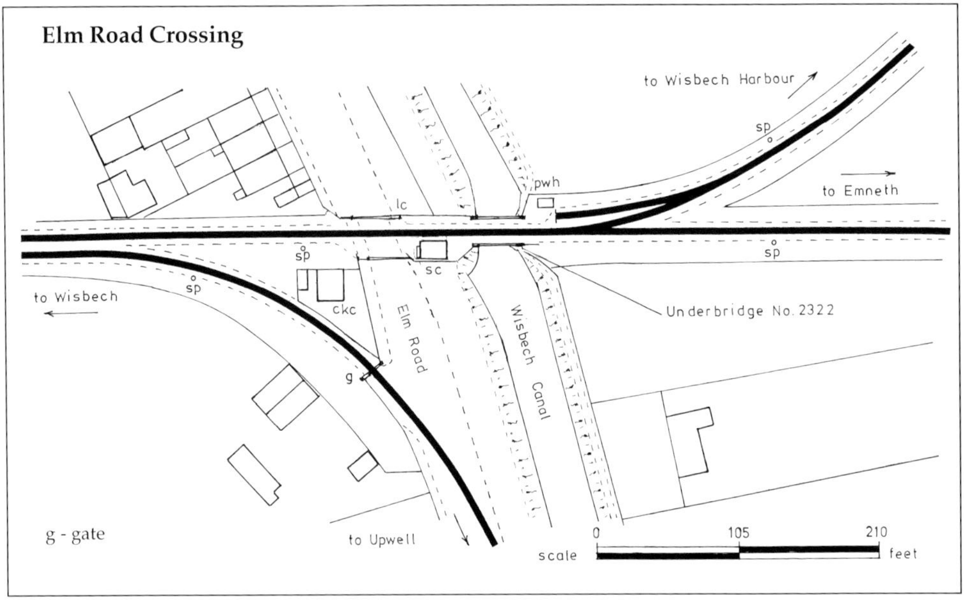

Elm Road Crossing

to Wisbech Harbour

sp

to Emneth

pwh

lc

to Wisbech

sp

sp

sp

sc

ckc

Elm Road

Wisbech Canal

Underbridge No. 2322

g

g - gate

to Upwell

scale

0   105   210

feet

The Upwell tramway curved to run alongside the Wisbech to Magdalen Road single line on the approach to Wisbech station. The stop signal protecting the tramway was worked by Wisbech Harbour Junction signal box No. 11 lever and acted as a sentinel for down trains approaching Elm Road tramway crossing.   *The late B.D.J. Walsh*

View from the cab of a Drewry 204 hp 0-6-0 diesel-mechanical shunting locomotive approaching Elm Road level crossing and Wisbech Harbour Junction showing the Upwell tramway diverging to the right past Harbour Junction No. 11 signal, which protected the tramway gate on Elm Road. The main line signals are single line to Emneth right arm and the left-hand shorter arm denoting to the Harbour Branch. *The late Dr I.C. Allen*

Elm Road tramway crossing No. 1 at 0 miles 31 chains from Tramway Junction and beyond that Elm Road main line crossing No. 3 on the line to Magdalen Road controlled by Wisbech Harbour Junction signal box. View from the cab of Drewry 204 hp 0-6-0 diesel-mechanical shunting locomotive No. 11101 as it is being flagged across the road on 9th July, 1955 by a railwayman standing by the gate adjacent to the ornate crossing keeper's cottage. *The late B.D.J. Walsh*

Wisbech canal bridge No. 2322 on the main line from Wisbech to Magdalen Road, spanning the stagnant waterway, with Wisbech Harbour Junction signal box to the left.   *Author's Collection*

In 1932 Newcommon bridge No. 2335 at 0 miles 48 chains from Wisbech, was replaced by an embankment over a concrete culvert, and the curvature and gradient of the tramway was greatly eased. This view looking along the Wisbech canal from the structure shows a bus wending its way along Elm Road *en route* to Wisbech on 23rd September, 1934.   *Author's Collection*

the first request stop for passenger trams. The line continued on a 1 in 812 falling gradient and past the half-mile point to run parallel with and along the east side of Elm Road, a low kerb separating the tarmac road from the railway trackbed. The dried-up bed of the disused Wisbech canal and its tree-lined bank was on the down side of the line as the tramway then fell at 1 in 480/133. The canal on this section formed the county boundary between Cambridgeshire and Norfolk. After the next crossroads the Royal Standard Inn corner, the second of the request passenger tram stops, the tramway climbed at 1 in 33/107 and then 1 in 38 on a sharp 15 chains left-hand curve to cross the canal by means of Newcommon bridge, a new brick and wrought-iron construction for both road and rail, measuring 25 ft wide with a 25 ft span which replaced the old brick bridge which had measured 16 ft in width and with a 16 ft span. This bridge, No. 2335 at 0 miles 48 chains, was hump-backed and set on a tight S bend with gradients on each approach and was notorious in times of adverse weather when the tram engines had difficulty hauling the loads. The bridge was subsequently rebuilt in 1932, the structure being replaced by an embankment over a concrete culvert when the gradients on the approaches were almost eradicated. It was whilst negotiating the curve on the Norfolk side of the bridge at the junction with Ramnoth Road, on a cold morning with hard frost coating the roadway and rails, that the locomotive of a down tram left the rails and ploughed a furrow through the hard ground. Fortunately, because of the low speed of the train, no other vehicle had derailed and after debating with his fireman and guard the driver decided to chance his luck and reverse the locomotive back through the furrow caused by the flanges to see if he could re-rail the engine. After gently persuading his steed into reverse and with the assistance of some baulks of timber the mission was completed and the train set off for Upwell with only moderate delay and the authorities none the wiser.

Beyond the bridge the line descended at 1 in 44 on the sharp 12 chains right-hand curve over ungated level crossing No. 2 at 0 miles 50 chains where Ramnoth Road converged from the north, to enter Norfolk and continued on the east side of Elm High Road, initially running alongside open fields and falling at 1 in 174 and then 1760. A 1 in 3300 rising gradient for three-eighths of a mile took the line on a long left-hand curve past the 1 mile point before reaching two further request stopping places at Rose Cottage, opposite the Paragon Garage and Brewery Siding where there was a 300 ft-long loop near Westfields House. The building, with its tall chimney on the down side of the tramway loop, was originally Emneth steam flour mill but in 1893 was converted to a brewery owned by Frederick Wood. After the disastrous fire on 24th May, 1911, part of the mill was rebuilt as a private residence and the tramway siding lifted. The railway then descended at 1 in 489 on straigth track as far as the Duke of Wellington Inn located on the down side of the line, which later became de-licensed in favour of the Blacksmith's Arms on the opposite side of the road. The Duke of Wellington location was mentioned in the Board of Trade bye-laws and was a compulsory stopping place for the tram. Proposals were mooted for a branch to diverge from this point to serve the villages of Elm and Friday Bridge but nothing came of the scheme. Here the line passed the 1¼ mile point, and curved sharply to the left away from the canal before crossing

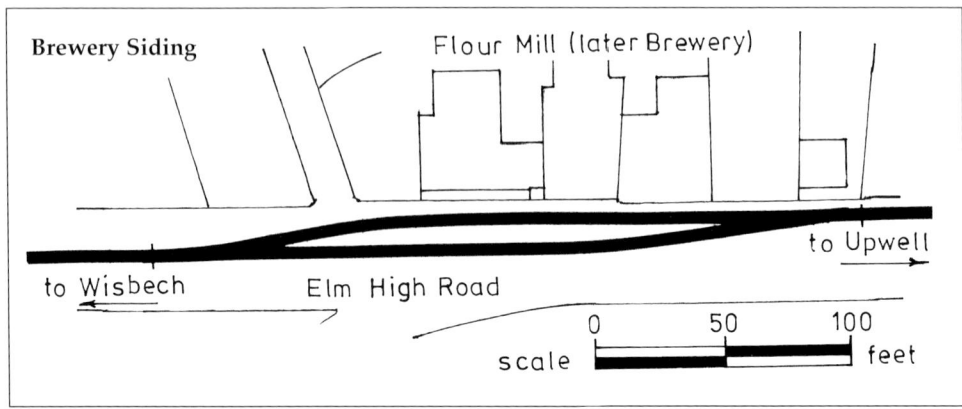

The Duke of Wellington crossing No. 3 looking towards Upwell and showing the tramway alongside the road in 1966.   *R. Powell*

to the right-hand or south side of the road by ungated level crossing No. 3 at 1 mile 28 chains. It then followed a straight west to east course passing Chapel Lane, another tram stop. The line then continued on 1 in 110/185 falling gradients before rising at 1 in 440/340 and 1 in 1889 to Elm Bridge depot.

Located at 1 mile 53 chains from Wisbech, the depot was situated on a sharp right-hand curve opposite the road leading to Emneth and in that parish and not in the parish of Elm. The track layout consisted of the main single line with the 420 ft-long inner loop line and 570 ft outside loop. The outside road was converted to a 430 ft-long siding when the points at the Upwell end of the line were removed, and at the same time the remaining loop was extended to a length of 500 ft. These sidings could accommodate 40 wagons. The amenities here consisted of a small brick-built goods office measuring 17 ft 8 in. by 12 ft 10 in., with a double door at one end, a single door at the opposite end and two windows on the front, the rear wall being blank. The structure was provided for the porter-in-charge and alongside was a glazed fronted waiting room, constructed in 1898 of brick and timber at a cost of £65. The glass frontage was later removed and the shed became open to the elements but had the added protection of an awning.

From Elm Bridge depot the line fell at 1 in 2640/689 in a southerly direction and followed the western verge of the Ely to Downham Market road on a tree-lined section before passing another request stop, the Weary Traveller. The railway and road curved slightly to the right as the line climbed at 1 in 1421 past the 2 mile point before passing the grounds of Inglethorpe Hall, another stopping point, on level track. The hall was at one time the home of Squire Francis Maltby Bland JP, a Director of Barclays Bank, who being a regular traveller on the tram required the driver to stop the train with the steps to a first class compartment directly opposite to where he was standing. If the driver failed to do so or the tram was late the engine crew were admonished, but Bland also had a kind heart and railway staff benefited especially at Christmas. Along this section after closure of the line a farm shop known as 'The Tramways' was established. As the Wisbech canal again approached on the up or west side of the line, the tramway curved to the left to run alongside the canal where the level track gave way to short sections of 1 in 2200/150 rising gradients. The line then fell slightly at 1 in 264 passing the request stop at the Prince of Wales Inn on the down side of the line and opposite Collett's bridge, which spanned the waterway. This structure, dating from 1797 and costing £226, was originally called Gosmere bridge and was shown on some maps as Emneth bridge. The dilapidated structure was replaced by a girder bridge costing £250 in 1931, and reopened on 4th December of that year. Running parallel to the Wisbech canal, the line continued past the 2½ mile point and along the western side of the road climbing initially at 1 in 754 before curving slightly to the left, with Collett's Bridge Farm on the opposite bank of the canal. The line then fell at 1 in 1320/861/780 until past the 3 mile post. The canal and railway again parted company at Shepherd's Cottage, another conditional stopping place. The railway continued alongside the south-western side of the road on rising 1 in 1584/ 251 gradients over occupational crossing No. 4 at 3 miles 22 chains to Boyce's Bridge depot, 3 miles 25 chains from Wisbech.

This depot, like Elm Bridge, was located on a sharp right-hand curve, known locally as Bird's Corner, and had a 400 ft-long inner loop line running parallel with

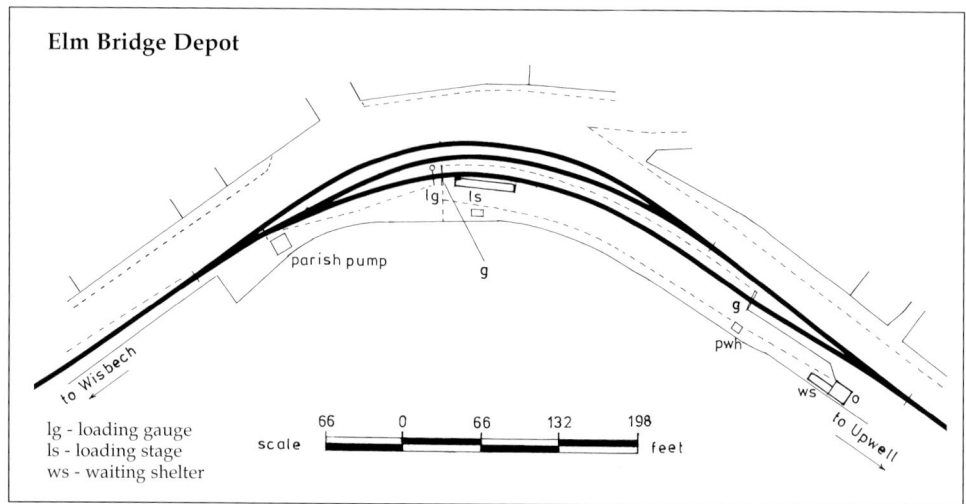

Elm Bridge Depot

parish pump

lg
ls
g

g
pwh
ws
o

to Wisbech

to Upwell

lg - loading gauge
ls - loading stage
ws - waiting shelter

scale

66   0   66   132   198

feet

Elm Bridge depot *circa* 1910 viewed facing towards Upwell. The main single line is clear of wagons and vans but as it is high summer the yard loop and inner siding are packed with vehicles, which are being prepared for loading.   *Author's Collection*

the main single line, together with a second loop siding 450 ft in length protected by a gate at the south end of the layout. This loop was also known as the back road and was invariably used as a siding, the space between the inner and outer loops being used as the depot yard road for loading and unloading freight traffic into and out of wagons. The amenities were completed by an office, together with a small waiting shelter for passengers, similar to the building at Elm Bridge. The depot being roughly halfway to Upwell was the designated passing place for trains especially when the passenger services operated. After the depot closed, on and from Monday 5th November, 1962, road improvements were planned to ease the situation for road traffic at Bird's Corner. In December 1963 the main line and loop were lifted and the path of the former inner siding became the main line.

Beyond the depot the tramway followed a southerly course and descended for a short section at 1 in 440 and then 1 in 720 following a straight section for a short distance to the 3½ mile point, before curving to the left to rejoin the canal at Boyce's Bridge. Here the tramway negotiated short switchback gradients of 1 in 480 falling, 1 in 188 rising, 1 in 88/848/2640 falling past the site of another request stop at Dial House Farm, which was to the north-east on the down side of the line. Just after Woodlands Farm near the 3¾ mile point, the A1101 public road diverged sharply to the left whilst the tramway followed a relatively straight course, running parallel to the north-west bank of the canal in a south-easterly direction and falling initially at 1 in 1320/377/220 behind an orchard on its own reserved track to the 4 mile point. It then climbed at 1 in 586 for the short distance to Outwell Basin depot.

Outwell Basin depot took its name from an adjacent widening of the canal, formerly used for berthing and turning barges and was 4 miles 10 chains from Wisbech. The track layout at the initial terminus of the tramway consisted of the main single line together with a run-round loop and a siding on the east side of the yard. When the tramway was extended to Upwell, the points were removed at the south end between the loop and main line, leaving the 530 ft-long inner siding and 450 ft outside road, so that the yard could only be shunted by up trains, all wagons having to be taken through to Upwell and returned. It was soon realized this presented a considerable operational inconvenience and the points and thus the loop were reinstated. The revised layout consisted of the 500 ft-long loop with a 200 ft headshunt at the south-east end and one long siding 520 ft in length, the loop and siding having accommodation for 45 wagons. A standard tramway brick-built office similar to others on the line was provided for the staff whilst an old coach body served as a passenger waiting room and later a store shed, the carriage reputedly used at one time in its life by Queen Victoria. The vehicle was in fact built by the GER in 1864 as family saloon No. 5 and was withdrawn in 1897. There was also a platelayers' hut located in this extensive layout. At the south end of the yard the main road had again swung alongside the railway and the entrance to the goods yard was by a gate leading directly from the road.

Immediately to the south of Outwell Basin depot the line climbed at 1 in 1980 and then steeply at 1 in 71/88/30 to cross the canal by Basin bridge No. 2336 at 4 miles 20 chains, a three-span iron bridge, which had gates at each end to prevent its use as a right of way by pedestrians or cattle, although later one set of gates was removed. Road and canal meandered to the east and from the bridge the line

Elm Bridge depot, 1 mile 53 chains from Wisbech, closed on and from 28th December, 1964, view facing towards Wisbech showing the former loop line remaining in use as the main running line. The former main line had been lifted to facilitate widening of the adjacent road and surplus sleepers await collection. *Stations UK*

Elm Bridge depot on 9th July, 1955 with covered vans occupying the dead end siding. To the left is the brick built depot building including office provided for the depot foreman and next to that the remains of the former passenger waiting shelter. The main single line and loop following a wide arcing course alongside the road in the background. *The late B.D.J. Walsh*

A sadly unkempt and overgrown Elm Bridge depot in 1964. The five vans are being loaded with fruit traffic. In the background the 430 ft-long inner siding has almost disappeared in the undergrowth. *Author's Collection*

Section of line near Inglethorpe Hall, facing towards Wisbech on 9th July, 1955, with an example of the hazard presented to tram locomotive drivers as road users drove their vehicles on to occupational crossings sometimes completely oblivious of the approaching train.
The late B.D.J. Walsh

The original Collett's bridge beside the tramway was also called Gosmere bridge and shown on some maps as Emneth bridge. It was built in 1797 at a cost of £226 to span the Wisbech canal. The bridge gave its name to a stopping place for the tramway passenger services but by 1931 the structure was in such a parlous state that it was replaced by a girder bridge costing £250 and opened on 4th December, 1931.   *Wisbech Fenland Museum*

The north end of Boyce's Bridge depot on 9th July, 1955, facing Wisbech with the 450 ft inner loop siding to the left and run-round loop running parallel to the main single line. Boyce's Bridge depot was the designated crossing point for trains on the single line especially when passenger services operated and later when extra trains ran during the busy fruit harvesting season.   *The late B.D.J. Walsh*

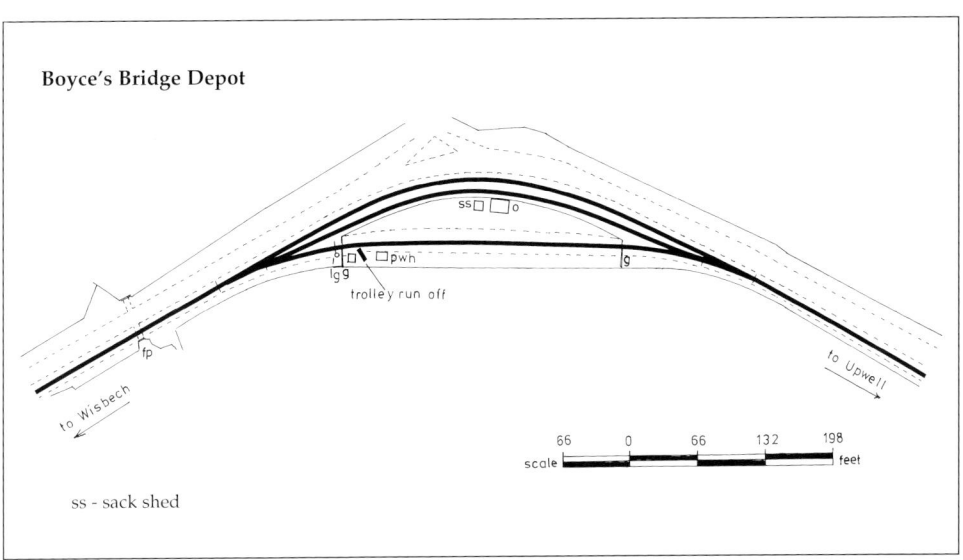

Boyce's Bridge Depot

ss□ □o

8□ □pwh

lg9

9

trolley run off

fp

to Wisbech

to Upwell

| 66 | 0 | 66 | 132 | 198 |

scale feet

ss - sack shed

The sharp curve of the main single line on the right and the parallel run-round loop at Boyce's Bridge depot, 3 miles 25 chains from Wisbech, viewed facing north. Beyond the depot office building the third siding is occupied by covered vans. *The late B.D.J. Walsh*

Section of line between Boyce's Bridge depot and Outwell Basin depot looking towards
Wisbech.   *The late B.D.J. Walsh*

Outwell Basin depot facing towards Upwell on 26th March, 1966 with the main single line to the
right and run-round loop alongside. The 520 ft back road siding is covered by weeds and can
only be identified by the location of the loading gauge.   *R. Powell*

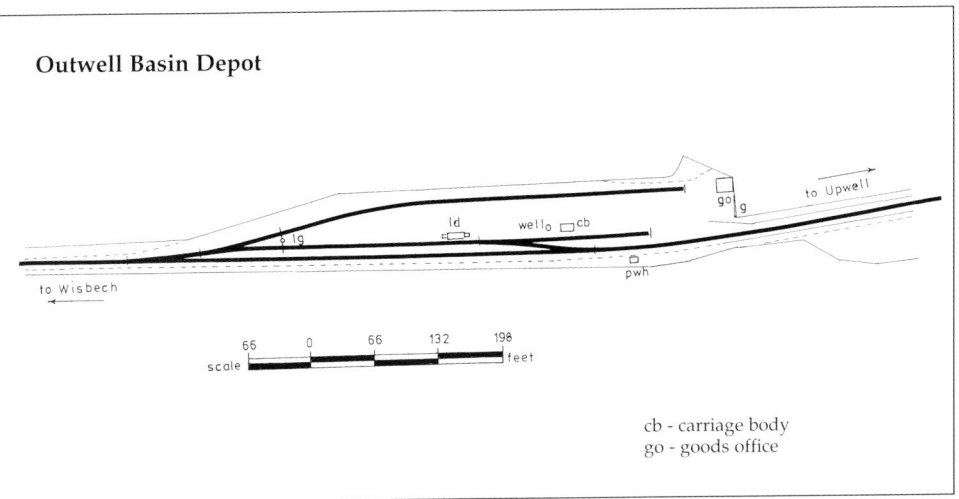

Outwell Basin Depot
to Upwell
go
g
ld
well
cb
lg
pwh
to Wisbech
66
0
66
132
198
scale
feet
cb - carriage body
go - goods office

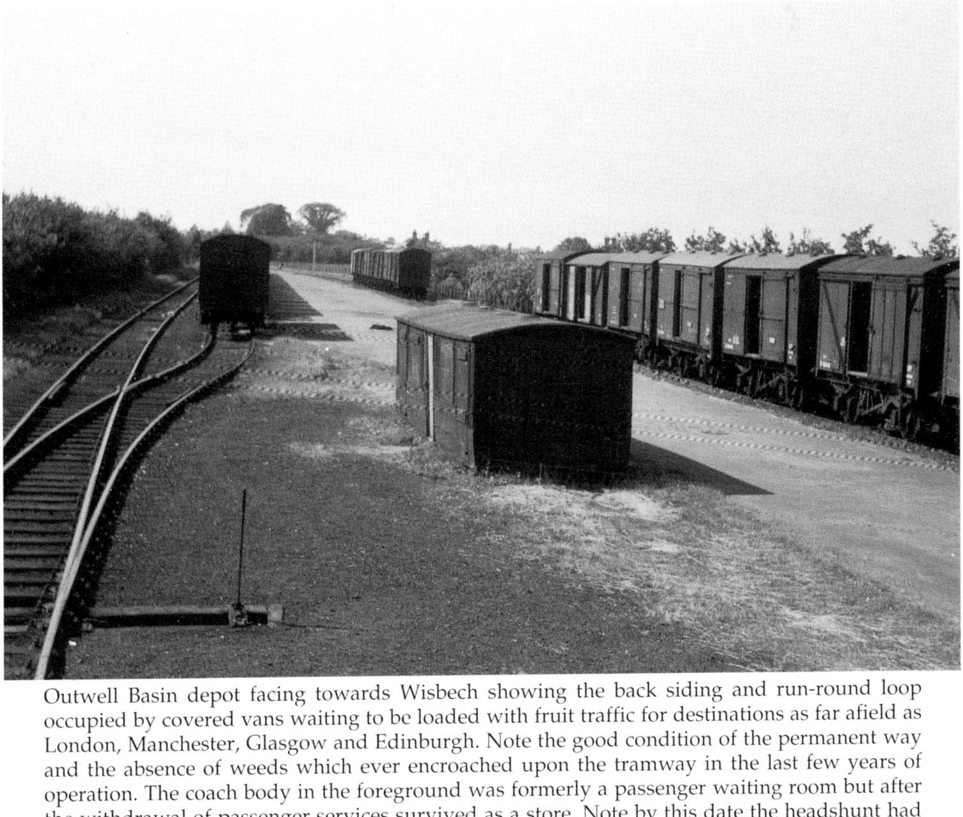

Outwell Basin depot facing towards Wisbech showing the back siding and run-round loop occupied by covered vans waiting to be loaded with fruit traffic for destinations as far afield as London, Manchester, Glasgow and Edinburgh. Note the good condition of the permanent way and the absence of weeds which ever encroached upon the tramway in the last few years of operation. The coach body in the foreground was formerly a passenger waiting room but after the withdrawal of passenger services survived as a store. Note by this date the headshunt had been removed. *The late B.D.J. Walsh*

The broad expanse of Outwell Basin depot facing towards Wisbech shortly before closure of the tramway. The main single line can be seen to the left passing the permanent way hut but the loop siding and back siding have both disappeared in the undergrowth.   *Stations UK*

Outwell Basin depot from the south just after closure on 5th October, 1964 with the yard bereft of wagons. The goods yard entrance gate and office are to the right.   *Stations UK*

Former GER family saloon coach No. 5 built to GER old diagram 4 in 1864 was withdrawn from traffic in 1897 and the body transferred to Outwell Basin depot to act as a passenger waiting room. After the withdrawal of the tramway passenger services in 1927 it served as a parcels shed but as shown here on 3rd August, 1961 its condition had considerably deteriorated. The body was later rescued for preservation in 1988. *J. Watling*

Outwell Basin bridge No. 2336 looking towards Upwell with the car straddled over the adjacent level crossing No. 5 at 4 miles 21 chains from Wisbech. *Author's Collection*

From Outwell Basin bridge No. 2336 at 4 miles 20 chains from Wisbech the single line descended at 1 in 83/73/330 on a straight section of reserved track where there were no less than one public and four occupational crossings. This view facing towards Wisbech and looking towards the bridge shows some of these crossings as the railway passed orchards on both sides of the line.
The late B.D.J. Walsh

The overgrown and disused Wisbech canal is immediately to the right of the single track tramway as it follows the Wisbech to Littleport/Ely A1101 road soon after the line had crossed the thoroughfare at Horn's Corner crossing. On the opposite side of the canal is the Wisbech to Downham Market A1122 road. View facing towards Wisbech on 9th July, 1955. *The late B.D.J. Walsh*

descended at 1 in 83/73 to re-enter Cambridgeshire and bisect a minor road at open level crossing No. 5 at 4 miles 21 chains. It then followed a straight course on reserved track, falling initially at 1 in 330 past the 4½ mile point and then a level section past allotments; this section was built to avoid unnecessary severe curves taken by the road and canal on the approach to Outwell. There were no less than one public and four occupational crossings on this section before the line again emerged on to the public highway on a 20 chains curve at Horn's Corner, another former request stop, with its adjacent cottage provided in 1914 by the GER for the goods foreman at Outwell Village depot. Here the road was crossed by level crossing No. 11 at 4 miles 51 chains, with a single gate on railway property, which, for as long as anyone could remember, was never closed across the line. The tramway then climbed initially at 1 in 370 and fell at 1 in 124/188 following the east side of the highway and parallel with the canal on the down side of the line past the 4¾ mile point. A short section of 1 in 188 falling and 1 in 352 rising took the line to the 360 ft-long loop siding at Outwell Sluice on a 1 in 2700 rising gradient. The loop road, positioned alongside the canal and adjacent lock gates, was used for many years as a coal siding by William Kingston so it was not possible for trains to pass at this point. Beyond the loop the tramway climbed at 1 in 281/188 on a sharp left-hand curve to cross Outwell bridge, another iron structure on the skew, No. 2337 at 4 miles 79 chains, where the line spanned the River Nene Old Course, which joined the Wisbech canal at this point. The line then descended a short 1 in 788 on a sharp 10 chains radius right-hand curve from the bridge and entered Outwell Village depot, 5 miles 00 chains from Wisbech. In the angle between the two waterways were four sidings and the offices. Initially the three sidings on the down side of the main line, 290 ft back road (160 ft siding, 130 ft headshunt), 250 ft middle road and the short 170 ft inner road were all dead-ended necessitating all wagons requiring to be taken in the up direction being first taken through to Upwell. This inconvenience was obviated by the later addition of an engine release crossover linking the back and middle roads and the sidings extended to 360 ft back road, 260 ft middle and 180 ft inner road. The 430 ft wharf or water road, the siding running alongside the River Nene, with trailing points from the main single line was for many years unique on the tramway for being equipped with lifebelts in case any unfortunate person fell into the water. The siding also had chutes for coal to be unloaded from rail to barge for distribution in the fens. The siding originally crossed the main single line and was bisected into two sections, 260 ft and the 170 ft where it curved alongside the bank of Well Creek to terminate at buffer stops. Trailing points from the main line also served the short stub end of the siding. After the first decade of the 20th century the siding was truncated short of the main single line to a length of 250 ft. The back and inner sidings and the water road all had cart loading tracks alongside. The passenger facilities included a small brick building for the foreman-in-charge, which included a ticket counter facing on to the village street, a passenger waiting shelter, similar to that at Elm Bridge depot and a van body, which was used as a store. By the early 1960s the depot exclusively handled coal class traffic for a local fuel merchant and only one of the four sidings survived. After representation from the Well Creek Trust, the tramway goods office was granted a grade two preservation order in October 1990.

Outwell Sluice siding located alongside the Wisbech to Littleport/Ely A1101 road and adjacent to Outwell lock gates on the Wisbech canal. The loop siding occupied by two coal wagons was the subject of a stream of complaints from the local clergy regarding the nuisance caused by the unloading of the coal wagons which culminated in a Board of Trade inspection. In this view facing Wisbech, the lorry is standing on the main single line. The loop siding was removed by 1955.   *Author's Collection*

The unkempt Well creek looking towards the lock at the entrance to the Wisbech canal at Outwell on 26th March, 1966.   *R. Powell*

Right: A aerial view of Outwell Village depot in August 1955 showing the main single line crossing the bridge over the River Nene (Old Course). Well Creek curves away past the yard and St Clement's church whilst the silted bed of the Wisbech canal is to the lower left. Well creek subsequently fell into disuse but was reopened for navigation by the Middle Level Commissioners on 1st June, 1975.   *Aerofilms*

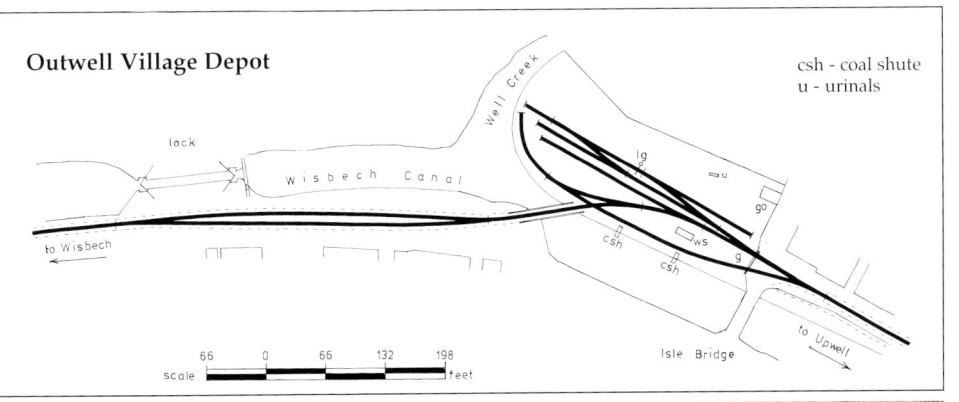

Outwell Village Depot

csh - coal shute
u - urinals

Well Creek

lock

Wisbech Canal

lg

u

go

to Wisbech

csh

ws

g

csh

66   0   66   132   198

scale   feet

Isle Bridge

to Upwell

At 4 miles 79 chains from Wisbech the single line of the tramway crossed the River Nene (Old Course) by Outwell Bridge No. 2337 to enter Outwell Village depot. This view on 9th July, 1955 facing towards Wisbech shows the meandering nature of the tramway as it followed the adjacent Wisbech to Littleport/Ely A1101 road and shows the site of the former Outwell Sluice siding. Where the railway parted company with the road the General Post Office located a public telephone box.   *The late B.D.J. Walsh*

The tramway approach to Outwell Village depot on 26th March, 1966, with the single line curving over Outwell Bridge No. 2337. The main road from Wisbech to Littleport/Ely A1101 parts company with the railway to run along the west bank of the waterway.   *R. Powell*

Drewry 204 hp diesel-mechanical locomotive BR class '04' No. D2201 standing at Outwell Village depot *en route* to Upwell. Outwell bridge No. 2337 is to the left whilst the former hoists used to transfer coal traffic from wagons in water siding to fen lighters are in the foreground.

The late Dr I.C. Allen

Outwell Village bridge No. 2337 at 4 miles 79 chains from Wisbech Tramway Junction in March 1966; the structure had three spans. *R. Powell*

Considerable rationalization was made to the track layout at Outwell Village depot in the last years of the tramway. In this view looking towards Wisbech on 26th March, 1966 only the main single line and one siding remain. The site of the former Wharf or Water siding serving the canal is to the left and the gun placement in the centre background is evidence of World War II defences.   *R. Powell*

The south end of Outwell Village depot on 26th March, 1966 showing the main single line in the foreground and the remaining single siding to the left. In the background is a covered van body used as a store alongside the depot office, which is now protected by a preservation order.
                                                                            R. Powell

Outwell Village depot, 5 miles 00 chains from Wisbech, from the south on 9th July, 1955, with a girl cyclist and a pedestrian crossing the railway by Church Terrace open level crossing No. 12 in the foreground. The main single line is to the centre and then curves to the left to cross the River Nene (Old Course). To the left is the connection to Wharf siding, 430 ft in length, which bisected the main single line near the bridge. Straight ahead are inner road, 170 ft in length, occupied by open wagons and then middle road 250 ft in length and 290 ft back road occupied by covered vans. *The late B.D.J. Walsh*

The southern approach to Outwell Village depot on 26th March, 1966 with the main single line entering the depot and the former connection to the former Wharf or Water siding fenced off. Isle bridge also known as Tuck's bridge spans the River Nene (Old Course) carrying Church Terrace across the waterway. *R. Powell*

View from Goodman's Corner crossing No. 13 at 5 miles 26 chains facing Wisbech showing the tramway running alongside the River Nene (Old Course). In the background is St Clement's Church at Outwell Village. On the opposite bank is the Wisbech to Littleport/Ely road.

R. Powell

From Goodman's Corner Crossing the tramway ran on reserved track towards the destination at Upwell. This view in March 1966 looking towards Wisbech shows the straight section leading to Small Lode, with the school field to the left.

R. Powell

Southwards from Outwell Village depot the tramway crossed Church Terrace by ungated level crossing No. 12 at 5 miles 02 chains leading from the Isle bridge, also known as Tuck's bridge, to the adjacent St Clement's Church and re-entered Norfolk. At busy periods shunting operations were occasionally executed across the road, much to the annoyance of local villagers. Beyond the crossing the line followed a meandering course on 1 in 88/322/493 falling gradients on the west side of the Outwell to Upwell road and alongside the River Nene (Old Course) past the 5¼ mile point before crossing the road by ungated level crossing No. 13 at 5 miles 26 chains to enter another section of reserved track, at Goodman's Corner, a request stop shown in the timetables as Goodman's Crossing. The line curved slightly to the left and followed a straight course in a south-south westerly direction falling at 1 in 247 before rising at 1 in 253 and falling at 1 in 539 over Wardrop occupational crossing No. 14 at 5 miles 41 chains. A short rise of 1 in 440 and then 1 in 273 falling then took the line over Pingle Bridge Road by ungated level crossing No. 15 at 5 miles 48 chains then Small Lode on timber bridge No. 2338 at 5 miles 49 chains, before crossing a by-road, Small Lode, by ungated level crossing No. 16 at 5 miles 50 chains, the final unofficial passenger halt. The tramway then continued the short distance curving to the right to reach the throat of the terminus at Upwell, on level track.

Upwell depot, 5 miles 72 chains from Wisbech, originally had seven sidings, the 800 ft-long passenger road serving the passenger ground level platform and 630 ft run-round loop, with 150 ft headshunt, containing the locomotive ash or inspection pit on the south-west side of the site. The two roads were connected by the engine release points near the buffer stops. The passenger station was a brick-built structure, larger than at other depots on the line, containing a waiting room, staff accommodation and parcels room, which after the withdrawal of passenger services was used as a store. The water tower, standing beside the buffer stops of the run-round road headshunt, was a GER locomotive tender mounted on timber trestles and served a water column for replenishing the tram engines, but these were removed in 1953 after the introduction of diesel traction. At the south-east corner of the depot situated alongside the A1101 road to Three Holes and Littleport was the house provided in 1901 by the GER for the foreman-in-charge. Road access to the yard was via gates in this road.

Three goods roads, the 660 ft-long No. 1, 670 ft No. 2 and 640 feet No. 3, fanned out in the centre of the yard with 60 ft, 130 ft and 40 ft headshunts respectively beyond the engine release points, which led from the outer roads to the middle road. Two outer roads, No. 4, 750 ft in length with a 150 ft headshunt beyond the engine release points and the 580 ft-long No. 5, with an 80 ft headshunt beyond the release points, completed the original layout. Carting roads for vehicular traffic were provided between the passenger road and No. 1 goods road and between Nos. 3 and 4 roads. A large low goods shed and coal grounds were also provided between Nos. 3 and 4 roads whilst a cattle dock and associated pens was served by the access to Nos. 4 and 5 sidings. A weighbridge and weighbridge office were located by the buffer stops at the end of No. 3 siding. With the ever-increasing traffic these facilities proved insufficient and four additional sidings Nos. 6, 7, 8 and 9 were installed in 1925. To accommodate the new sidings an additional approach was made from the points at the station throat and this divided into two, with the first subdividing into No. 6 road, 900 ft in length and

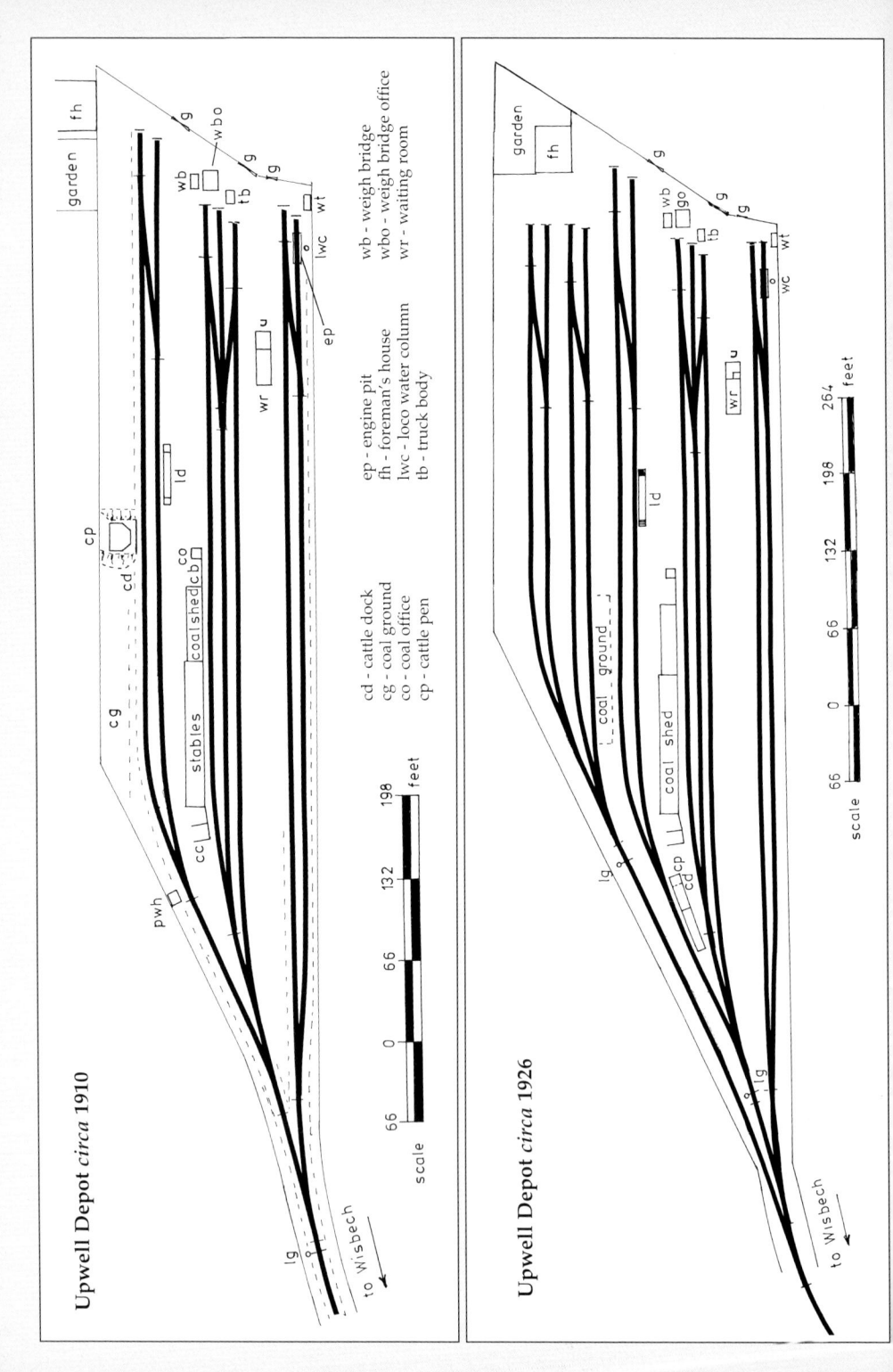

Upwell Depot *circa* 1910

Upwell Depot *circa* 1926

wb - weigh bridge
wbo - weigh bridge office
wr - waiting room

ep - engine pit
fh - foreman's house
lwc - loco water column
tb - truck body

cd - cattle dock
cg - coal ground
co - coal office
cp - cattle pen

garden

fh

to Wisbech

scale

feet

66   0   66   132   198   264

66   0   66   132   198

The entry points to Upwell depot in March 1966. The former passenger line and run-round loop are to the right whilst the loading gauge spans the approach to Nos. 1, 2 and 3 road sidings. The remainder of the total of 11 roads are to the left. In the distant background is the foreman's cottage provided by the GER in 1901.   *R. Powell*

Upwell depot yard facing the buffer stops with Drewry 204 hp 0-6-0 diesel-mechanical shunting locomotive No. D2201 waiting to depart for Wisbech on the former passenger line. The sidings in the foreground are right to left Nos. 1, 2 and 3 goods roads, 660, 670 and 640 feet in length respectively, with Nos. 4 and 5 goods roads to the left. Note the broad carting roads provided between the groups of sidings. Coal wagons stand on No. 5 road whilst Nos. 6 to 9 roads are behind the coal grounds. The foreman's cottage is the building with the tall chimney.

The late Dr I.C. Allen

Looking north towards the yard throat at Upwell with No. 3 road in the foreground and the cattle dock to the right. A goods brake van and three covered vans occupy the former passenger road and await to be collected by Drewry 204 hp 0-6-0 diesel locomotive No. D2202 for conveyance to Wisbech on 3rd September, 1964.   *Author's Collection*

Looking towards the yard throat at Upwell in March 1966. In the left foreground are the points leading to Nos 1, 2 and 3 goods roads with the connection to Nos. 4 and 5 roads serving the cattle dock and pens to the right.   *R. Powell*

An extremely dull, wet and windy Upwell depot on the occasion of the visit of the Railway Correspondence & Travel Society's 'Fensman No. 2 Railtour' on 9th September, 1956. Participants suitably clad in rainwear wander around the yard prior to the train returning to Wisbech and travellers to the comfort of the main line coaches. *Stations UK*

Upwell depot from across the perimeter fence with Drewry 204 hp diesel locomotive No. D2202 standing on the platform road with a brake van before shunting and making up the train for the return journey to Wisbech. *Stations UK*

The former passenger terminal building at Upwell on 9th July, 1955. The Railway Club brake van special train stands on the passenger road with the run-round loop alongside. The crossover in the foreground led to the loop road and a headshunt to the left, which contained an engine inspection pit.   *The late B.D.J. Walsh*

The former passenger terminal building at Upwell in 1966 with the goods yard entrance gates and wagon body in the background. After the withdrawal of the passenger services on and from 31st December, 1927 the depot foreman used the building as an office and store.   *R. Powell*

Drewry 204 hp 0-6-0 diesel-mechanical shunting locomotive No. D2202 waits with a train of covered vans at Upwell on 3rd September, 1964 before departing for Wisbech. Compared with earlier years traffic is declining and much of the yard is devoid of wagons.   *Author's Collection*

No. 7 road, 600 ft in length. The second approach then subdivided into No. 8 road, 920 ft in length and the 675 ft-long No. 9 road. The 11 sidings could accommodate 120 wagons. In the final months of operation the engine release points were removed from certain sidings and it was the normal procedure for the diesel locomotive of an arriving train to accelerate into one of the sidings and whilst approaching the points, the guard used his shunting pole to uncouple the following wagons. As the engine cleared, the points were altered so that the wagons rolled into the adjacent siding. Unfortunately on more than one occasion the speed governor on the locomotive applied the brakes before it entered the siding and the rolling wagons smashed into the buffer beam of the engine making it slide forward, fortunately without derailment.

Upwell depot 5 miles 72 chains from Wisbech from the buffer stops at the end of the former passenger road, with the crossover leading to the run-round loop to the left. The water crane stands by the run-round loop headshunt. This view taken soon after closure shows a deserted yard.   *Stations UK*

Chapter Seven

Regulations, Bye-Laws and Operating Instructions

Regulations

The Regulations under which the tramway was to operate were laid down by the Board of Trade and were very specific on certain points of safety. The Regulations and Bye-Laws produced in accordance with Clauses 55 to 60 of the 1881 Act and duly signed by Henry G. Calcraft, an Assistant Secretary for the Board of Trade on 6th September, 1884 specified the exact requirements:

> The Board of Trade, under and by virtue of the powers conferred upon them in this behalf do hereby state that the following Regulations for securing the Public reasonable protection against danger in the appointment by the Great Eastern Railway Company (hereinafter called 'the Company') of the powers conferred by Parliament upon the Company with respect to the use of steam power on all or any of the Tramways of the Company on which the use of such power had been authorised by the Great Eastern Railway Act 1881 (hereinafter called 'the Tramways') be substituted for all other Regulations in this behalf contained in any Tramway Act or Tramway Order confirmed by Act of Parliament, or in any order of the Board of Trade made thereunder.
>
> And the Board of Trade do also hereby rescind and annul all Bye-Laws heretofore made by them with regard to all or any of such Tramways aforesaid; and do hereby make the following Bye-Laws with regard to any of such Tramways.

1. The Engine or Engines to be used on the Tramway shall comply with the following requirements, that is to say
   a. Each coupled wheel shall be fitted with a brake block, which can be applied by a screw or treadle or by other means, and also by steam. (and also by compressed air. Six wheel coupled engines with brake blocks acting on four wheels may however be used.)
   b. A governor (which cannot be tampered with by the driver) shall be attached to each Engine, and shall be so arranged that at any time when the Engine exceeds a speed of Ten* miles per hour it shall cause the steam to be shut off and the brake applied.
   c. Each Engine shall be numbered and the number shall be shown in a conspicuous part thereof. [By 1906 amended to Each Engine shall be conspicuously numbered.]
   d. Each Engine shall be fitted with an indicator by means of which the speed is shown; with a suitable fender to push aside obstructions; and with a special bell to be sounded as a warning when necessary.
   e. Arrangements shall be made enabling the driver to command the fullest possible view of the road before him.
   f. Each engine shall be free from noise produced by blast and from the clatter of machinery, such as to constitute any reasonable ground of complaint either to the passengers or to the public; the machinery shall be concealed from view at all points above four inches from the level of the rails, and all fire used on such engines shall be concealed from view.
2. Every carriage used on the Tramways shall be so constructed as to provide for the safety of passengers and for their safe entrance to, exit from, and accommodation in such carriages, and for their protection from the machinery of any engine used for drawing or propelling such carriages.

---

* By 1906 amended to Fourteen miles per hour.

3. The Board of Trade and their officers may, from time to time, and shall on the application of the Local Authority of any of the districts through which the said Tramways pass, inspect such engines or carriages used on the Tramways and the machinery therein, and may, whenever they think fit, prohibit the use on the Tramways of any of them which in their opinion are not safe for use. [By 1906 this clause was deleted.]

4. The speed at which such Engines and Carriages shall be driven or propelled along the tramways shall not exceed the rate of EIGHT MILES AN HOUR, and the speed at which such engines and carriages shall pass through facing points, whether fixed or moveable, shall not exceed the rate of FOUR MILES AN HOUR.*

* By 1906 this clause renumbered 3 with the following amendment:
    The speed at which such engines and carriages shall be driven or propelled along the Tramways shall not exceed the rate of TWELVE MILES AN HOUR or such lower rate of speed as is specified below

The speed shall not exceed the rate of **Eight miles an hour**
a. At the Elm Road Crossing.
b. When crossing the New Common Bridge.
c. Between Elm Brewery siding and the Elm Goods Depot.
d. When crossing the road adjoining the Outwell Post Office on the inward journey†
    Four miles an hour
a. Through facing points, fixed or moveable.
b. When crossing the road adjoining Outwell Post Office on the inward journey.#

† and # later deleted from clause d 8 mph and placed under clause b 4 mph.

5. The Engines and Carriages shall be connected by double couplings. [By 1906 this clause renumbered 4.]

6. The speed of the Engines and Carriages shall not exceed the rate of four miles an hour on the narrow portion of the road near the point 15 chains from the commencement of Tramway No. 3. [By 1906 this clause was deleted.]

PENALTY

The Company or any person using steam power on the Tramways contrary to any of the above Regulations is, for every such offence, subject to a penalty not exceeding Ten Pounds: and also in the case of a continuing offence, to a further penalty not exceeding Five Pounds for every day after the first during which such offence shall continue.

Bye-Laws

1. The special bell shall be sounded by the Driver of the Engine from time to time when it is necessary as a warning.
2. No smoke or steam shall be emitted from the Engines so as to constitute any reasonable ground of complaint to the passengers or to the public.
3. Whenever it is necessary to avoid impending danger the Engine shall be brought to a standstill.
4. The entrance to and exit from the Carriages shall be by the hindermost or Conductor's platform.
5. The Engines and Carriages shall be brought to a standstill immediately before crossing at the following places
a. The road near the Duke of Wellington Inn, at a point 1 mile 23 chains from the commencement of tramway No. 1.

b.   The Canal Bridge on Tramway No. 2
c.   The road near the point 35 chains from the commencement of Tramway No. 2
d.   The roads near the points 5 chains, 27 chains and 51 chains respectively from the commencement of Tramway No. 3.

6.   The Company shall place and keep placed, in a conspicuous position inside each Carriage in use on the tramway, a printed copy of these Regulations and Bye-Laws.

By 1906 the Bye-Laws were amended, the clauses reduced to four and renumbered:

1.   No smoke or steam shall be emitted from the Engines so as to constitute any reasonable ground of complaint to passengers or to the public.
2   The entrance to and exit from carriages shall be by the hindermost or Conductor's platform.
3.   The engines and carriages shall be brought to a stand-still whenever it is necessary to avoid impending danger, and immediately before crossing at the following place.
                The road at Outwell Basin Goods Depot.
4.   The company shall place and keep placed, in a conspicuous position inside of each Carriage in use on the Tramways, a printed copy of these Regulations and Bye- Laws.

Later amended to:

1.   The special bell fitted to engines using the tramways shall be sounded by the driver whenever necessary as a warning.

All other byelaws revised by being renumbered from 2 to 5 inclusive.

PENALTY

Any person or corporation offending against or committing a breach of any of these Bye-Laws is liable to a penalty not exceeding Forty Shillings. The provisions of the Tramways Act 1870, with respect to the recovery of penalties is applicable to the penalties for the breach of these Regulations and Bye-Laws.

By 1906 the Penalty clause was amended:

Any person offending against or committing a breach of any of these Bye-Laws is liable to a penalty not exceeding Forty Shillings. The provisions of the Summary Jurisdiction Acts with respect to the recovery of penalties are applicable to the penalties for the breach of these Regulations or Bye-Laws.

Operating Instructions

The GER and later LNER also issued Working Instructions for the tramway in addition to the Regulations and Bye-Laws. The original instruction is shown in full with later amendments or replacement clauses shown in brackets.

This (The Wisbech and Upwell) Tramway has passing Loops and Goods Depots at Elm Bridge, Boyce's Bridge, Outwell Basin, Outwell Village and Upwell, but the crossing stations are **Wisbech, Boyce's Bridge and Upwell only**.

The Trams, which are to cross each other at Boyce's Bridge are so noted in the Working Timetables and these Booked Crossings must be strictly observed, except as provided for in the last paragraph of this Instruction. The man in charge of Boyce's Bridge Depot will be held responsible for unlocking and locking the points to allow the trams from opposite directions to cross each other.

The Tramcars will stop for the purpose of setting down or taking up passengers at any point along the line of route. When additional stoppages have to be made on the journey for which extra time is required, the time allowed in the Timetables may be exceeded, and the Tramcar Engine Driver and Conductor will not be taken up with for time so lost.

(Later amended to: The tramcars will stop at Elm Bridge, Boyce's Bridge, Outwell Basin and Outwell Village, but will only call if required, at the following points

        Elm Road Crossing
        New Common Bridge (Canal Bridge)
        Rose Cottage
        Duke of Wellington Junction
        Inglethorpe Hall
        Collett's Bridge
        Shepherd's Cottage (added in 1927)
        Dial House
        Basin Gate (added in 1927)
        Horn's Corner
        Goodman's Crossing
        Small Lode

The cars are not to stop at any other point along the line of route for the purpose of setting down and taking up passengers.)

(A telephonic communication is provided between Wisbech and Upwell, with a telephone at Elm Depot, Boyce's Depot, Outwell Basin and Outwell Village.)

No Coal or Dead Buffer trucks are to be worked by any of the booked Tramcars trains, but a Special trip must be run during the night for the working of such traffic. The Wisbech Station Master to arrange and advise all concerned.

After dusk and in foggy weather or during falling snow, each engine must carry one red light at the top of the smokebox and one white light in front in the centre of the buffer beam and the last vehicle one red light in rear.

Not exceeding 2 Through trucks from Wisbech to Upwell, and from Upwell to Wisbech, may be worked in the rear of a passenger tram.

The maximum loads of the trams are as under

Passenger Trams	9 vehicles
Mixed Trams	10 vehicles, 4 of which may be loaded Goods trucks.
Coal Trams	4 loaded Trucks in winter and 5 in summer

Note Tram Cars Nos. 5 and 7 to be counted as 2 vehicles each*
(Note Tramcars Nos. 7 and 8 to be counted as 2 vehicles each)†

---

* [For many years the GER Appendices to Working Timetables and Working Timetables referred to the bogie tramcars as Nos. 5 and 7. From rolling stock records and diagrams no reference has been found to bogie tramcar No. 5 and tramcar No. 5 was in fact a four-wheel tramcar to diagram 600. This was an error perpetuated and which was later corrected to No. 8.]
† Deleted by 1927.

WISBECH AND UPWELL TRAMWAY.

(5¾ miles, Single Line).

The Tramway is to be worked under the following Regulations and Bye-Laws issued by the Board of Trade:—

REGULATIONS.

1. The engine or engines to be used on the Tramways shall comply with the following requirements, that is to say:—

   (a) Each coupled wheel shall be fitted with a break block, which can be applied by a screw or treadle or by other means, and also by steam.

   (b) A governor (which cannot be tampered with by the driver) shall be attached to each engine, and shall be so arranged that at any time when the engine exceeds a speed of fourteen miles an hour it shall cause the steam to be shut off and the break applied.

   (c) Each engine shall be conspicuously numbered.

   (d) Each engine shall be fitted with an indicator by means of which the speed is shown; with a suitable fender to push aside obstructions; and with a special bell to be sounded as a warning when necessary.

   (e) Arrangements shall be made enabling the driver to command the fullest possible view of the road.

   (f) Each engine shall be free from noise produced by blast, and from the clatter of machinery, such as to constitute any reasonable ground of complaint either to the passengers or to the public; the machinery shall be concealed from view at all points above four inches from the level of the rails, and all fire used on such engines shall be concealed from view.

2. Every carriage used on the Tramways shall be so constructed as to provide for the safety of passengers, and for their safe entrance to, exit from, and accommodation in, such carriages, and for their protection from the machinery of any engine used for drawing or propelling such carriages.

3. **The speed at which such engines and carriages shall be driven or propelled along the Tramways shall not exceed the rate of TWELVE MILES AN HOUR, or such lower rate of speed as is specified below.**

   The speed shall not exceed the rate of

   Eight miles an hour:—

   (a) At the Elm Road Crossing.

   (b) When crossing the New Common Bridge.

   (c) Between the Elm Brewery Siding and the Elm Goods Depôt.

   Four miles an hour:—

   (a) Through facing points, whether fixed or movable.

   (b) When crossing the road adjoining the Outwell Post Office, on the inward journey.

4. The engines and carriages shall be connected by double couplings.

PENALTY.

The Company or any person using steam power on the Tramways contrary to any of the above Regulations is, for every such offence, subject to a penalty not exceeding **Ten Pounds**; and also, in the case of a continuing offence, to a further penalty not exceeding **Five Pounds** for every day after the first during which such offence continues.

BYE-LAWS.

1. No smoke or steam shall be emitted from the engines so as to constitute any reasonable ground of complaint to passengers or to the public.

2. The entrance to and exit from the carriages shall be by the hindermost or conductor's platform.

3. The engines and carriages shall be brought to a stand-still whenever it is necessary to avoid impending danger, and immediately before crossing at the following place:—

   The road at **Outwell Basin Goods Depot.**

4. The Company shall place and keep placed, in a conspicuous position inside of each carriage in use on the Tramways, a printed copy of these Regulations and Bye-laws.

PENALTY.

Any person or persons offending against or committing a breach of any of these Bye-laws is liable to a penalty not exceeding Forty Shillings.

The provisions of the Summary Jurisdiction Acts with respect to the recovery of penalties are applicable to the penalties for the breach of these Regulations or Bye-laws.

G. E. INSTRUCTIONS FOR WORKING.

This Tramway has passing Loops and Goods Depôts at Elm Depôt, Boyce's Depôt, Outwell Basin, Outwell Village, and Upwell, but the Crossing Stations are **Wisbech, Boyce's Depot, and Upwell only.**

The Trams which are to cross each other at Boyce's Bridge are so noted in the Working Time Tables, and these Booked Crossings must be strictly observed, except as provided for in the last paragraph of this Instruction. The man in charge of Boyce's Bridge Depôt will be held responsible for unlocking and locking the Points to allow the Trams from opposite directions to cross each other.

The Tram Cars will stop at Elm Depot, Boyce's Depot, Outwell Basin and Outwell Village, but will only call, if required, at the following points :—

> Elm Road Crossing.
> New Common Bridge (Canal Bridge).
> Rose Cottage.
> Duke of Wellington Junction.
> Inglethorpe Hall.
> Collett's Bridge.
> Dial House.
> Horn's Corner.
> Goodman's Crossing.
> Small Lode.

The Cars are not to stop at any other point along the line of route for the purpose of setting down or taking up passengers.

A Telephonic communication is provided between Wisbech and Upwell, with a telephone at Elm Depôt, Boyce's Depôt, Outwell Basin and Outwell Village.

No Coal or Dead Buffer trucks are to be worked by any of the booked Tram Car trains but a Special trip must be run during the night for the working of such traffic. The Wisbech Station Master to arrange and advise all concerned.

After dusk, and in foggy weather or during falling snow, each engine must carry one Red Light and one White Light in front, thus—

and the last vehicle one Red Light in rear.

Not exceeding **2 Through** trucks from Wisbech to Upwell, and from Upwell to Wisbech, may be worked **in the rear** of a Passenger Tram.

The maximum loads of the Trams are as under :—

> **Passenger Trams**—**9** vehicles.
> **Mixed Trams**—**10** vehicles, **4** of which may be loaded Goods trucks.
> **Coal Trams**—**4** loaded trucks in winter and **5** in summer.

NOTE.—Tram Cars Nos. **7** and **8** to be counted as 2 vehicles each.

In the event of a blockage on the Tram Line occurring from the failure of an engine or other cause, and another engine is required to be sent to assist the disabled engine or to clear the Line, a man with Hand and Detonating signals must be sent 800 yards in advance of the assistant engine.

In the event of a Tram having to proceed beyond its crossing point owing to the cancelling or stoppage of another Tram, the Guard, with Hand and Detonating signals, must proceed 900 yards in advance of his Tram.

Left & above: Regulations and bye-laws from GER Appendix to Working Timetables 1910.

In the event of a blockage on the Tram Line occurring from the failure of an engine or other cause, and another engine is required to be sent to assist the disabled engine or to clear the line, a man with Hand and Detonating signals must be sent 800 yards in advance of the Assistant engine.

In the event of a Tram having to proceed beyond its crossing point owing to the cancelling or stoppage of another Tram, the Guard with Hand and Detonating signals, must proceed 900 yards in advance of his Tram.

After the withdrawal of passenger services many of the instructions were superseded or modified by the LNER and in 1942 the Regulations, Bye-Laws and Local Instructions were a shadow of the former instructions.

This line is used for the running of Freight trains only and the tramway engines in use must comply with the regulations laid down by the Ministry of Transport.

The special bell fitted to the tramway engines must be sounded by the Driver whenever necessary as a warning.

No smoke or steam must be emitted from engines so as to constitute any reasonable ground of complaint to the public.

Trains must be brought to a standstill as soon as possible whenever it is necessary to avoid impending danger.

Crossing stations are Wisbech, Boyce's Depot and Upwell, and trains, which are to cross each other at Boyce's Depot, will be so noted in the Working Timetables or Special Notices. The man in charge at Boyce's Depot is responsible for unlocking and locking the points to allow trains to cross.

After dusk or during foggy weather or falling snow, each engine must carry one red light (at the top of the smokebox position) and one white light (in the centre of the buffer beam) in front, and the last vehicle one red light in rear.

In the event of a blockage of the line occurring from the failure of an engine or other cause, and another engine is required to be sent to assist the disabled engine or to clear the line, a man with hand and detonating signals must be sent 800 yards in advance of the assisting engine.

Should a train proceed beyond its crossing point owing the cancellation or stoppage of another train, the Guard, with hand and detonating signals, must proceed 900 yards in advance of his train.

Speed Limits on the tramway were as follows:

Wisbech & Upwell Tramway	Up and Down trains	12 mph
Wisbech & Upwell Tramway	Through all facing points	4 mph
Elm Road Crossing	Up and Down Trains	4 mph
New Common Bridge and Duke of Wellington Corner	Up and Down Trains	8 mph
Duke of Wellington Corner and Elm Goods Depot	Up and Down Trains	8 mph
Chapel Lane	Before crossing road	Stop
Outwell Village Post Office	Before crossing road adjoining	Stop

By 1956 BR had further reduced these instructions, which now commenced with reference to the crossing stations and deleted the first four paragraphs. An additional instruction advised 'Drivers of trams proceeding in the up direction must not cross the road at Elm Road until they receive a hand signal from the crossing keeper'.

These instructions remained in force until the closure of the tramway in May 1966.

Chapter Eight

Permanent Way, Signalling and Staff

Permanent Way

The tramway was constructed so that when running alongside the public roads it complied with the Board of Trade Regulations. The rails weighed 50 lb. per yard and were joined by fishplates weighing 40 lb. per pair. The rails were mounted on chairs weighing 38 lb. and were secured to the creosoted sleepers, measuring 8 ft 6 in. by 10 in. by 5 in., by iron spikes and wooden trenails. Where the tramway ran alongside the public highway the sleepers were covered with ballast to the level of the road. The tramway was so laid that at its minimum it was no nearer to the crown of the road that 8 ft and in most cases was a distance of 10 ft. The permanent way was designed to specifications laid down by John Wilson, the Engineer, which enabled the guard rail to be supplied where required or dispensed with when necessary, without interference with the chairs or fastenings. The construction of the tramway was not executed by contractors but carried out by a GER workforce under the direct supervision of Harry Jones, the Resident Engineer. The ballast consisted of ashes and clinker laid to the surface of the adjoining road on sections where the line ran alongside the public highway, but below sleeper level where it crossed railway-owned property.

The original pattern of rails remained in use until 1907 when the GER ordered a quantity of 75 lb. per yard tramway rails, some for use on the Upwell line, at a price of £10 15s. 0d. per ton. Allied to this order was a supply of cast chairs at a cost of £5 4s. 6d. per ton. From 1923 the LNER began replacing short length rails with lengths of 30 ft and 45 ft rails, whilst sleepers were increased in size.

From 1947 a piecemeal relaying programme commenced, using second-hand rails from the main line. Bullhead rails of 89, 90 and 92 lb. per yard in 45 and 60 ft lengths but weighing less because of previous use were installed and the task was completed by 1954. Throughout the life of the line ashes and clinker ballast was sufficient for the tramway, but conventional ballast was utilized on some sections where road side running required more substantial material.

During the harsh winters, frozen mud often accumulated between the running and the check rails, where the tramway bisected the many roads, causing locomotive adhesion problems on the slippery rails. Many cyclists were thrown from the saddle as their machines skidded on the surface whilst pedestrians also suffered, falling unsuspectingly on the black and impacted icy surface.

The maintenance and upkeep of the permanent way and infrastructure on the tramway in GER days was the responsibility of the district engineer, Cambridge and locally by the district inspector of No. 4 District at March. Of the permanent way staff who served on the tramway as well as the section of the main line through Wisbech, platelayer Charles Smith retired on 9th September, 1927, whilst Robert Hicks, ganger retired on 31st May, 1929 and passed away on 30th June, 1933; Robert Challis was sub-ganger until he retired on 6th May, 1932.

Platelayer Tommy Coulston died on 9th March, 1934 and lengthman Thomas Edgeley retired on 14th May, 1935. Four months later ganger J.W. Banks retired on 21st September, 1935 and died on 29th November, 1939. At the end of the 1935 John Singletary, who had served on the tramway for many years before retirement, died on 12th December. Another former ganger, George Banham, passed away on 29th November, 1937. John E. Softley a lengthman died on 6th January, 1940. Another member of the permanent way staff, Thomas Hutchinson retired in February 1946 after 46½ years service. He had entered service with the GER in 1899 and latterly served as an acting ganger for 18 months before being promoted to ganger for the last six years of his career. In 1936 a feasibility study showed that it was more economical to convey permanent way men responsible for maintaining the Coldham to Wisbech section of line and the Upwell tramway to site by motor lorry than by petrol driven rail motor. Authority was duly given for the provision of a road vehicle and, on introduction of the new scheme, the staff was reduced in number from 15 to 13 with a net saving of £109 per annum.

In addition to attending to routine track maintenance, the permanent way gang was responsible for cleaning toilets where no mains sewerage existed, as well as maintenance of fences and gates. On hot and dry summer days they also patrolled the tramway acting as beaters to extinguish any small fires caused by stray sparks from the locomotives.

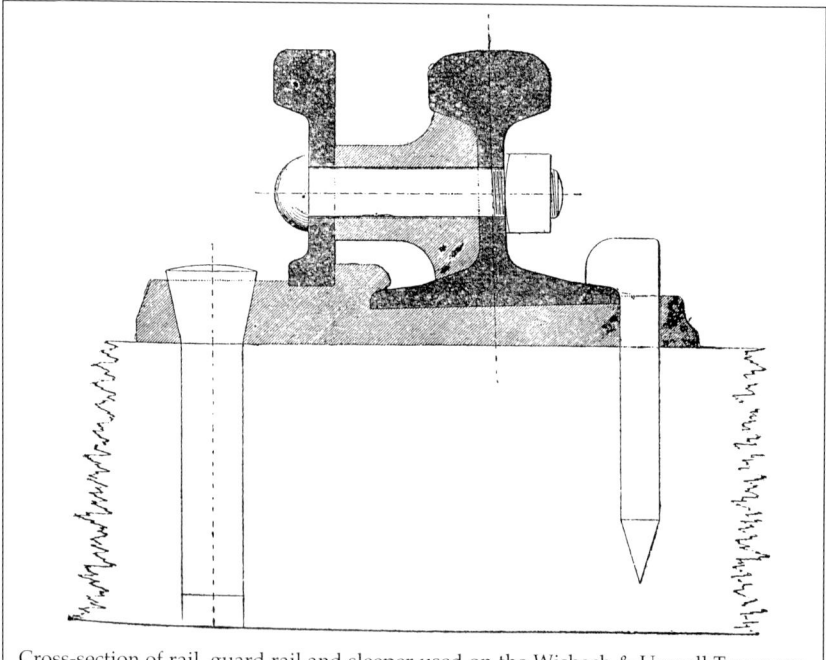

Cross-section of rail, guard rail and sleeper used on the Wisbech & Upwell Tramway.

Signalling

The tramway had few signals and those that applied to the line at Wisbech were under the control of the signalman in Wisbech Station signal box and to a lesser degree Wisbech Harbour Junction signal box. Although the line was single with authorized crossing places at Wisbech, Boyce's Bridge and Upwell no single line train staff or token was issued for permit to enter a single line section. The emergency procedures in the event of a late running service or blockage of the line were included in the Working Instructions (the last two paragraphs shown on page 145).

The initial Wisbech Station signal box involved with train movements on the tramway was of brick and timber construction, located on the down or north side of the line at the west end of the platform and adjacent to Victoria Road level crossing. With the rebuilding of the station it was necessary to re-locate the signal box to the south side of the line and west of the level crossing. This new timber signal box dating from 1888, and measuring 22 ft by 10 ft 5 in. with the operating floor 6 ft 6 in. above rail level, was provided with a Saxby & Farmer 32-lever Rocker frame with 5 in. centres with 21 working and 11 spare levers, later 26 working and six spares. The working floor of the original box was abolished and the ground floor retained as a store until finally demolished in 1899. Wisbech Station signal box was renamed to Wisbech East from 27th September, 1948. After the closure of the tramway on 21st May, 1966 the signals and points were retained until the removal of the tramway connections and all sidings on the up side of the station was completed on 24th July, 1967. Wisbech East Station signal box which then retained its 32-lever frame but with 23 working and nine spares was abolished when the Wisbech East Junction to Magdalen Road line was closed on 9th September, 1968.

The original Wisbech Harbour Junction signal box provided in 1884 was located on the up side of the single line from Emneth opposite the actual junction to Wisbech Harbour and on the east side of the Wisbech canal bridge No. 2322. Six years later in 1890 it was re-sited west of the bridge on the up side of the line adjacent to, but east of, Elm Road level crossing No. 3. The new signal box measuring 16 ft by 10 ft 4 in. with the operating floor 5 ft 8 in. above rail level and located 32 chains distant from Wisbech Station signal box, contained a 16-lever Saxby & Farmer Duplex frame with 4 inch centres initially with 13 working and 3 spare levers, later amended to 14 working and 2 spare levers, and then to all 16 working. Its sole claim to involvement with the Upwell tramway was that lever No. 11 operated a down stop signal which protected Elm Road tram crossing No. 1 and was to advise the driver of a down tram working that the gates across the railway and protecting Elm Road were open for the passage of the train. The Wisbech Harbour Junction signalman was also responsible for advising the signalman in Wisbech Station signal box of an approaching train from Upwell as there were no telephones linking the tramway depots and the signal boxes at Wisbech. Similarly when a tram departed Wisbech for Upwell the signalman in Wisbech Station signal box advised the signalman at Harbour Junction. The latter would open the gates protecting the tramway at Elm Road and advise the driver accordingly by lowering his No. 11 signal and then either close the gates on the

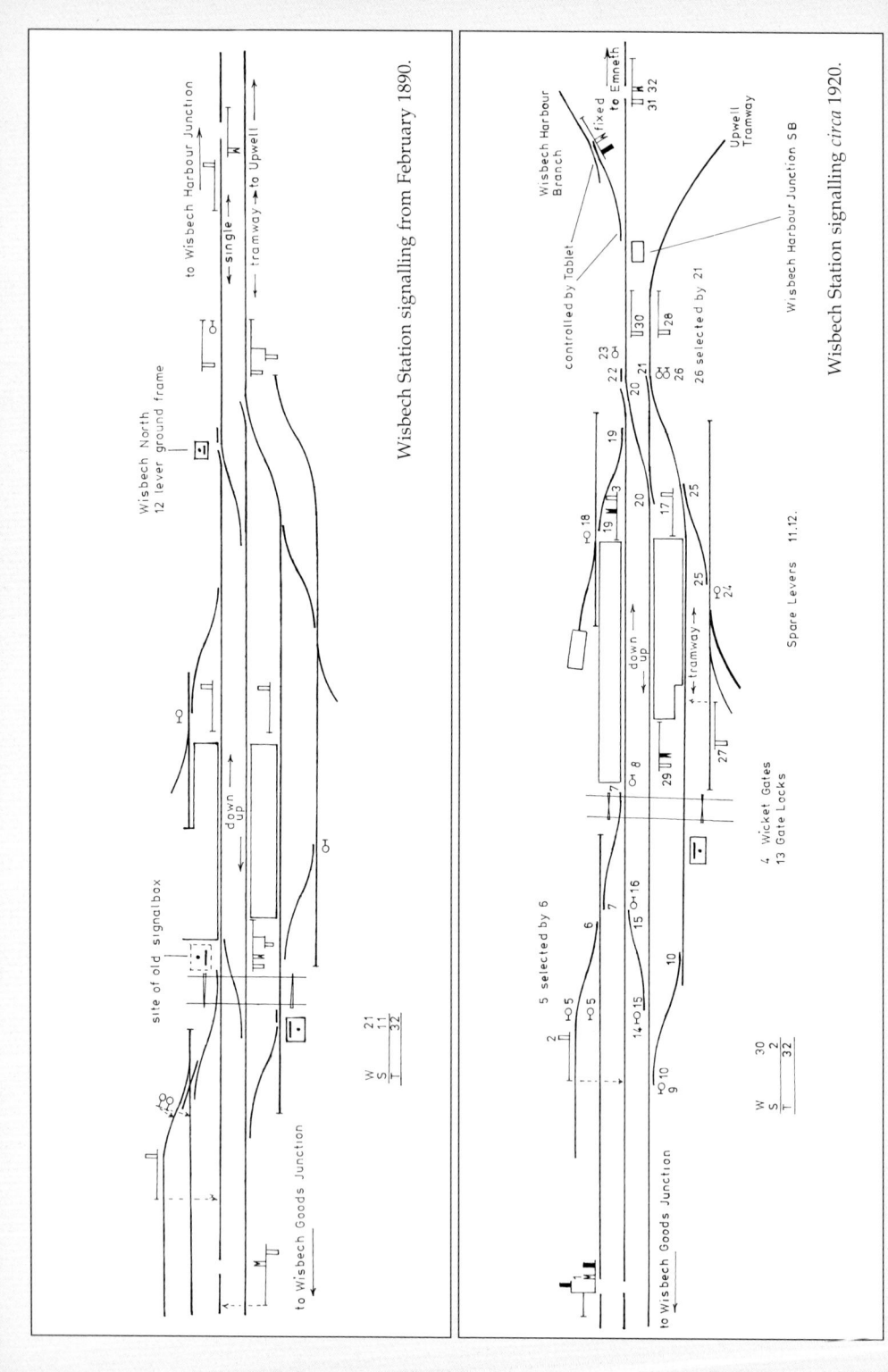

Wisbech Station signalling from February 1890.

Wisbech Station signalling *circa* 1920.

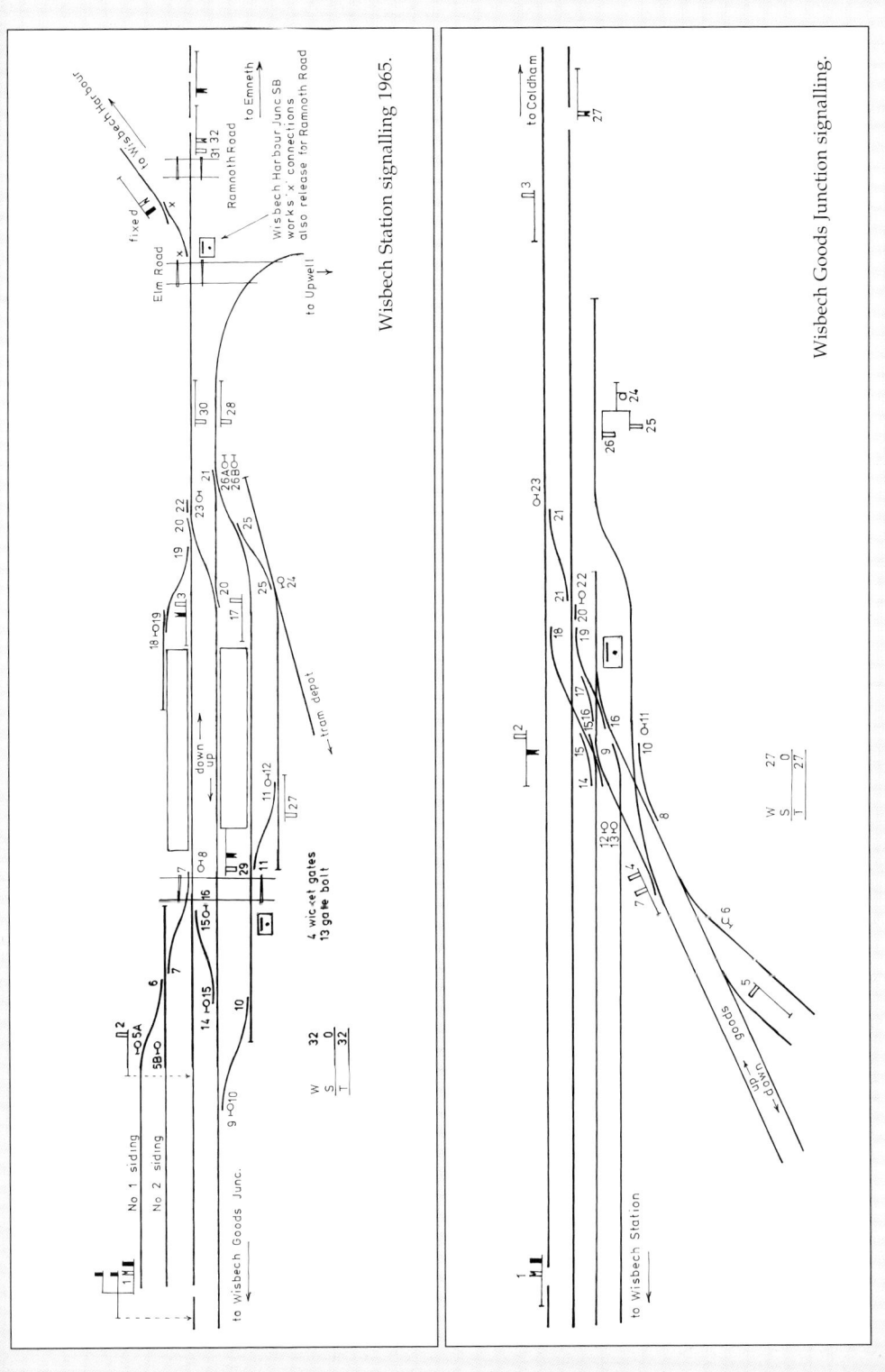

Wisbech Station signalling 1965.

Wisbech Goods Junction signalling.

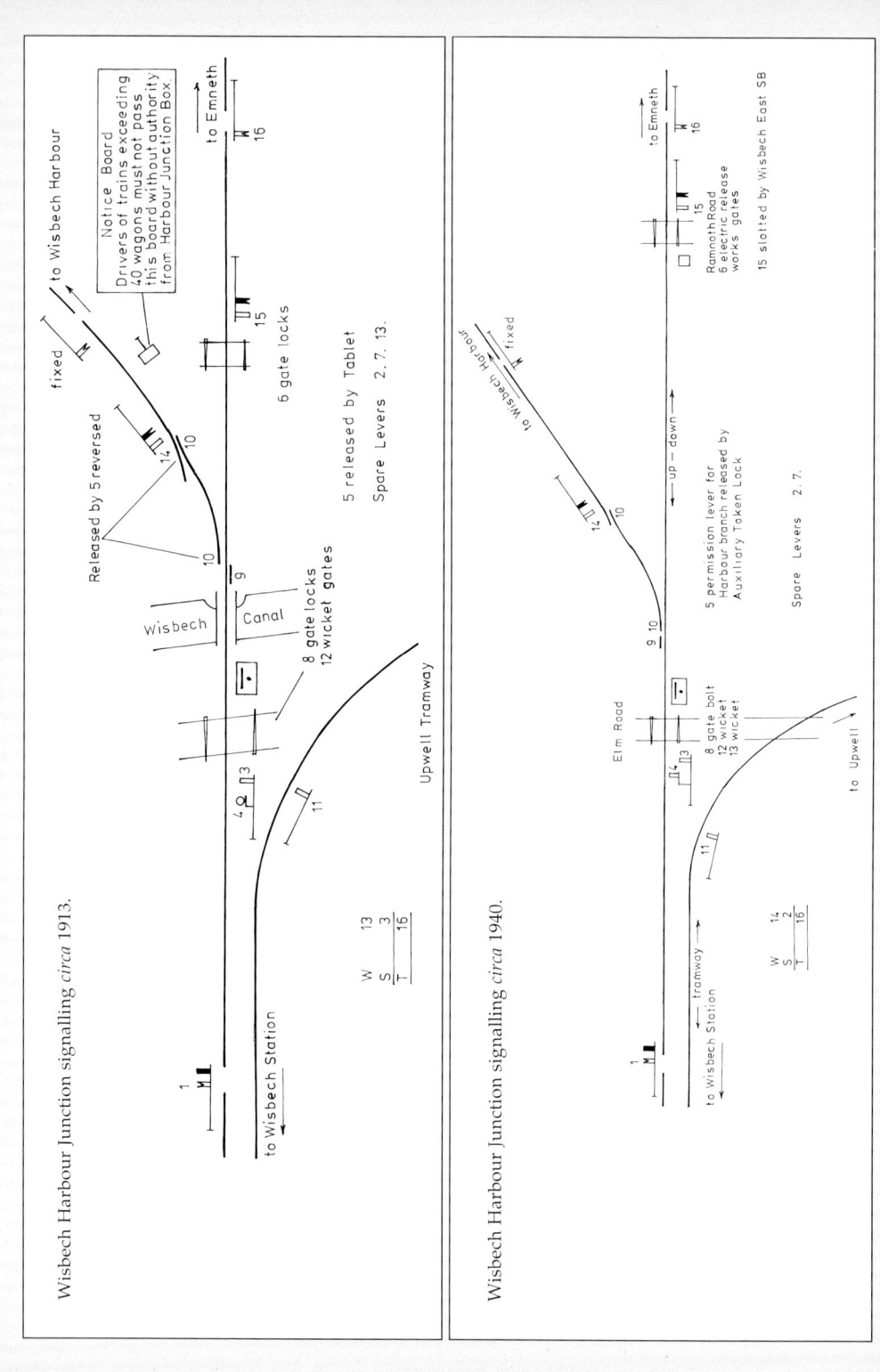

Wisbech Harbour Junction signalling *circa* 1913.

Notice Board
Drivers of trains exceeding
40 wagons must not pass
this board without authority
from Harbour Junction Box

to Emneth

16

15

fixed

to Wisbech Harbour

Released by 5 reversed

14
10

10

6 gate locks

5 released by Tablet

Spare Levers   2. 7. 13.

9

Wisbech   Canal

8 gate locks
12 wicket gates

3

11

Upwell Tramway

to Wisbech Station

W	13
S	3
T	16

Wisbech Harbour Junction signalling *circa* 1940.

to Emneth

16

15

Ramnoth Road
6 electric release
works gates

15 slotted by Wisbech East SB

to Wisbech Harbour

fixed

12
10

up — down

5 permission lever for
Harbour branch released by
Auxiliary Token Lock

9 10

Spare Levers   2. 7.

Elm Road

8 gate bolt
12 wicket
13 wicket

4
3

11

to Upwell

← tramway →

to Wisbech Station

W	14
S	2
T	16

'J70' class 0-6-0 tram locomotive No. 7136 passing Wisbech Station signal box with a transfer freight from Wisbech goods yard to the tramway on 15th June, 1938. The train is coming off the up main line on to the Upwell line at Tramway Junction, which was the zero point for all mileages on the tramway.   *Author's Collection*

Wisbech Goods Junction signal box initially containing a 25-lever Saxby & Farmer frame, later enlarged in stages to 27, then 29 and subsequently to 31 levers controlled points and signals leading to and from Wisbech Goods station occupying the site of the original ECR Wisbech station. The connections to Wisbech goods are straight ahead whilst the main line to Wisbech East curves to the right. View taken in 1962.   *G. Murfitt*

Wisbech Harbour Junction signal box and crossing gates of Elm Road. The signal box containing a 16 lever Saxby & Farmer Duplex frame controlled points and signals on the main single line to Emneth and the connection to the Wisbech harbour branch. The signalman also had control of one signal on the Wisbech & Upwell Tramway.   *R. Powell*

main line or go along Elm Road and stop road traffic to allow the tram the right of way across the thoroughfare. In the latter years the operating instructions required tramway trains working in the up direction to stop and obtain a hand signal from the signalman or crossing keeper before proceeding across Elm Road. Wisbech Harbour Junction signal box was abolished on 9th September, 1968, latterly having only been used as a gate box, although the Harbour branch had closed on 12th September, 1966 and with the junction was officially taken out of use on 20th September, 1967.

Wisbech Goods Junction signal box was only involved with movements of tramway traffic working to and from the goods yard. This box, opened in 1889 as a replacement for an earlier structure, measured 16 ft 5 in. by 10 ft 4 in. with the operating floor 8 ft above rail level and initially contained a 25-lever Saxby & Farmer Duplex frame with all levers working. The frame was subsequently enlarged to 27 levers with 26 working and 1 spare and was again enlarged to 29 levers in 1954. By 1st January, 1967 the frame was again enlarged to 31 levers but on and from 9th September, 1968 the lines towards Wisbech station were designated sidings and the number of working levers reduced. The signal box was finally closed on 18th March, 1969.

In GER days Wisbech Station, Wisbech Harbour Junction and Wisbech Goods Junction signal boxes were open continuously on weekdays and were closed on Sundays between the running of booked trains and later open for trains specially advised. By 1926 the three signal boxes were open continuously from 6.00 am on Monday until 2.00 am the following Sunday, or after the booked trains were 'Out of Section', and then open on Sundays for the running of trains shown in the Working Timetable and for trains specially advised. The same timings prevailed in 1939 but by 1952 Wisbech East and Wisbech Harbour Junction signal boxes were open from 6.00 am Monday until 'Train out of Section' was received for 11.10 pm Saturdays only Whitemoor to King's Lynn freight train and then for the running of trains shown in the Working Timetable and for trains specially advised on Sundays. Wisbech Goods Junction box opened from 5.00 am to 9.00 pm Mondays to Saturdays only. By 1961 Wisbech East signal box was open continuously, whilst the Harbour branch points were controlled by the token for the Wisbech East to Emneth single line section as the signal box had been reduced in status to a gate box. After closure the 32-lever frame from Wisbech East Station signal box was removed by volunteers from the North Norfolk Railway on Sunday 1st June, 1969 together with ground shunt signals and point rodding, for further use on the preserved line linking Sheringham and Holt.

Station Masters and Traffic Staff

In 1883 Deacon Bowker was station master at Wisbech and took up responsibility for the day to day running of the tramway. For the increase in responsibility the post was regraded. Succeeding station masters included George Ablitt in 1901 and F.J. Beales, the latter promoted to station master at Wisbech in 1921 from a similar position at Swavesey where he had served since 1915. He commenced his railway career at Saffron Walden in 1886 and was chief booking clerk at Wisbech from 1899 to 1915. During his time at Wisbech he served as a member of the Town Council and the Isle of Ely County Council. He retired due to ill health at the age of 57 on 17th August, 1929 and subsequently passed away on 25th January, 1937 aged 65. Beales was replaced by F. Maude who stayed at Wisbech until December 1931 when he gained promotion to station master Ardsley on the former Great Northern Railway near Leeds. In November 1933 J. Plant gained promotion from station master Worksop to take charge at Wisbech. His tenure was relatively short for he was promoted to Leicester Central in April 1937 and was superseded by S.J. Hiner. Hiner remained at Wisbech and served through the difficult war years until his retirement on 14th January, 1947. At a social arranged by local staff he was presented with a leather dressing case and wallet in recognition of his 45 years' service by G.M. Willson, the chief goods clerk. The last serving official during the lifetime of the tramway was station master Curson who was recorded in charge in 1963.

From the opening of the tramway, at each of the depots a depot foreman was appointed to issue tickets and handle all the loading and unloading of parcels as well as supervising the loading and unloading of wagons. One of the longest serving was Thomas Reeve who worked at Elm Bridge depot from its opening in 1883 until 1922 when he was succeeded by Fred Blake. Along the line at Outwell Village, Ernie Gretton was foreman for 30 years before retiring on Saturday 13th August, 1960. Charlie Barker superseded Gretton and remained in the position until the depot closed on 20th May, 1966.

Charles Dorrington was working foreman at Outwell depot in 1914 and was resident in the railway cottage where he paid an annual rent of £11 5s. 4d. Dorrington moved to the new cottage erected by GER on 21st November paying a rent of 4s. 4d. per week. He transferred away from Outwell on 19th July, 1924 and the foreman's position was covered by relief staff until Reginald George Rowe was appointed on 1st December, 1924. In 1926 the rent of the cottage had been reduced to £10 14s. 6d. per annum. When Outwell Basin depot closed on 5th October, 1964 the incumbent foreman Newman was transferred to Wisbech East Harbour goods depot.

Michael O'Shea was working foreman at Upwell in 1914 and resided in the railway owned cottage for which he paid an annual rent of £10 8s. 0d. William Gray was appointed porter at Upwell depot in December 1914 but quickly enlisted in the colours. On demobilisation he returned to his post, but in September 1920 was transferred to Kings Lynn where he unfortunately suffered fatal injuries in a shunting accident on 25th September of the same year. Arthur W. Clow was working foreman at the depot in 1924 and paid £14 4s. 8d. annual rent for the cottage, which was increased to £16 0s. 8d. per annum the following year. Wilson Peacock was subsequently appointed to the vacancy at Upwell in 1926 and served at the terminus until retirement on 21st September, 1946 after a total of 36 years' service. He had commenced his railway career as a porter at Chatteris Dock in March 1910 before transferring to Upwell as working foreman. On his retirement Alderman Hunter Row presented Peacock with gifts on behalf of local traders and farmers.

Wisbech guards worked the tramway services and were initially in the tram link although some worked main line services when required. Josiah Rollison and William Collett were early appointees, whilst in December 1923 William Frederick Blake, who had served for five years as a conductor-guard before becoming ticket collector at Wisbech station, retired from service. William Warman had been promoted to guard in 1906 and retired on 3rd June, 1929 after 47 years' service with the GER and LNER. He did not enjoy a long retirement for he passed away on 9th July, 1930. Harry Salmon, who also served as a conductor-guard on the tramway before retirement, died on 11th October, 1937. H.B. Fletcher who had served as a conductor-guard and later as a goods guard on the line retired on 21st June, 1940. Amongst other goods guards who worked the branch over the years were Fred Cole, Arthur Blake, and Tim Downes. The latter worked the final train across the tramway on Friday 20th May, 1966.

Station foreman Fordham of Wisbech retired after nearly 50 years' service with the GER and LNER on 28th September, 1946. He had commenced his railway service as a gate and lamp lad at Swaffhamprior on the Cambridge to Mildenhall branch in 1897 and then served at Whittlesea, March, York and Lincoln before returning to March as a goods guard in 1907. In 1922 he was transferred to Wisbech and served on the tramway before taking up duties as station foreman. At his retirement station master Hiner presented Fordham with a gift of money contributed by his colleagues. Alma Cook, a goods porteress at Wisbech, was presented with an oak clock on 3rd February, 1930 on the occasion of her marriage.

The arrival of the fruit and vegetable traffic at Wisbech meant much shunting and regrouping of wagons for outwards services. The responsibility for much of this work lay with the yard inspector. In the early years Henry E. Quantrill served at Wisbech and recalled the days when loading proceeded from early morning until late in the evening as specials trains brought vans off the tramway and local pick-up goods added to the confusion. He had served as a signalman at Emneth and Wisbech before becoming inspector at Wisbech in 1912. He retired on 8th October, 1927 just before the withdrawal of the tramway passenger services, after 45 years' service. He passed away on 9th March, 1933. Another member of staff involved with the transfer of traffic to and from the tramway, goods foreman George Oglesby passed away on 2nd June, 1938.

Of the signalmen serving at Wisbech Harbour Junction and responsible for hand signalling the tram across Elm Road, mention must be made of James Smith who died in March 1927 at the early age of 40 and John Scott who spent many years in the box and who died in retirement on 1st April, 1930. Another signalman William Brown retired on 22nd April, 1941. On the last day of operation Signalman Harry Kidd performed the honours as No. D2201 headed her train back to Wisbech on Friday 20th May, 1966.

The local staff often arranged social functions at Wisbech and on one such occasion a whist drive, arranged by the clerks of the GE, GN and M&GN companies on Wednesday 18th January, 1911 was attended by over 100 players. The whist drive was followed by a dance. Later in the year on Sunday 13th August the clerical staff of the goods department, which included the staff who travelled on the tramway goods services to attend to consignment notes, organised an annual outing to Yarmouth. A special saloon coach was attached to the 8.13 am excursion train from Wisbech and the return was made on the 8.10 pm special from the Norfolk resort, which arrived back at Wisbech at 11.00 pm.

Chapter Nine

Timetables and Traffic

The GER management always considered the Wisbech & Upwell Tramway as the precursor of an experimental foray into the provision of cheaply built and operated systems, which could tap the hinterland of and provide additional revenue to the main lines and provide useful contributions to the overall receipts of the company. It was always envisaged that freight would provide the largest proportion of traffic but adequate provision was made for passenger traffic, although from the census figures given below the line failed to facilitate an increase in the population, which only increased marginally after the withdrawal of the passenger services. As it turned out the experiment was unique in East Anglia and was not repeated.

The population of the towns and villages served by the Tramway were:

	1871	1881	1891	1901	1911	1921	1931	1951	1961
Wisbech, St Peter	9,362	9,249	9,395	9,381	10,822	11,321	12,006	17,432	17,528
Elm	1,803	1,795	1,779	1,798	2,140	2,738	2,570	2,402	2,492
Emneth	1,048	1,001	922	960	1,082	1,810	1,406	1,956	1,886
Outwell, Cambs	399	343	351	374	376	483	456	576	433
Outwell, Norfolk	894	869	882	846	959	1,084	1,022	1,586	1,736
Upwell, Cambs	2,059	1,855	1,952	1,858	2,064	2,114	2,122	1,639	1,401
Upwell, Norfolk	1,925	2,082	2,107	2,094	2,229	1,917	1,894	2,100	2,439
Total excl. Wisbech	8,128	7,945	7,993	7,930	8,850	10,146	9,470	10,259	10,387
Total incl. Wisbech	17,490	17,194	17,388	17,311	19,672	21,467	21,476	27,691	27,915

The timetable operative from October 1883 showed six trains in each direction on weekdays only and as well as stopping at each of the intermediate depots, the trams were permitted to pick up or set down passengers at any point *en route*. The initial timetable was:

Down		am	am	am	pm	pm	pm
Wisbech Station	dep.	7.10	9.30	11.40	2.40	4.45	6.45
Elm Bridge	dep.	7.28	9.50	12.00	2.58	5.05	7.03
Boyce's Bridge	dep.	7.42	10.05	12.15	3.12	5.20	7.17
Outwell Basin	arr.	7.50	10.15	12.25	3.20	5.30	7.25

Up		am	am	pm	pm	pm	pm
Outwell Basin	dep.	8.00	10.40	1.35	3.40	5.50	7.45
Boyce's Bridge	dep.	8.08	10.48	1.45	3.50	5.58	7.53
Elm Bridge	dep.	8.22	11.02	2.00	4.05	6.12	8.25
Wisbech Station	arr.	8.40	11.20	2.20	4.25	6.30	8.25

The timetable for May 1884 showed the following amended passenger service, weekdays only with extended running times:

Great Eastern Railway

Office of Superintendent of the Line,
Liverpool Street Station.
June 4th 1885

WORKING TIME TABLE OF TRAMCARS

BETWEEN

WISBECH STATION AND UPWELL.

On Monday, 8th June, 1885, and every Week day until further notice, Tramcars will run between Wisbech Station and Upwell as under :—

Miles		1	2 Mixed.	3 Mixed.	4	5	6	
		a.m.	a.m.	a.m.	p.m	p.m.	p.m.	
	Wisbech Station	6 45	9 28	11 40	2 30	5 40	7 50	...
1¾	Elm Bridge	7 3	9 46	12 0	2 48	5 57	8 8	...
3¼	Boyce's Bridge	7 17	10 0	12 15	3 2	6 10	8 22	...
4¼	Outwell Basin	7 25	10 8	12 25	3 10	6 17	8 30	...
5	Outwell Village	7 35	10 18	12 35	3 20	6 26	8 40	...
5¼	Upwell	7 45	10 28	12 45	3 30	6 35	8 50	...

No. 4. An extra Engine, Break, and Guard to leave Wisbech for Upwell attached to No. 4 Trip, and work No. 5 Trip from Upwell to Wisbech.
No. 5 not to leave Wisbech until No. 5 from Upwell has arrived.

Miles		1	2	3 Mixed.	4 Mixed.	5 Fruit & Gds.	6	7
		a.m.	a.m.	p.m.	p.m.	p.m.	p.m.	p.m.
	Upwell	7 55	10 35	12 55	3 35	4 35	6 40	9 0
¼	Outwell Village	8 5	10 45	1 5	3 44	4 45	6 49	9 10
1¼	Outwell Basin	8 15	10 55	1 15	3 53	4 55	6 53	9 20
2¼	Boyce's Bridge	8 23	11 3	1 25	4 0	5 3	7 5	9 28
4	Elm Bridge	8 37	11 17	1 40	4 13	5 17	7 18	9 42
5¼	Wisbech Station	8 55	11 35	2 0	4 30	5 35	7 35	10 0

The Tramcars will stop for the purpose of setting down or taking up Passengers at any point along the line of route.

When additional stoppages have to be made on the journey for which extra time is required, the time allowed in the above Tables may be exceeded, and the Tramcar Engine Driver and the Conductor will not be taken up with for time so lost.

No Coal or Dead Buffer Trucks are to be worked by any of the above Tramcar Trains. A Special Trip is to be run for the working of such Traffic.

For the Regulations and Bye Laws for the Working of the above Tramway, see Special Order, No. R. 1672, of 22nd September, 1884.

For the present only one engine in steam is to be allowed on the Tramway Line at one time, and the engine, after dusk, is to carry one Red Light and one White Light in front, and the last Vehicle is to carry one Red Light in rear.

JAMES ROBERTSON,

Superintendent of the Line

GER working timetable 1885.

Down		am	am	am	pm	pm	pm
Wisbech	dep.	7.15	9.43	11.45	2.30	5.00	7.55
Elm Bridge	dep.	7.33	10.01	12.03	2.48	5.18	8.13
Boyce's Bridge	dep.	7.47	10.15	12.17	3.02	5.32	8.27
Outwell Basin	arr.	8.05	10.33	12.35	3.20	5.50	8.45

Up		am	am	pm	pm	pm	pm
Outwell Basin	dep.	8.15	10.38	1.00	3.25	6.25	8.50
Boyce's Bridge	dep.	8.23	10.48	1.10	3.35	6.35	9.05
Elm Bridge	dep.	8.39	11.02	1.24	3.50	6.55	9.25
Wisbech	arr.	9.05	11.28	1.50	4.15	7.15	9.46

Later from 8th September, 1884 the line was opened throughout from Wisbech to Upwell with journey times of one hour or over.

Down		am	am	am	pm	pm	pm
Wisbech Station	dep.	6.45	9.15	11.40	2.15	5.10	7.50
Elm Bridge	dep.	7.03	9.35	12.00	2.35	5.28	8.05
Boyce's Bridge	dep.	7.17	9.50	12.13	2.47	5.42	8.22
Outwell Basin	dep.	7.25	10.00	12.25	2.53	5.50	8.30
Outwell Village	dep.	7.35	10.10	12.35	3.05	6.00	8.40
Upwell	arr.	7.45	10.20	12.45	3.15	6.10	8.50

Up		am	am	pm	pm	pm	pm
Upwell	dep.	7.55	10.30	12.55	3.40	6.25	9.00
Outwell Village	dep.	8.05	10.40	1.05	3.50	6.35	9.10
Outwell Basin	dep.	8.15	10.50	1.15	4.00	6.45	9.20
Boyce's Bridge	dep.	8.23	10.58	1.25	4.10	6.55	9.26
Elm Bridge	dep.	8.37	11.12	1.40	4.25	7.07	9.42
Wisbech Station	arr.	8.53	11.30	2.00	4.45	7.25	10.00

The tramcars stopped for the purpose of setting down or picking up passengers at any point along the line of route.

The working timetable from June 1885 showed six trains in the down direction. Only one engine in steam was allowed on the tramway at any one time, with the exception for an extra engine and brake van with guard attached to the 2.30 pm down train to specifically work the 4.35 pm fruit and goods train from Upwell. The 5.40 pm down service was not permitted to depart Wisbech until the arrival of the 4.35 pm up train scheduled at 5.35 pm, thus maintaining the 'one engine in steam' method of operation. The tramcars were permitted to stop at any point on the route for the purposes of setting down or taking up passengers. When additional stoppages were made on the journey, for which extra time was required over and above the timetable timings, no action was to be taken against the tramcar engine driver or conductor for time lost *en route*. No coal or dumb buffer wagons were permitted to be conveyed by the scheduled services and special trips were made to work such traffic across the tramway.

TIME TABLE OF TRAMCARS & GOODS TRIPS BETWEEN WISBECH STATION & UPWELL.

(Single Line between Wisbech and Upwell).

Week Days.

Miles.	FROM	1	2	3	4	5	6	7	8	9	10	11	12	13
							A	A	A	B	A	B		
		Gds.	Pass.	Pass.	Gds.	Pass.	Gds.	Gds.	Pass.	Pass.	Pass.	Pass.	Pass.	
		a.m.	a.m.	a.m.	a.m.	a.m.	p.m.	p.m.	p.m.	p.m.	p.m.	p.m.	p.m.	
—	Wisbech Station ......dep.	6 45	7 15	9 43	10 25	11 45	2 0	2 10	2 28	3 0	4 50	5 0	8 0	.....
1¾	Elm Bridge .... ,,	7 2	7 26	9 55	10 42	11 58	2 15	2 25	2 41	3 13	5 3	5 12	8 13	...
3¼	Boyce's Bridge ......arr.	7 15	7 40	10 3	10 55	12 11	2 28	2 38	2 54	3 26	5 16	5 25	8 26	.....
	dep.	7 25	7 41	10 9	11 5	12 12	2 32	2 42	2 55	3 27	5 17	5 26	8 27	...
4¼	Outwell Basin .... ,,	7 33	7 49	10 17	11 18	12 21	2 43	2 53	3 4	3 36	5 26	5 35	8 36	.....
5	Outwell Village ...... ,,	7 49	7 57	10 25	11 30	12 27	2 54	3 4	3 10	3 42	5 32	5 41	8 42	...
5¾	Upwell......................arr.	7 55	8 5	10 33	11 36	12 35	3 0	3 10	3 16	3 50	5 40	5 49	8 50	.....

A Nos. 6, 7, 8, and 10. Not on Saturdays. **B** Nos. 9 and 11. Saturdays only.

The Tramcars will stop for the purpose of setting down or taking up Passengers at any point along the line of route. When additional stoppages have to be made on the journey for which extra time is required, the time allowed in the above Tables may be exceeded, and the Tramcar Engine Driver and the Conductor will not be taken up with for time so lost.

No Coal or Dead Buffer Trucks are to be worked by any of the above Tramcar Trains. A Special Trip is to be run for the working of such Traffic.

The Engine, after dusk, is to carry one Red Light and one White Light in front, and the last vehicle is to carry one Red Light in rear.

For the Regulations and Bye Laws for the working of the above Tramway see pages 269 and 270 of the "Appendix."

Week Days.

Miles.	FROM	1	2	3	4	5	6	7	8	9	10	11	12	13
					D		E	D	D	E	D			
		Pass.	Gds.	Pass.	Gds.	Pass.	Gds.	Pass.	Gds.	Pass.	Gds.		Pass.	Pass.
		a.m.	a.m.	a.m.	p.m.	p.m.	p.m.	p.m.	p.m.	p.m.	p.m.		p.m.	p.m
—	Upwell ....dep.	8 15	8 40	10 38	12 40	1 0	1 50	3 19	3 30	3 55	4 40	.....	6 5	8 55
¾	Outwell Village ...... ,,	8 23	8 51	10 46	12 51	1 8	2 1	3 27	3 43	4 3	4 55	...	6 13	9 3
1¼	Outwell Basin .... ,,	8 31	9 2	10 54	1 2	1 16	2 12	3 35	3 55	4 11	5 0	.....	6 21	9 11
2½	Boyce's Bridge ......arr.	8 39	9 10	11 3	1 10	1 22	2 20	3 42	4 3	4 18	5 8	...	6 28	9 17
	dep	8 40	9 12	11 4	1 13	1 23	2 22	3 43	4 8	4 19	5 18	.....	6 31	9 18
4¼	Elm Bridge .... ,,	8 53	9 25	11 17	1 28	1 37	2 35	3 56	4 33	4 32	5 33	...	6 43	9 32
5¾	Wisbech Station ......arr.	9 5	9 37	11 28	1 40	1 50	2 50	4 8	4 45	4 45	5 45	.....	6 55	9 45

D Nos. 4, 7, 8, and 10. Not on Saturdays. **E** Nos. 6 and 9. Saturdays only;

N.B.—Not exceeding 2 **Through** Trucks from Wisbech to Upwell, and from Upwell to Wisbech may be worked **in rear** of any of the above Passenger Trams.

When required, SPECIAL TRIPS for conveying the Coal Traffic, will be run between Wisbech and Upwell during the night. The Wisbech Station Master to arrange and advise all concerned.

The Loads of the Wisbech and Upwell Trams will be as under .—

Passenger Trams.—Not to exceed 9 vehicles.
Mixed Trams.—Not to exceed 10 vehicles, 4 of which may be loaded Goods Trucks.
Coal Trams.—Not to exceed 4 loaded Trucks in Winter and 5 in Summer.

Tram Cars Nos. 5 and 7 each to be counted as 2 vehicles.

GER Working Timetable 1897.

The public timetable for 1892 showed the following weekday service:

Down		am	am	am	pm	pm	pm
Wisbech	dep.	7.15	9.43	11.45	2.30	5.00	7.55
Elm Bridge	dep.	7.26	9.55	11.58	2.43	5.12	8.08
Boyce's Bridge	dep.	7.41	10.09	12.12	2.57	5.26	8.22
Outwell Basin	dep.	7.49	10.17	12.21	3.06	5.35	8.31
Outwell Village	dep.	7.57	10.25	12.27	3.13	5.41	8.37
Upwell	arr.	8.05	10.33	12.35	3.20	5.50	8.45

Up		am	am	pm	pm	pm	pm
Upwell	dep.	8.15	10.38	1.00	3.25	6.25	8.50
Outwell Village	dep.	8.23	10.46	1.08	3.33	6.33	8.58
Outwell Basin	dep.	8.31	10.54	1.16	3.41	6.41	9.06
Boyce's Bridge	dep.	8.40	11.04	1.23	3.49	6.51	9.13
Elm Bridge	dep.	8.53	11.17	1.37	4.05	7.03	9.32
Wisbech	arr.	9.05	11.28	1.50	4.15	7.15	9.46

The 1897 working timetable showed a service of six passenger and four goods trains in each direction on Mondays to Fridays and six passenger and two goods trains each way on Saturdays. Passenger trains were allowed 50 minutes running time and goods trains between 60 and 70 minutes for the 5 miles 72 chains journey. In addition to the scheduled stops at the intermediate depots, the passenger tramcars were permitted to stop for the purpose of setting down or taking up passengers at any point on the line of route. When such additional stops were made, the scheduled time could not be maintained and the driver and conductor were not held responsible for any late running. Passenger trains could convey at the rear of the formation not exceeding two trucks through from Wisbech to Upwell or vice versa. No coal or dumb buffer wagons were to be worked by scheduled tram services and such traffic was to be worked by special train. When required these special trains were worked between Wisbech and Upwell during the night, with the Wisbech station master responsible for making the necessary local arrangements. The loads on the passenger trams were not to exceed nine vehicles, mixed trams 10 vehicles, of which four may be loaded goods trucks, and coal trams were not to exceed four loaded trucks in winter and five loaded in summer. Bogie tramcars Nos. 5 and 7, later 7 and 8 were to be counted as two vehicles.

The 1899 public timetable showed the following service:

Down					SX	SO		
		am	am	am	pm	pm	pm	pm
Wisbech	dep.	7.15	9.43	11.45	2.28	3.00	5.00	8.00
Elm Bridge	dep.	7.26	9.55	11.58	2.41	3.13	5.12	8.13
Boyce's Bridge	dep.	7.41	10.09	12.12	2.55	3.27	5.26	8.27
Outwell Basin	dep.	7.49	10.17	12.21	3.04	3.36	5.35	8.36
Outwell Village	dep.	7.57	10.25	12.27	3.10	3.42	5.41	8.42
Upwell	arr.	8.05	10.33	12.35	3.16	3.50	5.49	8.50

SX – Saturdays excepted.
SO – Saturdays only.

Up

		am	am	pm	SX pm	SO pm	pm	pm
Upwell	*dep.*	8.15	10.38	1.00	3.19	3.55	6.05	8.55
Outwell Village	*dep.*	8.23	10.46	1.08	3.27	4.03	6.13	9.03
Outwell Basin	*dep.*	8.31	10.54	1.16	3.35	4.11	6.21	9.11
Boyce's Bridge	*dep.*	8.40	11.04	1.23	3.43	4.19	6.31	9.18
Elm Bridge	*dep.*	8.53	11.17	1.37	3.56	4.32	6.43	9.32
Wisbech	*arr.*	9.05	11.28	1.50	4.08	4.45	6.55	9.45

The 1907 working timetable continued to show six passenger and four goods trains in each direction on Mondays to Fridays and six passenger and two goods trains each way on Saturdays. Passenger trams were allowed 39 minutes running time, whilst the goods trips varied between 56 minutes and 1 hour 35 minutes for the journey.

Down
6.45 am (goods), 7.30, 9.43, 10.25 (goods), 11.45, 12.30 pm SX (goods), 2.10 SX (goods), 2.28 SX, 3.00 SO, 5.20, 8.10.

Up
8.26 am, 8.40 (goods), 10.49, 12.40 pm SX (goods), 1.11, 1.50 SO (goods), 3.21 SX, 3.30 SX (goods), 4.00 SX (goods), 4.06 SO, 6.16, 8.55.

All trams called at all intermediate depots, except the 3.30 pm (SX) goods ex-Upwell which omitted calling at Outwell Village and the 4.00 pm (SX) goods which only called at Outwell Village and Boyce's Bridge. Boyce's Bridge depot was used as the crossing point for the 10.25 am down goods train and the 10.49 am up passenger tram and also Saturdays excepted for the crossing of the 12.30 pm (SX) down goods and the 1.11 pm up passenger service. The 2.10 pm (SX) goods ex-Wisbech also shunted at Boyce's Bridge depot for the following 2.28 pm (SX) passenger tram ex-Wisbech to pass. In addition to stopping at the timetabled tram depots passenger services were authorized to stop at Elm Road Crossing, Newcommon bridge, Rose Cottage, Duke of Wellington Junction, Inglethorpe Hall, Collett's bridge, Dial House, Horn's Corner, Goodman's Crossing and Small Lode for the purpose of taking up or setting down passengers. The tramcars were not permitted to stop at any other points *en route*. No coal or dead buffer trucks were to be worked by timetabled services and special trips were arranged to work such wagons. When required, special trips for the conveyance of coal traffic were to run during the night with the Wisbech station master making the necessary arrangements. Passenger trains were permitted to take not exceeding two wagons as a tail load between Wisbech and Upwell and vice versa but not to the intermediate depots. The working timetable for 1908 was identical.

In 1913 the working timetable for the tramway showed the usual six passenger and four goods trains in each direction, Saturdays excepted, and six passenger and two goods trains each way, Saturdays only.

Down
6.45 am (goods), 7.30, 9.45, 10.25 (goods), 11.45, 12.30 pm SX (goods), 2.10 SX (goods), 2.36 SX, 3.00 SO, 5.20, 8.10 SX, 8.30 SO.

Up
8.26 am, 8.40 (goods), 10.49, 12.40 pm SX (goods), 1.11, 1.50 SO (goods), 3.21 SX, 3.30 SX (goods), 4.00 SX (goods), 4.06 SO, 6.16, 8.55 SX, 9.15 SO.

There were no alterations to the stopping patterns or special arrangements and similar instructions to those applicable in 1907 remained in operation.

The working timetable for 1916 continued to show a service of six passenger and four goods train in each direction, Saturdays excepted, and six passenger and two goods services each way, Saturdays only. All trains called at all depots *en route* except the 3.30 pm (SX) goods ex-Upwell which omitted calling at Outwell Village and the 4.00 pm (SX) goods ex-Upwell which called at Outwell Village and Boyce's Bridge depot only. Two down and three up services were booked to cross other trains at Boyce's Bridge depot. Passenger services also called at the same authorized stopping points shown in the 1907 timetable. Not exceeding two trucks were permitted as a tail load on passenger trains provided they were worked through from Wisbech to Upwell or Upwell to Wisbech. No coal or dead buffer wagons were to be worked by the booked timetabled trains with the arrangements for clearing these as before. Passenger services were allowed 39 minutes for the 5 miles 72 chains journey, whilst goods train timings varied between 55 minutes and 90 minutes.

In 1919 there were six passenger services each way, weekdays only.

The final GER working timetable for 1922 showed an increased service of seven passenger and four goods trains in each direction, Saturdays excepted, and seven passenger and three goods trains each way, Saturdays only. There was also an additional 'Q' goods train path in each direction which ran only when required, Saturdays excepted.

Down
6.30 am (goods), 7.55, 9.30, 10.55 SX, 10.55 SO (goods), 11.05 SX (goods), 11.30 SO (goods), 11.55 SO, 12.40 pm SX, 12.45 SX, 2.13 SX (goods), 2.25 SX (Q) (goods), 2.45 SX, 3.05 SO, 5.32, 6.45 SX, 7.20 SO, 8.00 SX, 8.30 SX 9.00 SO.

Up
8.35 am, 9.15 (goods), 10.15, 11.40 SX, 1.03 pm SO, 1.25 SX (pass), 1.25 SO (goods), 1.25 (Q) SX (goods), 1.50 SO (goods), 3.32 SX, 3.35 SX (goods), 3.50 SX (goods), 4.06 SO, 4.15 SX (goods), 6.16, 7.32 SX, 8.05 SO, 8.50 SX, 9.20 SX, 9.45 SO.

Q - Runs when required.

Similar arrangements were in force for the working of coal traffic and for the additional stopping points for passenger services as in previous timetables.

The LNER public timetable for July 1923 showed seven passenger trains each way, Saturdays excepted, and eight, Saturdays only. Running times remained at 39 minutes and in addition to stopping at the depots, the tram was shown to call if required at the following intermediate points to set down or pick up passengers; Elm Road Crossing, Newcommon bridge (canal bridge), Rose Cottage, Duke of Wellington Junction, Inglethorpe Hall, Collett's bridge, Shepherd's Cottage, Dial House, Basin Gate, Horn's Corner, Goodman's Crossing and Small Lode. Trams would not stop at any other place along the line of route.

By 1926 the service had been increased to eight passenger trains each way, with one less in the summer season when there was more goods traffic.

The LNER working timetable from 11th July, 1927, the last summer of passenger train operation, showed in the down direction a weekdays only service of seven passenger trains, Saturdays excepted, eight passenger trains,

WISBECH AND UPWELL TRAMWAY. *Tram Cars run as under:—*

WEEK DAYS.

								Sats. only.			
WISBECH STATION	dep.	7 30	9 45	11 45			4 0	5 20	8 10		
Elm Depot											
Boyce's Depot											
Outwell Basin											
Outwell Village											
UPWELL	arr.							5 59	8 49		

					NotSats.		Sats. only.		
UPWELL	dep.	8 26	9 45	11 22			4 16	6 16 8 55	
Outwell Village									
Outwell Basin									
Boyce's Depot									
Elm Depot									
WISBECH STATION	arr.	9 5	11 23					6 55 9 34	

In addition to the above stopping places, the Tram Cars will also stop at the following points in Upwell, but for the purpose of taking up or setting down Passengers, viz.: — Elm Road Crossing, New Common Bridge (Canal Bridge), Rose Cottage, Duke of Wellington Junction, Inglethorpe Hall, Collett's Bridge, Horn's Corner, Goodman's Crossing, and Small Lode. The Tram Cars will not stop at any other points along the line of route.

FARES.

	Wisbech.			Elm Depot.		
	1st Class.	2nd Class.		1st Class.	2nd Class.	
Elm Depot	1d.	1d.	Boyce's Depot	1d.	1d.	Outwell Village
Boyce's Depot	2d.	2d.	Outwell Basin	2d.	1d.	1st Class. 2nd Class.
Outwell Basin	3d.	2d.	Outwell Village	2d.	2d.	2d. 1d.	Upwell
Outwell Village	4d.	3d.	Elm Depot.			
Upwell		4d.	1st Class.	2nd Class.		

GER public timetable 1910.

GER working timetable 1916.

TIME TABLE OF TRAMCARS & GOODS TRIPS BETWEEN WISBECH STATION & UPWELL.

Single Line. For regulations and bye laws for working this tramway see "Appendix" to the Working Time Tables.

M.C.	WEEK DAYS.		1 Gds.	2 Pass.	3 Gds.	4 Pass.	5 Gds.	6 Pass.	7 Gds. NS	8 Pass. SO	9 Gds. NS	10 Pass.	11 Pass. NS	12 Pass. SO
			a.m.	a.m.	a.m.	a.m.		p.m.	p.m.	p.m.	p.m.	p.m.	p.m.	p.m.
	Wisbech Stn. (S)	dep.	6 45	7 30	9 45	10 25	11 45	2 30	2 30	3 0	5 32	8 0	8 30	
1 53	Elm Depot		7 7	7 41	9 56	10 42	11 56	2 39	2 35	3 15	5 43	8 11	8 41	
3 25	Boyce's Depot (S)	arr.	7 12	7 50	10 5	10 52	12 5	2 45	2 35	3 20	5 52	8 20	8 50	
		dep.	7 25	8 12	6 12		12 49	2 49		3 25	5 53	8 21	8 51	
4 12	Outwell Basin		7 33	8 57	10 12			2 55		3 27	5 59	8 27	8 57	
4 79	Outwell Village		7 49	8 10	10 18	11 33	12 18	3 0		3 33	6 3	8 33	9 3	
5 72	Upwell (S)	arr.	7 55	8 10	10 24	11 39	12 24	3 3		3 39	6 11	8 39	9 9	

In addition to the above stopping places, the tram cars will also stop at the following points if required, for the purpose of taking up or setting down passengers, viz.:— Elm Road Crossing, New Common Bridge (Canal Bridge), Rose Cottage, Duke of Wellington Junction, Inglethorpe Hall, Collett's Bridge, Dial House, Horn's Corner, Goodman's Crossing, and Small Lode. The tram cars will not stop at any other point along the line of route.

No coal or dead buffer trucks are to be worked by any of the above tram-car trains. A special trip is to be run for the working of such traffic.

The engine, after dusk, is to carry one red light and one white light in front, and the last vehicle is to carry one red light in rear.

TIME TABLE OF TRAMCARS & GOODS TRIPS BETWEEN WISBECH STATION & UPWELL.

WEEK DAYS.		1 Pass.	2 Gds.	3 Pass.	4 Pass.	5 Gds. NS	6 Pass. SO	7 Gds. SO	8 Gds. NS	9 Pass.	10 Gds.	11 Pass.	12 Pass. SO	13 Pass. SO
		a.m.	a.m.	a.m.	a.m.	p.m.	p.m.	p.m.	p.m.	p.m.	p.m.	p.m.	p.m.	p.m.
Upwell (S)	dep.	8 26	8 40	10 49		1 30	1 30		3 21	4 0	4 6	6 16	8 50	9 20
Outwell Village "		8 32	8 51	10 55	12 51	1 9	2 0		3 27	4 12	4 30	6 22	8 56	9 26
Outwell Basin "		8 38	9 2	11 0	1 1	1 15	2 7		3 33	4 18		6 28	9 2	9 32
Boyce's Depot (S)	arr.	8 43	9 7	11 6	1 7	1 20	2 13		3 38	4 23		6 33	9 7	9 37
	dep.	8 44	9 12	11 7	1 13	1 21	2 22		3 39	4 24	4 39	6 34	9 8	9 38
Elm Depot "		8 54	9 25	11 17	1 25	1 31	2 41		3 49	4 34		6 44	9 18	9 48
Wisbech Stn. (S)	arr.	9 5	9 36	11 28	1 39	1 42	2 44		4 0	4 45		6 55	9 29	9 59

N.B.— Not exceeding 2 Through trucks from Wisbech to Upwell, and from Upwell to Wisbech may be worked in rear of any of the above passenger trams.

When required, SPECIAL TRIPS for conveying the coal traffic will be run between Wisbech and Upwell during the night. The Wisbech Station Master to arrange and advise all concerned.

The loads of the Wisbech and Upwell trams will be as under:
Passenger trams.—Not to exceed 9 vehicles.
Mixed trams.—Not to exceed 10 vehicles, 4 of which may be loaded goods trucks.
Coal trams.—Not to exceed 4 loaded trucks in Winter and 5 in Summer.

Tram Cars Nos. 7 and 8 each to be counted as 2 vehicles.

Saturdays only, four goods trains, Saturday excepted, three goods trains, Saturdays only, augmented by an additional goods train which ran as required Saturdays excepted. Passenger services were allowed 39 minutes running time between Wisbech and Upwell and goods services up to 90 minutes for the 5 miles 72 chains journey. In addition to stopping at the intermediate depots, passenger services were authorized to call if required at Elm Road Crossing, Newcommon bridge (canal bridge), Rose Cottage, Duke of Wellington Junction, Inglethorpe Hall, Collett's bridge, Shepherd's Cottage, Dial House, Basin Gate, Horn's Corner, Goodman's Crossing and Small Lode for the purposes of picking up or setting down passengers. No other stopping points were allowed. No coal trucks were to be worked by any of the services, a special train being arranged to convey such loads as before. Not exceeding four through trucks could be worked on the rear of passenger trains from Wisbech to Upwell or Upwell to Wisbech. Boyce's Bridge depot was used extensively as a crossing point on the single line and no less than five services passed one another at this station.

The running time of 39 minutes could not be improved and was too slow to compete against rival bus services. Passenger trains were withdrawn on and from Saturday 31st December, 1927 and the following Monday, 2nd January, 1928, the bus services were improved and a replacement service operated in place of the tram.

The working timetable for 1928 showed four goods trains, Saturdays excepted, and three Saturdays only, in each direction. Trains only called at Elm Depot, Boyce's Bridge, Outwell Basin and Outwell Village if required. Timings varied between 1 hour 5 minutes and 1 hour 30 minutes. By 1937 the working timetable showed three (SX) and two (SO) only trains in each direction. Trains only called at the intermediate depots when required to pick up or set down traffic. Parcels and Miscellaneous traffic and livestock at passenger rates were conveyed by these services. The engine after dusk carried one red light and one white light on the front, whilst the last vehicle carried on red light on the rear.

In 1939 two services ran in the down direction each weekday departing Wisbech station, the 2.10 pm (SX) being double-headed to enable the second locomotive to work an additional up service from Upwell. In the up directions three trains ran (SX) and two (SO). All trains called at the intermediate depots only if required. The engine of the 11.15 am (SO) from Upwell after arrival at Wisbech at 12.15 pm performed shunting duties at Wisbech goods yard until 2.00 pm. Timings varied between 60 minutes and 90 minutes *en route*.

The 1944 working timetable showed a service of three (SX) and two (SO) trains in each direction, each calling at the intermediate depots only if required. The first down train of the day conveyed the usual passenger van for the conveyence of parcels, fish and small traffic for local shops, whilst the 12.45 pm (SX) ex-Wisbech cleared Outwell Village of traffic for forwarding by the 4.15 pm (SX) up train from Upwell. The 3.20 pm (SX) from Upwell conveyed the passenger van to clear parcels from the depots and cleared all goods traffic from Outwell Basin, Boyce's Bridge depot and Elm Bridge depot. As in previous years, timings varied between 60 minutes and 90 minutes for the journey.

The 1946 working timetable continued to show the same number of Saturdays excepted and Saturdays only trains. These only called at the intermediate depots if required:

TIME TABLE OF TRAMCARS & GOODS TRIPS BETWEEN WISBECH & UPWELL.

Single Line. For regulations and bye laws for working this tramway see "Appendix" to the Working Time Tables.

DOWN WEEK DAYS.

Miles M.C.			1 Gda. a.m.	2 Pass. a.m.	3 Pass. a.m.	4	5 Pass. a.m.	6 Pass. a.m.	7 Pass. a.m.	8 Pass. a.m.	9 Gda. SO a.m.	10 Gda. SO a.m.	11	12 Pass. p.m.	13	14 Gda. NS p.m.	15 W.R. NS Gda. p.m.	16 Gda. NS p.m.	17 Pass. NS p.m.	18 Pass. NS p.m.	19	20 Pass. SO p.m.	21	22	23 Pass. p.m.	24	25 Pass. NS p.m.	26 Pass. SO p.m.	27 Pass. p.m.	28
	Wisbech Station	dep.	6 30	8 15	7 30	—	9 30	10 55	10 55	11 28	11 5	11 45	—	12 40	—	12 45	—	2 12	2 15	2 30	—	4 25	—	—	6 20	—	8 30	9 0	—	
1 53	Elm Depot		6 50	8 21	7 41	—	9 41	11 6	11 6	11 15	11 40	11 45	—	12 51	—	1 15	—	2 30	2 41	3 10	—	4 36	—	—	6 31	—	8 41	9 11	—	
3 25	Boyce's Depot	arr.	7 5	8 27	7 47	—	9 50	11 15	11 15	11 22	11 51	11 55	—	1 1	—	1 25	2 32	2 39	2 51	3 11	—	4 50	—	—	6 40	—	8 50	9 20	—	
		dep.	7 20	8 31	7 51	—	9 51	11 16	11 16	11 29	11 58	12 10	—	1 7	—	1 50	—	2 44	3 17	—	—	4 56	—	—	6 47	—	8 57	9 27	—	
4 12	Outwell Basin		7 54	8 43	8 3	—	10 3	11 28	11 28	12 18	12 24	12 20	—	1 13	—	2 4	—	2 59	3 23	—	—	5 3	—	—	6 53	—	9 3	9 33	—	
4 79	Outwell Village		8 0	8 54	8 9	—	10 9	11 34	11 34	12 30	12 46	12 40	—	1 19	—	2 9	—	3 3	3 28	—	—	5 8	—	—	6 59	—	9 9	9 39	—	
5 72	Upwell	arr.	8 0													2 15	2 52													

UP WEEK DAYS.

Miles M.C.			1 Pass. a.m.	2 Pass. a.m.	3 Gda. a.m.	4 Gda. a.m.	5	6 Pass. a.m.	7 Pass. a.m.	8	9 Pass. p.m.	10 Gda. WB p.m.	11	12 Gda. SO p.m.	13	14 Pass. NS p.m.	15 Gda. SO p.m.	16 Gda. NS p.m.	17 Gda. NS p.m.	18 Gda. NS p.m.	19 Gda. NS p.m.	20 Pass. SO p.m.	21 Pass. p.m.	22	23 Pass. p.m.	24	25 Pass. NS p.m.	26 Pass. SO p.m.	27 Pass. p.m.	28
	Upwell	dep.	8 15	—	9 30	9 30	—	10 11	10 11	—	1 25	1 26	—	1 50	—	3 15	3 35	3 35	3 50	4 15	4 25	5 15	—	—	7 5	—	9 15	9 45	—	
73	Outwell Village		8 21	—	9 36	9 36	—	10 21	10 21	—	1 31	1 31	—	2 15	—	3 21	3 41	3 50	4 10	4 25	4 30	5 21	—	—	7 11	—	9 21	9 51	—	
1 60	Outwell Basin		8 27	—	9 40	9 40	—	10 27	10 27	—	1 37	1 37	—	2 25	—	3 27	3 47	4 14	4 30	4 35	4 35	5 27	—	—	7 17	—	9 27	9 57	—	
2 47	Boyce's Depot	arr.	8 33	—	9 45	9 45	—	10 33	10 33	—	1 42	1 42	—	2 35	—	3 33	3 53	4 20	4 35	5 0	4 61	5 33	—	—	7 23	—	9 33	10 3	—	
		dep.	8 33	—	9 53	9 53	—	10 33	10 33	—	1 43	1 50	—	3 12	—	3 43	4 8	4 61	5 0	5 10	—	5 33	—	—	7 33	—	9 33	10 10	—	
4 19	Elm Depot		8 43	—	10 18	10 18	—	10 43	10 43	—	1 53	2 4	—	3 22	—	3 43	3 5	5 19	5 20	5 30	—	5 43	—	—	7 44	—	9 43	10 13	—	
5 72	Wisbech Station	arr.	8 54	—	10 30	10 30	—	10 54	10 54	—	2 1	2 11	—	3 33	—	3 54	4 14	5 30	5 40	6 10	—	5 54	—	—		—	9 54	10 24	—	

In addition to the above stopping places, the tram cars will also stop at the following points if required, for the purpose of taking up or setting down passengers, viz.—Elm Road Crossing, New Common Bridge (Canal Bridge), Rose Cottage, Duke of Wellington Junction, Inglethorpe Hall, Collett's Bridge, Shepherd's Cottage, Dial House, Basin Gate, Horn's Corner, Goodman's Crossing, and Small Lode. The tram cars will not stop at any other point along the line of route.

No coal trucks are to be worked by any of the above tram-car trains. A special trip is to be run for the working of such traffic.

When required, SPECIAL TRIPS for conveying the coal traffic will be run between Wisbech and Upwell during the night. The Wisbech Station Master to arrange and advise all concerned.

The loads of the Wisbech and Upwell Passenger trams must not exceed 9 vehicles.

Loads of Goods and Coal trains.—The loads of goods and coal trains over the Wisbech and Upwell Tramway may be increased as under :—

For ordinary purposes, four-coupled tram engine loads :—

10 mineral; 15 goods: 22 empties.

and for six-coupled tram engines for ordinary purposes the loads should be :—

15 mineral; 22 goods; 33 empties.

These loads may, however, be increased to meet special exigencies. The D.S.O. to arrange.

Tram Cars Nos. 7 and 8 each to be counted as 2 vehicles.

N.B.—Not exceeding 4 Through trucks from Wisbech to Upwell, and from Upwell to Wisbech may be worked in rear of a passenger tram.

The engine, after dusk, is to carry one red light and one white light in front, and the last vehicle is to carry one red light in rear.

LNER working timetable 1927.

TIME TABLE OF GOODS TRIPS BETWEEN WISBECH & UPWELL.

Single Line. For regulations and bye laws for working this tramway see "Appendix" to the Working Time Tables.

Parcels and Miscellaneous traffic and live stock at passenger rates will also be worked by goods service.

Miles.	DOWN WEEK DAYS.			1 Gds.	2	3 Gds.	4	5 Gds. SO	6	7 Gds. NS	8	9 Gds. NS	10
M. C.				a.m.		a.m.		a.m.		p.m.		p.m.	
— —	Wisbech Station ... Ⓢ	dep.		6 30	.....	11 5	.....	11 25	.....	12 45	.....	2 10	.....
1 53	Elm Depot	„		*	—	*	—	*	—	*	—	*	—
3 25	Boyce's Depot .... Ⓢ	{ arr. dep.		*	.....	*	.....	*	.....	*	.....	▶ *	.....
4 12	Outwell Basin	„		*	.....	*	.....	*	.....	*	.....	*	.....
4 79	Outwell Village	„		*	—	*	—	*	—	*	—	*	—
5 72	Upwell .... Ⓢ	arr.		8 0	.....	12 30	.....	12 30	.....	2 15	.....	3 10	.....

Miles.	UP WEEK DAYS.			1 Gds. NS	2 Gds. SO	3	4 Gds. NS	5 Gds. SO	6	7 Gds. SO	8 Gds. NS	9	10 Gds. NS
M. C.				a.m.	a.m.		p.m.	p.m.		p.m.	p.m.		p.m.
— —	Upwell .... Ⓢ	dep.		8 50	9 15	.....	1 0	1 28	.....	1 50	3 20	.....	4 15
73	Outwell Village	„		*	*	—	*	*	—	*	*	—	*
1 60	Outwell Basin	„		*	*	—	*	*	—	*	*	.....	*
2 47	Boyce's Depot .... Ⓢ	{ arr. dep.		*	*	—	*	*	—	*	*	.....	*
4 19	Elm Depot	„		*	*		*	*	—	*	*		*
5 72	Wisbech Station ... Ⓢ	arr.		10 0	10 35	.....	1 40	2 35	.....	2 50	4 35	.....	5 40

Loads of Goods and Coal trains.—The loads of goods and coal trains over the Wisbech and Upwell Tramway may be increased as under :—

For ordinary purposes four-coupled tram engine loads :—

     10 mineral ; 15 goods ; 22 empties.

and for six-coupled tram engines for ordinary purposes the loads should be :—

     15 mineral ; 22 goods ; 33 empties.

These loads may, however, be increased to meet special exigencies. The District Superintendent to arrange.

Tram Cars Nos. 7 and 8 each to be counted as 2 vehicles.

The engine, after dusk, is to carry one red light and one white light in front, and the last vehicle is to carry one red light in rear.

LNER working timetable 1928.

TIME TABLE OF GOODS TRIPS
BETWEEN WISBECH & UPWELL.

Single Line. For regulations and bye laws for working this tramway see "Appendix" to the Working Time Tables.

Parcels and Miscellaneous traffic and live stock at passenger rates will be conveyed by goods service.

Miles. M. C.	**DOWN WEEK DAYS.**			1 Gds. S O a.m.	2 Gds. S X a.m.	3	4	5 Gds. S O a.m.	6 Gds. S X p.m.	7	8 Gds. S X p.m.	9	10	11
— —	Wisbech Station ...	Ⓢ	dep.	6 30	9 0	.....	.....	11 25	12 45	.....	2 10	.....	.....	
1 53	Elm Depot	"		*	*	—	—	*	*	—	*	.....		
3 25	Boyce's Depot	Ⓢ	{arr. {dep.	*	*	.....	.....	*	*	.....	*	.....		
4 12	Outwell Basin	"		—	—	.....	.....	—	—	.....	—			
4 79	Outwell Village	"		*	*	.....	—	*	*	.....	*			
5 72	Upwell	Ⓢ	arr.	8 0	10 15	.....	.....	12 30	3 0	.....	3 10	.....	.....	

Miles. M. C.	**UP WEEK DAYS.**			1 Gds. S O a.m.	2 Gds. S X a.m.	3	4	5	6 Gds. S O p.m.	7 Gds. S X p.m.	8 Gds. S X p.m.	9	10	11
— —	Upwell	Ⓢ	dep	9 15	11 0	.....	.....	.....	1 50	3 20	4 15	.....	.....	
73	Outwell Village	"		*	*	—	—	—	*	*	*	.....	.....	
1 60	Outwell Basin	"		*	*	—	—	—	*	*	*	—	—	
2 47	Boyce's Depot	Ⓢ	{arr. {dep.	*	*	—	—	—	*	*	*	—	—	
4 19	Elm Depot	"		*	*	.....	.....	.....	*	*	*	—	—	
5 72	Wisbech Station ...	Ⓢ	arr.	10 35	12 0	.....	.....	.....	2 50	4 35	5 15	.....	—	

Loads of Goods and Coal trains.—The loads of goods and coal trains over the Wisbech and Upwell Tramway may be increased as under :—

For ordinary purposes four-coupled tram engine loads :--
10 mineral; 15 goods; 22 empties.

and for six-coupled tram engines for ordinary purposes the loads should be :—
15 mineral; 22 goods; 33 empties.

These loads may, however, be increased to meet special exigencies. The District Superintendent to arrange.

The engine, after dusk, is to carry one red light and one white light in front, and the last vehicle is to carry one red light in rear.

LNER working timetable 1937.

TIME TABLE OF GOODS TRIPS
BETWEEN WISBECH & UPWELL.

Single line. For regulations and bye-laws for working this tramway see " Appendix."
Parcels and miscellaneous traffic and live stock at passenger train rates will
be conveyed by goods service.

Miles from Wisbech.	DOWN WEEK DAYS.		1	2	3	4	5	6	7	8	9	10	11
			Gds.				Gds.		Gds.		Gds.		
			S O		S X		S O		S X		S X		
			a.m.	.	a.m.		a.m.		p.m.		p.m.		
M. c.	Wisbech Station	dep.	7 0	....	9 0	....	11 25	....	12 45	....	2 10	....	....
1 53	Elm Depot	„	*	—	*	—	*	—	*	—	*	—	....
3 25	Boyce's Depot	{arr.	*	....	*	....	*	....	*	....	*	....	....
		{dep.	—	—	—	—	—	—	—	—	—	—	
4 12	Outwell Basin	„	*	—	*	—	*	—	*	—	*	—	
4 79	Outwell Village	„	*	—	*	—	*	—	*	—	*	—	
5 72	Upwell	arr.	8 30	....	10 15	....	12 30	....	2 0	....	3 10	....	....

1 & 3 To convey passenger van with parcels, fish, etc.

7 To clear Outwell Village of traffic for forwarding by 9 up.

Miles from Upwell.	UP WEEK DAYS.		1	2	3	4	5	6	7	8	9	10	11
			Gds.		Gds.		Gds.		Gds.		Gds.		
			S O		S X		S O		S X		S X		
			a.m.		a.m.		p.m.		p.m		p.m.		
M. c.	Upwell	dep.	9 15	....	11 15	....	1 15	....	3 20	....	4 15	....	....
— 73	Outwell Village	„	*	—	*	—	*	—	*	—	*	—	—
1 60	Outwell Basin	„	*	—	*	—	*	—	*	—	*	—	
2 47	Boyce's Depot	{arr.	*	—	*	—	*	—	*	—	*	—	
		{dep.	....		....		....		....		....		
4 19	Elm Depot	„	*	—	*	—	*	—	*	—	*	—	
5 72	Wisbech Station	arr.	10 35	....	12 15	....	2 15	....	4 35	....	5 15	....	....

7 To convey passenger van to clear parcels, etc., traffic from all depots and clear all goods
traffic from Outwell Basin, Boyce's Depot and Elm Depot.

Loads of Goods and Coal trains.—The loads of goods and coal trains over the Wisbech
and Upwell Tramway may be increased as under :—

For ordinary purposes four-coupled tram engine loads :—
10 mineral ; 15 goods ; 22 empties.

and for six-coupled tram engines for ordinary purposes the loads should be :—
15 mineral ; 22 goods ; 33 empties.

These loads may, however, be increased to meet special exigencies. The District
Superintendent to arrange.

**The engine, after dusk, is to carry one red light and one white light in front,
and the last vehicle is to carry one red light in rear.**

LNER working timetable 1944.

TIME TABLE OF GOODS TRIPS BETWEEN
WISBECH EAST AND UPWELL

Single Line. For regulations and bye-laws for working this tramway see "Appendix."
Parcels and Miscellaneous traffic and live stock at passenger train rates will be conveyed by Goods Service.

DOWN — WEEKDAYS

Miles from Wisbech		No.	1	2	3	4	5	6	7	8	9	10	11	12	13	14	15
		Class			K		K						K			K	
		Description															
M. C.					SO		SX						SX			SX	
					am		am						PM			PM	
	Wisbech East Station				10 0		10 15						12 55			1 50	
1 53	Elm Depot				✳		✳						✳			✳	
3 25	Boyce's Depot				✳		✳						✳			✳	
4 12	Outwell Basin				✳		✳						✳			✳	
4 79	Outwell Village				✳		✳						✳			✳	
5 72	Upwell				11 15		11 30						2 10			2 50	

3 & 5 To convey passenger van with parcels, fish, etc.

11 To clear Outwell Village of traffic for forwarding by 14 up.

UP — WEEKDAYS

Miles from Upwell		No.	1	2	3	4	5	6	7	8	9	10	11	12	13	14	15
		Class					K			K			K			K	
		Description															
M. C.							SX			SO			SX			SX	
							am			PM			PM			PM	
	Upwell						11 50			12 15			3 20			4 15	
73	Outwell Village ..						✳			✳			✳			✳	
1 60	Outwell Basin						✳			✳			✳			✳	
2 47	Boyce's Depot						✳			✳			✳			✳	
4 19	Elm Depot						✳			✳			✳			✳	
5 72	Wisbech East Station						12 50			1 15			4 35			5 15	

11 To convey passenger van to clear parcels, etc., traffic from all depots and clear all goods traffic from Outwell Basin, Boyce's Depot and Elm Depot.

Loads of Goods and Mineral Trains. The maximum loads of goods and mineral trains over the Wisbech East and Upwell Tramway are to be:—

Between Wisbech East and Outwell Basin and between Upwell and Wisbech East.

Four-coupled tram—15 Mineral, 23 Goods, 30 Empties.
Six-coupled tram—20 Mineral, 30 Goods, 40 Empties.

Between Outwell Basin and Upwell :

Four-coupled tram—12 Mineral, 18 Goods, 24 Empties.
Six-coupled tram—17 Mineral, 25 Goods, 34 Empties.

The engine, after dusk, is to carry one red light and one white light in front, and the last vehicle is to carry one red light in rear.

BR (ER) working timetable 1952.

BR (ER) working timetable 1961.

WISBECH AND UPWELL TRAMWAY — WEEKDAYS

		K	K						K	K
DOWN						**UP**				
Mileage		SO	SX		Mileage				SO	SX
M C		am	PM		M C				am	PM
0 0	WISBECH EAST ...... dep	10 0	12 25		0 0	Upwell .... dep			11 45	3 30
1 53	Elm Depot	R	R		0 73	Outwell Village			R	R
3 25	Boyce's Depot	R	R		1 40	Outwell Basin			R	R
4 32	Outwell Basin	R	R		2 47	Boyce's Depot			R	R
4 79	Outwell Village	R	R		4 19	Elm Depot			R	R
5 72	Upwell .. .. .. arr	11 15	12 55		5 72	WISBECH EAST.. arr			12 45	4 3

Down
7.00 am SO, 9.00 SX, 11.25 SO, 12.45 pm SX, 2.10 SX

Up
9.15 SO, 11.15 SX, 1.15 pm SO, 3.20 SX, 4.15 SX

In the down direction the 7.00 am (SO) and 9.00 am (SX) ex-Wisbech conveyed a passenger van with parcels, fish and small traffic, whilst the 12.45 pm (SX) ex-Wisbech cleared Outwell Village of all traffic for forwarding by the 4.15 pm up train from Upwell. In the up direction the 3.20 pm (SX) conveyed the passenger van to carry parcels and smalls traffic and was booked to clear all goods traffic from Outwell Basin, Boyce's Bridge depot and Elm Bridge depot.

By 1949 eight trips were scheduled to run across the branch on Mondays to Fridays and three each way on Saturdays during the summer months. The winter timetable showed a drastic reduction with down trains departing Wisbech East at 9.45 am, 12.55 pm (SX) and 1.50 pm (SX) and returning from Upwell at 11.50 am (SX), 1.15 pm (SO), 3.20 pm (SX) and 4.15 pm (SX). Calls were only made as required at the intermediate depots and the 9.45 am down train conveyed the passenger van with parcels and fish traffic, whilst the 12.55 pm (SX) cleared Outwell Village of traffic for forwarding by the 4.15 pm (SX) up train. The 3.20 pm (SX) ex-Upwell conveyed the passenger van to clear the branch of parcels and also took all goods traffic from Outwell Basin, Boyce's Bridge depot and Elm Bridge depot. The working timetable for June 1950 continued to show the reduced service, with only three trains in each direction on Mondays to Fridays and one each way on Saturdays in similar timings to 1949. Running times varied between 60 minutes and 75 minutes.

In 1951 the last full year of full steam operation on the tramway, three down trains departed Wisbech at 10.15 am (conveying a parcels van for passenger rated parcels traffic including fish), 12.55 pm (SX) and 1.50 pm (SX). The 12.55 pm (SX) was required to clear all up traffic from Outwell Village by taking the traffic to Upwell to be returned to Wisbech by the 3.20 pm (SX) departure. The up services departed Upwell at 11.50 (SX), 12.15 pm (SO), 3.20 pm (SX) and 4.15 pm (SX). Trains operated on weekdays only. By 1952 the morning down departure from Wisbech East was altered to 10.00 am (SO) and 10.15 am (SX) whilst other times remained unaltered. All trains ran as class K and only called at the intermediate depots if required.

The competition from road transport gradually took its toll and by 1961 the tramway was served by just one train in each direction on weekdays only. The 10.00 am (SO) train was allowed 75 minutes whilst the 12.25 pm (SX) was booked a mere 30 minutes to Upwell. Both up services were allowed 60 minutes for the journey and all trains only called at the intermediate depots if required. Little had changed by 1964 with only one train scheduled across the tramway Mondays to Fridays departing Wisbech at 1.30 pm and returning at 3.30 from Upwell. The Saturday service departed Wisbech at 10.00 am and returned from Upwell at 11.45. During the final months of operation the SX timings were unaltered but the Saturday working only ran if required, departing Wisbech at the later time of 11.00 and returning from Upwell at 12.00 noon. The final train ran on Friday 20th May, 1966.

Fares

When the tramway terminated at Outwell Basin, uniform fares were charged of 3*d.* first class and 2*d.* third class for any distance. By 1884 when the extension to Upwell opened the following single fare structure showing first and second class only was introduced and was still operative in 1900, although from 1st January, 1893 second class was abolished and the tramway accommodation down graded to third class.

	First	Second
Wisbech and Outwell Village or Upwell	4*d.*	3*d.*
Elm Bridge and Upwell	4*d.*	3*d.*
Wisbech and Elm Bridge, Boyce's Bridge or Outwell Basin	3*d.*	2*d.*
Elm Bridge and Boyce's Bridge, Outwell Basin or Outwell Village	3*d.*	2*d.*
Boyce's Bridge and Outwell Village or Upwell	3*d.*	2*d.*
Outwell Basin and Boyce's Bridge, Outwell Village or Upwell	2*d.*	1*d.*
Outwell Village and Upwell, Wisbech	2*d.*	1*d.*

The single fare structure on the tramway in 1915 was:

	First	Third
Wisbech to Elm Depot	2*d.*	1*d.*
Elm Bridge Depot to Boyce's Bridge	2*d.*	1*d.*
Boyce's Depot to Outwell Basin	2*d.*	1*d.*
Outwell Basin to Outwell Village or Upwell	2*d.*	1*d.*
Outwell Village to Upwell	2*d.*	1*d.*
Wisbech to Boyce's Depot	3*d.*	2*d.*
Elm Depot to Outwell Basin	3*d.*	2*d.*
Boyce's Depot to Outwell Village or Upwell	3*d.*	2*d.*
Wisbech to Outwell Basin	5*d.*	3*d.*
Elm Depot to Outwell Village or Upwell	5*d.*	3*d.*
Wisbech to Outwell Village or Upwell	6*d.*	4*d.*

In the final year of GER operation the fare structure was:

	First	Third
Wisbech to Elm Depot	3½*d.*	2*d.*
Elm Depot to Boyce's Bridge	3½*d.*	2*d.*
Boyce' s Bridge to Outwell Basin	3½*d.*	2*d.*
Outwell Basin to Outwell Village or Upwell	3½*d.*	2*d.*
Outwell Village to Upwell	3½*d.*	2*d.*
Wisbech to Boyce's Depot	5½*d.*	3½*d.*
Elm Depot to Outwell Basin	5½*d.*	3½*d.*
Boyce's Depot to Outwell Village and Upwell	5½*d.*	3½*d.*
Wisbech to Outwell Basin	9*d.*	5½*d.*
Elm Depot to Outwell Village or Upwell	9*d.*	5½*d.*
Wisbech to Outwell Village or Upwell	10½*d.*	7*d.*

Third class return market tickets were issued to Wisbech on Thursdays and Saturdays from Upwell and Outwell Village at 10*d.* and Outwell Basin at 8*d.* by leaving Upwell on the 8.35, 10.15, 11.40 am (ThO), 1.03 (SO) and 1.25 pm (ThO) trains.

During the final year of passenger train operation in 1927 the single fares had been reduced and the following structure was in operation:

	First	Third
Wisbech Station to Elm Depot	2½d.	1½d.
Elm Depot to Boyce's Bridge	2½d.	1½d.
Boyce's Bridge to Outwell Basin	2½d.	1½d.
Outwell Basin to Outwell Village	2½d.	1½d.
Outwell Village to Upwell	2½d.	1½d.
Wisbech to Boyce's Depot	5d.	3d.
Elm Depot to Outwell Basin	5d.	3d.
Boyce's Depot to Outwell Village or Upwell	5d.	3d.
Wisbech to Outwell Basin	7½d.	4½d.
Elm Depot to Outwell Village or Upwell	7½d.	4½d.
Wisbech to Outwell Village or Upwell	10d.	6d.

Return Third class market tickets were also available from Upwell, Outwell Village and Outwell Basin to Wisbech at a price of 8d. by cars leaving Upwell at 8.15, 10.15, 11.40 am and 1.25 pm on Thursdays and by the 1.25 pm train on Saturdays.

Daily takings from the tramway depots were sent to Wisbech station in leather cash bags with the depot name stamped thereon on a brass plate, the guard being responsible for their safekeeping.

Excursions

The GER offered limited excursion facilities to the inhabitants of the villages served by the tramway, when compared to other branch lines. Weekly cheap fares were available to Wisbech on market days, whilst half-day trips to the seaside were available several times a year in the summer months for the relatively short journey to Hunstanton, with passengers changing to the main line service at Wisbech. Infrequent offers were made to destinations further afield including Yarmouth, Lowestoft and Cromer, but these tended to be full day excursions requiring an early start and a late return, when special connecting services operated on the tramway.

Facilities were also available for local organizations, such as on 24th March, 1897 when a concert was held in the Railway Benevolent Institute at Wisbech. To cater for patrons attending the event, a special train was run to Upwell departing Wisbech at 10.45 pm calling at all depots. In the summer months the Anglican and three Methodist Churches in Outwell organized joint excursions to the coast, hiring a special tram to Wisbech, where they boarded a main line train for Hunstanton. Wisbech Horse Show was always a special attraction and return tickets at single fares and a third were issued from many stations in the area including the Upwell tramway depots. On 2nd July, 1913 a special tramcar returned excursionists departing Wisbech at 11.15 pm calling at all depots to Upwell.

The excursion programme was severely curtailed after World War I and ceased altogether with the withdrawal of the passenger train service.

G. E. R.

WISBECH HORSE SHOW

WEDNESDAY, 2nd JULY, 1913,

RETURN TICKETS

AT A

Single Fare and a Third

(no less charge than 1s. for an Adult Passenger)

WILL BE ISSUED TO

WISBECH

by any train, from Peterboro', King's Lynn, St. Ives, Cambridge, Ely, and intermediate Stations; also from Godmanchester, Ramsey, Warboys, Somersham, Chatteris, Wimblington, Spalding, and intermediate Stations (G.N. & G.E. Joint Line), available for return the same day, by any train.

Fractional parts of a penny are charged as one penny.

Children under 3 years of age, free; above 3 and under 12, half-price. No luggage allowed.

A SPECIAL TRAM CAR

WILL LEAVE

AT
p.m.

WISBECH

FOR

11.15 UPWELL

London. May, 1913.

WALTER H. HYDE, General Manager.

Printed at the Company's Works, Stratford.

Excursion poster for Wisbech Horse Show on Wednesday 2nd July, 1913.

Goods Traffic

Before the advent of the railway, local carriers' carts were a common sight on the roads linking the towns and villages of the area with the market centre of Wisbech. As early as 1847, a regular carrier service from The Griffin, Market Place, Wisbech to Upwell was operated by Thomas Whitehead on Mondays, Wednesdays, Fridays and Saturdays, returning the same day. Wiles and Cawthorne operated an additional return service to Wisbech from Upwell on Tuesdays, Thursdays and Saturdays. By the time the tramway opened to traffic in 1883 carriers' waggons operating from Wisbech included Whitehead from The Griffin to Elm, Emneth, Outwell and Upwell on a daily basis, whilst Boyce operated from The Ship to Outwell and Upwell on Tuesdays, Thursdays and Saturdays. Bensley travelled from The Royal Hotel to the same destinations on Tuesdays and Saturdays, with an extension thereon to Tipp's End via Christchurch. Bensley was still providing a carrier service over the same road in 1896, whilst Whitehead was travelling to Wisbech each weekday.

The Wisbech & Upwell Tramway, conceived and built as a feeder service to the main line, like many branches of the GER soon assumed the role of a farmers' line, providing an effective outlet for growers in the area and a railhead for connecting waterway services into and out of the fens, especially from Outwell Village. Traffic quickly transferred from the Wisbech canal lighters and the carriers' carts to the railway for rapid transport to and from Wisbech, King's Lynn, Peterborough, Cambridge and Ely markets, other destinations throughout the country and indeed abroad, confirming the optimism and ultimate gamble taken by the GER Directors.

When the tramway opened for traffic on 20th August, 1883, the rates for the conveyance of coal from Wisbech to Elm Bridge was 2*d*. per ton, Boyce's Bridge 3*d*. per ton and Outwell Basin 4*d*. per ton. Coal was always the main import traffic with merchants based at all tramway depots but chiefly at Outwell Village and Upwell depots. Dixon was at Elm Bridge, William Kingston at Outwell Sluice and Outwell Village, and Thomas Coote and Sons at Upwell where a coal ground was established in 1902, dealing with domestic and horticultural supplies. The firm later amalgamated with F. Warren and Company Limited to become Coote and Warren. In 1914 the annual rental was £5 0s. 0d. In 1909 over 40 fenland pumping stations were receiving coal supplies by lighter from Outwell Village depot. Coal was received from Sherwood, Newstead, Kirkley, Bestwood, Hucknall, Sheepbridge, Stanton, Shirebrook, Clipstone, Worksop and Blidworth collieries amongst others. The wagons usually travelled via Peterborough, where the Stanground sidings acted as a Clearing House for empty wagons returning to the collieries and loaded ones *en route* to the tramway. Other coal traffic was routed over the GN & GE Joint Railway via Spalding and March. In the 1920 and 1930s coke was conveyed for horticultural purposes, but in the latter years this was taken by road.

The *Wisbech Advertiser* also reported on the opening of the tramway that: 'The road surveyors along the line will derive a great benefit inasmuch as Leicestershire and other granite will be conveyed to the sides of their roads, at a mere trifling cost beyond Wisbech station rates. One surveyor stated that he estimates the Tramway will relieve and benefit his ratepayers to the extent of at least 1*d*. in the £.' Certainly up the late 1920s and early 1930s many of the fenland roads remained unmetalled - dust tracks in summer and muddy morasses in winter. County Councils then undertook a rolling programme of road improvements, which involved levelling the surface before covering with granite chippings and tarmacadam. Much of the material was delivered by rail to the depots, from where the material was offloaded and taken to site by horse and waggon. The granite and tarmacadam was then levelled by steam roller. Although the conveyance of these commodities brought much needed revenue to the railway company, the end product was improved facilities for the competitive road industry, which ultimately sounded the death knell of the Upwell tram.

The chief outward traffic was vegetables, potatoes, hay, straw, corn and other agricultural produce. In addition to the root crops conveyed, including potatoes, carrots, swedes, parsnips, turnips and mangold wurzels, from the early 1920s sugar beet was increasingly grown in the fens. Considerable loads were transferred from fen tumbrels and horse-drawn waggons to railway wagons at the depot sidings for conveyance to the British Sugar Corporation sugar processing factories at Ely, South Lynn, Wissington and Peterborough. By the late 1950s much of this traffic had transferred to road haulage for direct delivery from farm to factory, but until closure in 1966 some sugar beet was conveyed on the tramway.

Another product of the local fields were flowers which were gathered and sent daily to London and provincial cities and towns, usually loaded in fully brake-fitted covered vans so that the vehicles could be forwarded attached to passenger trains for onward transit beyond Wisbech.

Milk was regularly dispatched from the depots and conveyed to dairies at Wisbech and Kings Lynn in the familiar 17 gallon churns, two loads being dispatched in the summer months by the first up train and then again in the late afternoon. During winter months the milk was forwarded by the first up train only. This area of the fens was not noted for its dairy farming and the relatively small amounts were lost to road transport in the late 1930s when the milk churns were collected by lorry from the farms and delivered direct to the dairies.

Fruit traffic was an essential part of the tramway's exports, especially apples. Considerable tonnages were transported including Bramley Seedling's but after World War II the trend was towards dessert apples, including Cox's Orange Pippins, Worcester Pearmain and other varieties. The apples were loaded into crates and put into the wagons for transit. Before World War II apples were exported to the continent in French, Belgian and German ferry wagons and dispatched via Harwich and Dover. The method of transit was different from the home market for in this case the ferry wagons were lined with straw and cardboard and the fruit tipped out of the crates. On arrival at the foreign channel ports the fruit was loaded into boxes for onward transit.

By far the greatest tonnage conveyed was summer fruits including raspberries, gooseberries, redcurrants, blackcurrants and not the least strawberries for which the Wisbech area and the tramway were renowned. The remarkably fertile area of Cambridgeshire and Norfolk attracted large numbers of fruit growers and the soft fruit season lasting from mid-June to mid-August was extremely busy on the tramway. From early June fruit pickers were recruited from the East End of London and some 2,000 were conveyed to the area at regular intervals for a weekly or fortnightly stint, many returning year after year with their families. They were accommodated in bunkhouses and during the day female undergraduates from Girton and Newnham Colleges at Cambridge organized crèches for the under 10-years-old children. The students slept in tented camps scattered around the fruit farms and smallholdings. In addition the staff complement at Wisbech goods depot were augmented by some 60 loaders and checkers, usually transferred temporarily from other fenland stations. Once the fruit had reached its appointed ripeness the strawberries, including such varieties as Paxton, Laxton, Royal Sovereign and Duke, were picked. Initially the soft fruit was loaded into 7 lb. baskets or 12 lb. sieves but after World War I fruit was packed in chip baskets, trays and tubs, the chips averaging from 3 to 4 lb. in weight each and tubs varying in weight according to size. One commentator said, 'the whole area exudes fruit; men talk of it, the women eat it and the trains smell of it'. The strawberry chips required specialist packing and they were loaded in a pyramid in the vans to prevent the chips sliding during shunting. Baker of Emneth was one large fruit grower.

Harvesting continued from almost first light until early evening and at the height of the season the growers' horse-drawn carts and waggons and later motor lorries, augmented in later years by railway road vehicles, conveyed the produce to the local tram depots, resulting in a steady stream of vehicles through the gates leading to the sidings. At the depots loading commencing from mid-morning supervised by the depot foreman and the produce was loaded into vans suitably labelled to the London markets and destinations in the Midlands and the North such as Birmingham, Wolverhampton, Leeds, Bradford, Liverpool and Manchester. Vans loaded and dispatched from Wisbech by 3 pm were guaranteed delivery in Glasgow and Edinburgh by 7 am the following day. The vans were worked down to the depots each morning and later during the day once the first flight of loaded vans had been dispatched to Wisbech. At the beginning of each season growers were advised as to the latest times for loading to various destinations with the last departure around 8.00 pm from Upwell. This advanced notice did not always prevent growers, eager to get their produce to market, from flouting the regulations and tempers became frayed as traders often arrived at the last minute to find the train departing to time, so that connections at Wisbech and later Whitemoor Yard could be maintained. The last up tram at about 8.00 pm conveyed vans bound for Spitalfields and wagons from the branch were united with vans from Kings Lynn and intermediate stations at Wisbech for onward dispatch to March and thence to London arriving in Spitalfields and Covent Garden Markets by 4 am the following morning. During the fruit growing season the tram would convey a fruit traffic office van from Wisbech each morning, with one clerk alighting at each of the depots to complete consignment notes for growers. Two clerks usually remained on the tram to Upwell where they waybilled as much traffic as possible before the last tram returned. Consignments notes not dealt with were waybilled in the van on the return journey before arrival at Wisbech. The clerks at the intermediate depots were also collected on the last up run. At the height of the season it was estimated over 5½ million chip baskets of strawberries were dispatched via Wisbech. Vagrants taking advantage of the empty vehicles sometimes used the fruit vans as sleeping cars. Between June and October 1922, 15,609 tons of fruit traffic were dispatched from Wisbech by passenger and goods trains, much of it originating from the Upwell tramway depots. The strawberry traffic usually required extra trains but was exhausted within a four to six week period, depending on the weather. During both World War I and World War II any available vehicle was used to transport the fruit away to the home markets, and coal wagons, high side opens, cattle wagons, horseboxes and plate wagons were pressed into use to augment the covered vans.

From the outset livestock handled on the tramway was two-way traffic. The potential of the railway for the speedy transit of animals was quickly realised and horses were regularly conveyed in wagons or horseboxes. Cattle wagons were a common feature until the early 1950s for the conveyance of livestock to Wisbech, Kings Lynn and Ely markets held on Thursday, Tuesday and Thursday respectively. Some animals were sent further afield to Cambridge, Peterborough and Huntingdon. Trade declined with the relaxation of petrol rationing after World War II when all livestock traffic was lost to road transport. Thursday was Wisbech market day and most early trains would convey cattle wagons with animals for trading whilst the late afternoon services would return with calves and heifers bought by farmers for fattening. Loading and offloading at the tramway depots was somewhat difficult as only Upwell was provided with cattle pens and a loading dock.

In the latter years traffic dwindled alarmingly. The receipts from the conveyance of coal and seed potatoes was nullified when contracts were negotiated for the bulk haulage of fruit and flowers by road to Wisbech for onward transit by train, removing over £10,000 revenue from the tramway. Conveyance by this method was short-lived for the produce was soon transported through to the final destination by road.

The following facilities were available at the stations and depots on the Tramway:

Wisbech	Loading gauges
	3 Cattle pens
	Watering facilities for cattle in transit
	Loading dock
	Fixed crane 6 tons capacity
	4 Fixed cranes 1 ton capacity (later removed)
	Truck weighbridge 20 tons capacity
	Cart weighbridge 7 tons capacity
	Weighing machine 1 ton 2 cwt capacity
	Weighing machine 2 cwt capacity (later removed)
	7 weighing machines 11 cwt capacity (later removed)
	Goods shed with capacity to store 1,200 quarters of grain, later reduced to 500 qtrs
	Lock up for small packages
	Wagon turntable
	Facilities for loading round timber and lifting vans requiring crane power by special arrangement.
	Cartage conveyed by the GE company

Elm Bridge	Loading gauge	
	2 Weighing machines	11 cwt capacity (later reduced to one)
	Lock-up for small packages	

Boyce's Bridge	Loading gauge	
	Weighing machine	10 cwt capacity
	Lock-up for small packages	
	Facilities for loading round timber and	
	lifting vans requiring crane power by special arrangement	

Outwell Basin	Loading gauge	
	Weighing machine	11 cwt capacity
	Lock-up for small packages	

Outwell Village	Loading gauge	
	Weighing machine	10 cwt capacity
	Lock-up for small packages	
	Facilities for loading round timber and lifting	
	vans requiring crane power by special arrangement	

Upwell	Loading gauge	
	Cattle pen	
	Cart weighbridge	5 ton capacity
	3 Weighing machines	10, 11 and 12 cwt
	capacities (later reduced to one x 11 cwt)	
	Lock-up for small packages	
	Facilities for loading round timber and lifting	
	vans requiring crane power by special arrangement.	

The latest times for receipt of goods for transit the same day were:

Wisbech 6.00 pm (SX), 3.00 pm (SO); later amended to 4.00 pm
Elm Bridge 5.00 pm (SX), 2.00 pm (SO); later amended to 4.00 pm
Boyce's Bridge 4.30 pm (SX), 2.00 pm (SO); later amended to 4.00 pm (3.40 pm June-October)
Outwell Basin 4.30 pm (SX), 2.00 pm (SO) ⎫ Later amended to
Outwell Village 4.15 pm (SX), 1.30 pm (SO) ⎬ 4.00 pm (3.30 pm July-October)
Upwell 4.00 pm (SX), 1.30 pm (SO) ⎭

In 1897 the load limits for the tram locomotives between Wisbech and Upwell were:

Passenger Trams	Not exceeding 9 vehicles. Tramcars Nos. 5 and 7 were to be counted as two vehicles.
Mixed trams	Not exceeding 10 vehicles, 4 of which may be loaded goods trucks.
Coal Trams	Not to exceed 4 loaded trucks in winter and 5 loaded in summer.

From the 1908 working timetable tramcars Nos. 5 and 7 were renumbered 8 and 7 and each continued to count as two vehicles.

By 1928 the wagon loads permitted for ordinary purposes were:

		Minerals	*Goods*	*Empties*
Y6 class	0-4-0T	10	15	22
J70 class	0-6-0T	15	22	33

Curiously enough although the passenger service had been withdrawn, the branch loading continued to show passenger tramcars Nos. 7 and 8 to be counted as two vehicles. The loads could, however, be increased to meet special exigencies, especially in the soft fruit harvesting season and on the instructions of the district superintendent. These loadings continued in operation (minus the reference to the passenger vehicles which had been transferred to the Kelvedon to Tollesbury Light Railway) throughout the 1930s and up to 1945.

The load limits of wagons for the tramway locomotives were revised in 1946:

		Wisbech to Outwell Basin Upwell to Wisbech		
Class		Minerals	Goods	Empties
Y6	0-4-0T	15	23	30
J70	0-6-0T	20	30	40
		Outwell Basin to Upwell		
Class		Minerals	Goods	Empties
Y6	0-4-0T	12	18	24
J70	0-6-0T	17	25	34

From 1952 and in the latter years of operation the Drewry 204 hp diesel-mechanical locomotives were restricted to a tail load of 38 wagons in both directions on the Upwell tramway.

We may well imagine the expletives uttered by the enginemen on Drewry 204 hp 0-6-0 diesel locomotive No. D2202 as the progress of the Upwell to Wisbech train is impeded by a van alongside Elm High Road on the approach to the Duke of Wellington crossing. Compared with the present day the absence of road traffic is most noticeable.

Author's Collection

Chapter Ten

Locomotives

Steam Tram Locomotives

When the GER embarked on the ambitious plan to provide the tramway between Wisbech and Upwell, running for a greater part alongside public roads, it was realised that special rolling stock would have to be provided. Consideration was given to operating the line by electricity with tramcars but the necessity to operate goods traffic, to make the scheme viable, ruled against such proposals and the company resorted to working the line with steam traction. A close liaison was maintained with the Board of Trade for guidance and the assistance of Major General C.S. Hutchinson, who specialised in roadside tramways, was especially valuable. He commented on and approved of the various plans at all stages of progress. The company already possessed a four-wheel tram locomotive, purchased from Kitson & Company on 4th November, 1878 at a cost of £650, as a replacement for the 2-2-0 well tank locomotive *Ariel's Girdle* on the Millwall Extension Railway. The diminutive machine received the number 230 and was the last GER engine to regularly work on the Millwall line, as from 1880 the operation was taken over by the Millwall Dock Company. The use of this lightweight machine on the embryonic Upwell tramway was quickly ruled out as more substantive motive power was deemed necessary to handle the fenland passenger and freight traffic. No. 230 was withdrawn in 1884 and stored for five years before being converted in 1889 to work a steam traverser in Stratford works carriage shops.

On 16th January, 1883 T.W. Worsdell, the locomotive superintendent, submitted a plan he had prepared of a steam tram locomotive to the Way and Works Committee, as required by the Land and Construction Committee at their meeting on 3rd October, 1882. After discussion, it was resolved to construct three locomotives, 'in accordance with such a plan, at the Stratford Shops, for use on the Wisbech and Upwell Tramways'. The small inside-cylinder 0-4-0 steam tram engines were duly built at Stratford in the same year as GER class 'G15', and numbered 130, 131 and 132. As much of the route lay alongside public roads, the locomotives complied with Board of Trade Regulations which stated: 'the machines shall be concealed from view at all points above four inches from the level of the rails and all fires used on such engines shall be concealed from view'. Thus the wheels were enclosed by steel plate aprons at the side and cowcatchers at the front and rear. The upper part of the locomotive was encased in a wooden body resembling a goods brake van, whilst a governor, driven from a pulley on the left-hand leading wheel, limited the speed of the vehicle. A warning bell was mounted on the roof and the locomotives had duplicate controls enabling them to be driven from either end. Side chains were also fitted as well as screw couplings, but when first introduced into traffic the engines had no continuous brakes. The boiler had a raised firebox, on which was a dome surmounted by a pair of Ramsbottom

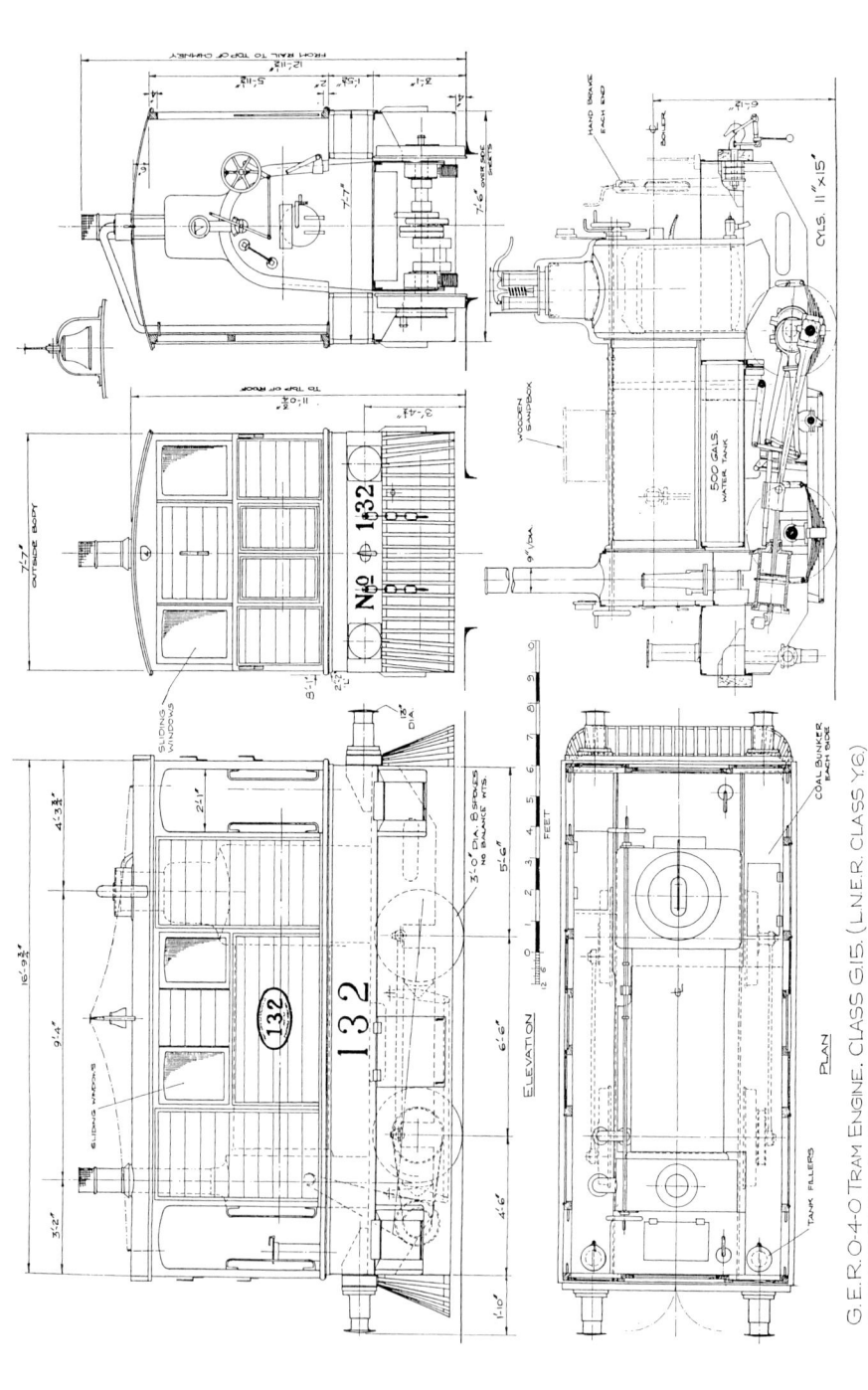

G.E.R. 0-4-0 TRAM ENGINE. CLASS G15. (L.N.E.R. CLASS Y.6)

BUILT STRATFORD, 130-132 – 1883., 126 & 138 – 1885., 125-127 – 1891., 133 -134 – 1897.

Plan of GER class 'G15', LNER 'Y6' 0-4-0 tram locomotive.

Courtesy of the GER Society

safety valves which discharged into a receiver, which led by way of a pipe across the roof and down into the well tank. The chief purpose of this fitting was to quieten the discharge from the safety valves to prevent horses and other animals taking fright. Spark arresters were also fitted to the top of the chimney throughout the life of the class. The engines also had disc wheels and twin slide bars to each cylinder. The new locomotives were to be loaded to a maximum of nine vehicles on a passenger train and 10 on a mixed train, four of which could be loaded with goods and for a coal train five vehicles loaded in summer months and four in winter months. The *Cambridge Chronicle* described the tram engine as 'a perfect model of an ordinary locomotive but it is encased in teak which gives it the appearance of a luggage van, thus reducing the chances of frightening horses on the road to a minimum'.

After introduction into traffic the three locomotives gave satisfactory service and in 1885 the GER built a further two locomotives, Nos. 128 and 129, for use on the Yarmouth Union tramway between Yarmouth Vauxhall station and the fish wharf. As traffic increased on the Wisbech & Upwell line a further three engines, Nos. 125, 126 and 127 were introduced in 1891 and 1892, to be followed by Nos. 133 and 134 in 1897. Over the years the locomotives were transferred from their original depots and by the turn of the century Nos. 126, 130 and 133 were working from Yarmouth, whilst the remaining seven were allocated to the Kings Lynn division but out-based at Wisbech.

As traffic and loadings increased on the Upwell tramway so it became imperative to introduce more powerful tram engines to haul the loads. In 1903 James Holden introduced his six-coupled 'C53' class locomotives into traffic and these were especially popular on the goods services. As a result some of the 'G15' class were placed in store at Wisbech and No. 131 was withdrawn from traffic as early as July 1907. Another of the original trio No. 130 was scrapped in December 1909, whilst Nos. 128 and 127 were withdrawn from traffic in March and December 1913 respectively. In 1921 Nos. 125, 126 and 129 were transferred to the GER duplicate list and were renumbered 0125, 0126 and 0129. Their original numbers were reused on the last three 'C53' class 0-6-0 tram engines under construction at that time. When the LNER took over at Grouping in 1923 the 'G15' class 0-4-0s was redesignated to 'Y6' with route availability 1. No. 134 was stationed at Ipswich for working the dock line with the other five based at Wisbech, by now in the Cambridge district, where they were soon joined by No. 134. The passenger traffic on the tramway continued to be worked by the 'Y6' class in preference to the 0-6-0s, by now re-designated to class 'J70', which were preferred on the goods services. With a surplus of 0-4-0 tram locomotives at Wisbech, Nos. 0125E and 0129E were transferred to Neasden in December 1924, in connection with work at the Wembley Exhibition but they were returned to the Cambridgeshire shed in May 1925. No. 7133 travelled north in July 1925 to take part in the Stockton & Darlington Railway Centenary procession as exhibit 35.

The withdrawal of passenger services from the Upwell tramway on 31st December, 1927 and the introduction of the 'Y10' class Super Sentinel locomotives in 1930 meant few duties could be found for the 'Y6' 0-4-0s. No. 7132 was withdrawn in 1931 and No. 07129 suffered a similar fate two years

'G15' class 0-4-0 tram locomotive No. 131 in full GER livery complete with polished teak bodywork and blue side tanks with black beading and 'G. E. R.' on the side tanks. The locomotive also has the obligatory cow catchers and side aprons. It was built in 1883 and had external sliding side windows. *Author's Collection*

GER 'G15' class 0-4-0 tram locomotive No. 129 entered service in October 1885 at Yarmouth but by the turn of the century had been transferred to Wisbech for service on the Upwell tramway. It received a duplicate No. 0129 in January 1921 to make way for a new 0-6-0 tram locomotive then under construction, which confusingly received the number 129. No. 0129 had window frames with rounded top corners and sliding side windows inside the body. *Author's Collection*

later. The remaining four engines were placed in store and usually only returned to traffic to supplement the 'J70s' on the tramway during the busy fruit season. The two locomotives on the duplicate list, Nos. 07125 and 07126, were withdrawn from traffic in February 1940, whilst Nos. 7133 and 7134 were loaned to the Wissington Light Railway, which formed a junction with the nearby Downham to Stoke Ferry branch at Abbey, in July 1941. Their visit was not a success for derailments were frequent on the lightly-laid track, especially on the sharp curves leading to the sugar beet factory and they were soon replaced by two 'J70' class 0-6-0s. The pair duly returned to Wisbech but in November 1943 No. 7134 found employment with the United States Army Transportation Corps at Burton-on-Trent. In July 1944 it was transferred to the War Department and shunted at the Royal Army Ordnance Corps depot at Sinfin Lane, Derby. The engine was returned to the LNER in October 1944 and with No. 7133 again took up duties on the Upwell tramway. Nos. 7133 and 7134 were renumbered to 8082 and 8083 in the LNER 1946 renumbering scheme and entered service with British Railways in 1948 to be renumbered again to 68082 and 68083 respectively with the power classification '0F'. The former was withdrawn from traffic in 1951 whilst No. 68083 was withdrawn in November 1952. After travelling to Stratford No. 68083 was stored in the paint shop for nearly a year awaiting possible preservation, but the attempt failed and it was subsequently put to the cutter's torch.

GER No.	Built	LNER 1924 No.	LNER 1946 No.	BR No.	Withdrawn
130	June 1883	–	–	–	December 1909
131	June 1883	–	–	–	July 1907
132	August 1883	7132	–	–	October 1931
128	March 1885*	–	–	–	March 1913
129	April 1885†	07129	–	–	April 1933
125	December 1891	07125	–	–	February 1940
126	January 1892	07126	–	–	February 1940
127	January 1892	–	–	–	December 1913
133	August 1897	7133	8082	68082	May 1951
134	August 1897	7134	8083	68083	November 1952

* not placed into traffic until December 1885
† not placed into traffic until October 1885

The leading dimensions of the locomotives as built were:

Cylinders	2 inside	11 in. x 15 in.
Motion		Stephenson with slide valves
Boiler	Max. diameter outside	2 ft 9¾ in.
	Barrel length	6 ft 10 in.
	Firebox outside length	3 ft 2 in.
Heating surface	Firebox	43.4 sq. ft
	Tubes	265.5 sq. ft
	Total	308.9 sq. ft
Tubes		82 x 1¾ in.
Grate area		9.5 sq. ft

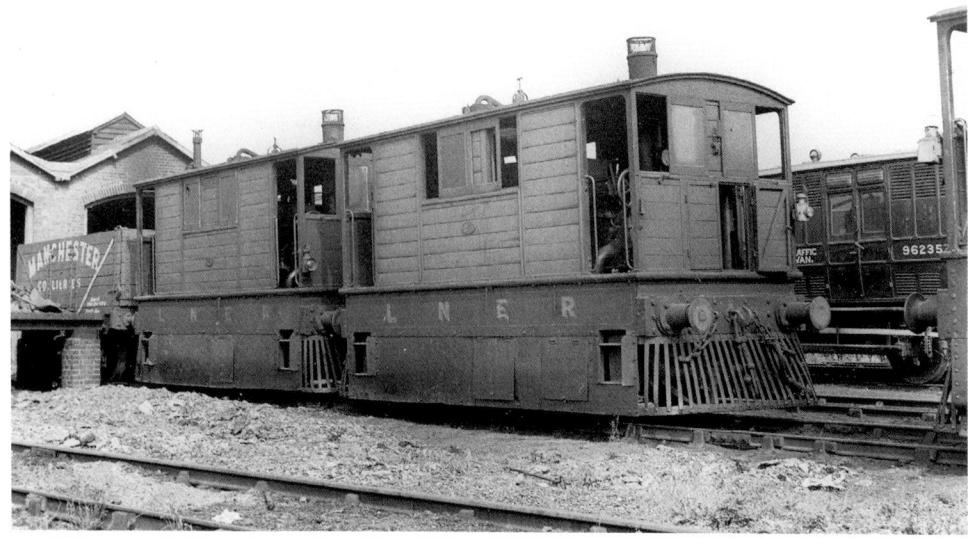

'Y6' class 0-4-0 tram locomotives Nos. 7133 and 7134 standing outside Wisbech shed on 24th July, 1943. Behind the locomotives is a Manchester Collieries private owner coal wagon and in the background fruit traffic office van No. 962352. *L.W. Perkins/Kidderminster Railway Museum*

'Y6' class 0-4-0 tram locomotive No. 68082 with cowcatchers and side aprons removed standing by the buffer stops on back road at Wisbech shed on 25th August, 1950. Plans were formulated to preserve sister locomotive No. 68083 as last of the class when she was withdrawn from service but ultimately met with failure. *The late H.C. Casserley*

Boiler pressure	120 psi
Coupled wheels	3 ft 0 in.
Tractive effort	5,003 lb.
Length over buffers	20 ft 2½ in.
Wheelbase	6 ft 6 in.
Weight	20 tons 19 cwt
Max. axle load	11 tons 2 cwt
Water capacity	500 gallons
Coal capacity	10 cwt

When Nos. 133 and 134 were built in 1897 they had the following detailed differences:

Heating surface	*Firebox*	43.24 sq. ft
	Tubes	306.22 sq. ft
	Total	349.46 sq. ft
Tubes		102 x 1⅝ in.
Grate area		9.7 sq. ft
Boiler pressure		140 psi
Coupled wheels		3 ft 1 in.
Tractive effort		5,837 lb.
Weight in working order		21 tons 5 cwt
Max. axle load		11 tons 14 cwt

They also had steel wheels with eight spokes, which resulted in the diameter being one inch greater than the disc wheels and had single slide bar motion. These engines were built with the Westinghouse brake, whilst the earlier locomotives were fitted with this equipment in 1891. The train pipe connection was located below the bufferbeam and protruded through the cowcatcher. The first five engines, Nos. 130, 131, 132, 128 and 129, were built with buffers having a square base whilst the engines constructed from 1891 had the later GER pattern with a circular base.

The remaining locomotives were re-boilered with the exception of No. 131, which was withdrawn in 1907, and these were the standard dimensions at Grouping. In 1929 No. 07129 received a new boiler of the pattern fitted to the 'J70s' and ultimately all 'Y6s', except No. 7132, received these boilers, albeit pressed to 140 psi instead of 180 psi. The specific differences were·

Heating surface	*Firebox*	42.08 sq. ft
	Tubes	306.00 sq. ft
	Total	348.08 sq. ft
Tubes		102 x 1⅝ in.
Grate area		9.2 sq. ft
Boiler pressure		140 psi
Tractive effort		5,837 lb.
Weight in working order		21 tons 5 cwt
Max. axle load		11 tons 14 cwt

The engines that survived the Grouping were all fitted with the 3 ft 1 in. diameter spoked wheels.

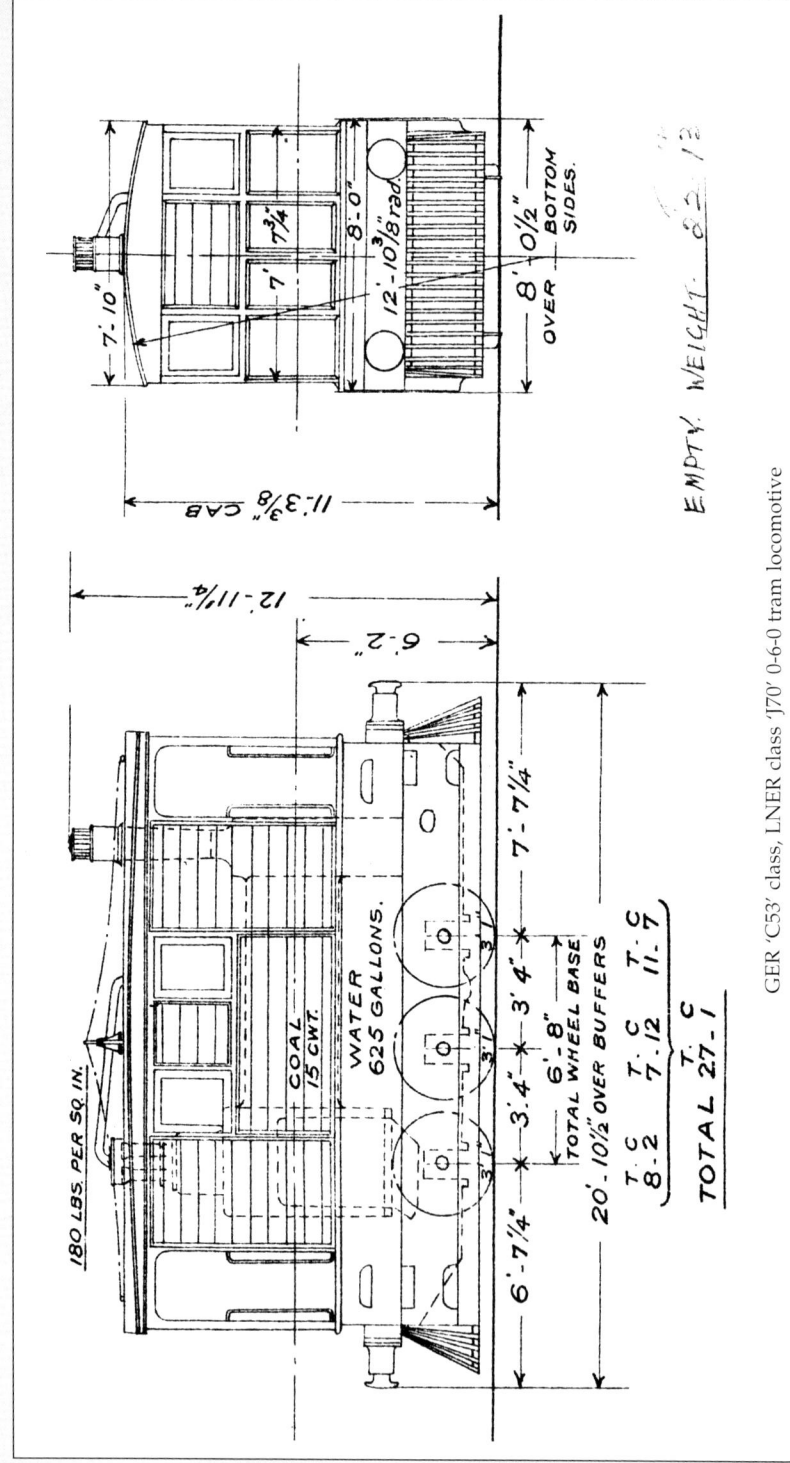

GER 'C53' class, LNER class 'J70' 0-6-0 tram locomotive

The tram engines were fitted with a feed pump because of their limited water capacity, the tank water was liable to heat very quickly. The 0-6-0Ts were also equipped with emergency dumping valves to allow the tank water to be discharged and replaced with a fresh supply if the water overheated.

In 1903 James Holden designed a more powerful six-coupled tram engine with outside cylinders and Walschaerts valve gear, and two locomotives, Nos. 135 and 136 of GER class 'C53' entered traffic the same year. The wheelbase at 6 ft 8 in. was only two inches longer than the four-wheel tram locomotives whilst the same size of boiler was fitted but with more tubes and a higher working pressure. The boiler had a raised firebox surmounted by a dome, on which were the Ramsbottom safety valves. The wooden body and general appearance was similar to the 0-4-0 tram engines especially when the side skirts and cowcatchers were fitted. The six-coupled engine could be distinguished by the three slotted footsteps at each end of each side, the topmost being in the deep framing, and also by the recessed foot to the side skirtings. Like the earlier 'G15' class, the 'C53' class had to comply with BoT regulations and when working on the tramway were provided with cowcatchers, protective skirting over the wheels, warning bells, a spark arrester on top of the chimney and a governor to limit the speed to 8 mph, later altered to 12 mph. To restrict noise, especially when running alongside a public highway, the steam from the safety valves was discharged into a receiver, which carried it by way of a pipe over the roof and back into the tanks, where it was condensed. Duplicate controls, including screw reverser were fitted to each end of the locomotive. Safety chains were fitted on the buffer beams and the locomotives were equipped with the Westinghouse brake from new. The boiler feed was by an injector and a single-acting feed pump.

The first two locomotives Nos. 135 and 136 were, surprisingly, not sent to the Wisbech & Upwell Tramway but were put to work on the dock lines at Ipswich. It was five years before another three 'C53' class tram engines emerged from Stratford works and Nos. 137 and 138, when released to traffic, were sent to Yarmouth Vauxhall to work the local dock lines. The third new engine, No. 139, was the first to be allocated to Wisbech. A further new locomotive, No. 130, was released to traffic in 1910 followed by Nos. 127, 128 and 131 in 1914. After World War I the final three of the class emerged in 1921, as Nos. 125, 126 and 129. At the end of 1921 Ipswich had six of the class, Yarmouth Vauxhall, three and Wisbech the remaining three.

At Grouping the LNER reclassified the 'C53' 0-6-0 tram locomotives to class 'J70' and added 7,000 to the running numbers and classified them to Route Availability 2. In November 1928 No. 7136 was allocated to Colchester shed where it was used as a replacement for 'Y5' class 0-4-0 tank locomotive No. 7231 on shunting work at Hythe Quay. A Sentinel shunting locomotive then took over the work and in April 1929 No. 7136 was transferred away. Five years later in October 1934, another 'J70', No. 7125, was allocated to Colchester and thereafter, until the final withdrawal, one of the class was allocated to the Essex depot. At the beginning of 1935 the Wisbech allocation had been increased to five, with another five at Ipswich and a single member of the class at Yarmouth. After the withdrawal of the passenger service between Wisbech and Upwell on 31st December, 1927, two tram locomotives were found adequate to cope with

The first two 'C53' class 0-6-0 tram locomotives Nos. 135 and 136 on introduction into traffic were initially employed at Ipswich dock. Here No. 136 leads sister locomotive over a bridge built by the local firm of Ransomes & Rapier. Both engines later served on the Wisbech & Upwell Tramway.   *Author's Collection*

The secrets of a tram locomotive revealed. GER 'C53' class 0-6-0 No. 125 under construction at Stratford works on 5th February, 1921.   *LCGB/Ken Nunn Collection*

'J70' class 0-6-0 tram locomotive No. 7136 standing at Upwell in 1937. The locomotive was built as GER class 'C53' No. 136 and entered traffic in November 1903. It later became LNER No. 7136 after Grouping, then 8217 in the 1946 renumbering programme and finally BR No. 68217 before being withdrawn in March 1953.   *J.G. Dewing*

The secret of what was concealed within the box body of a tram locomotive. The interior view of 'J70' class 0-6-0 No. 68217 at Wisbech on 25th August, 1950.   *The late H.C. Casserley*

'J70' class 0-6-0 tram locomotive No. 68217 working a down service to Upwell stands at Small Lode level crossing No 16, with the adjacent Small Lode stream underbridge No. 2338 in the foreground. *The late H.C. Casserley*

With side aprons removed, 'J70' class 0-6-0 tram locomotive No. 68225 stands on the back road at Wisbech shed. She was built as GER class 'C53' No. 126 in March 1921 and later became LNER No. 7126 and 8225 in the 1946 renumbering scheme. It was renumbered 68225 by BR before being withdrawn in March 1955. *Author's Collection*

the daily freight service on the tramway, except during the fruit season when additional power was required to handle the extra traffic. During such times, and at the discretion of the driver, the normal maximum load of 12 wagons of coal was often exceeded and No. 7131 was once recorded leaving Upwell with 48 covered vans, which if laden with fruit, weighed nearly 400 tons! No. 7131 subsequently ran short of water at Elm Bridge and had to run light to Wisbech to top up the tanks, before returning to the wagons and continuing the journey.

During World War II, two 'J70' class tram locomotives were loaned to the Wissington Light Railway from 1943 to 1944 and worked all over the fen. They replaced two 'Y6' class 0-4-0s, which derailed on the tightly-curved track. At nationalisation in 1948 Wisbech maintained an allocation of five 'J70s', which were allocated to power class '0F' by BR, but their reign was relatively short-lived for the Drewry 204 hp diesel-mechanical 0-6-0 shunting locomotives arrived at Wisbech in 1952. The last steam-hauled working on the tramway was scheduled to run on 4th July, 1952, but in the event the availability of the new motive power was not as high as expected and 'J70' class No. 68222 was retained as a spare engine and used on a number of occasions whenever a diesel locomotive was unavailable. The other 'J70s' Nos. 68217, 68223 and 68225, were initially stored at March shed. No. 68222 finally left Wisbech in June 1953 and was transferred to Colchester before moving on to Ipswich in November of the same year. At the beginning of 1954 the four remaining 'J70s' were No. 68226 at Colchester, Nos. 68222 and 68225 at Ipswich and 68223 at Yarmouth Vauxhall but all were subsequently replaced by Drewry diesel-mechanical shunting locomotives and were condemned in 1955.

GER No.	Built	LNER 1924 No.	LNER 1946 No.	BR No.	Withdrawn
135	October 1903	7135	8216	68216	November 1953
136	November 1903	7136	8217	68217	March 1953
137	September 1908	7137	8218	68218	September 1949
138	September 1908	7138	–	–	January 1942
139	October 1908	7139	8219	68219	August 1953
130	April 1910	7130	8220	68220	February 1953
127	June 1914	7127	8221	68221	May 1951
128	June 1914	7128	8222	68222	January 1955
131	June 1914	7131	8223	68223	July 1955
125	March 1921	7125	8224	68224	March 1952
126	March 1921	7126	8225	68225	March 1955
129	March 1921	7129	8226	68226	August 1955

The principal dimensions of the 'J70s' were:

Cylinders	2 outside	12 in. x 15 in.
Motion		Walschaerts with slide valves
Boiler	Max. diameter outside	2 ft 10½ in.
	Barrel length	6 ft 10 in.
	Firebox length outside	3 ft 2 in.
Heating surface	Firebox	42.08 sq. ft
	Tubes (102 x 1⅝ in.)	306.00 sq. ft
	Total	348.08 sq. ft

Grate area	9.2 sq. ft
Boiler pressure	180 psi
Coupled wheels	3 ft 1 in.
Tractive effort	8,931 lb.
Length over buffers	20 ft 10½ in.
Wheelbase	6 ft 8 in.
Weight in working order	27 tons 1 cwt
Max. axle load	11 tons 7 cwt
Water capacity	625 gallons
Coal capacity	15 cwt

Liveries

The tram engines at first glance appeared to resemble a large goods brakevan and therefore from the outset the livery was a little different from the conventional locomotive. The wooden body was always repaired and maintained by the Carriage & Wagon department and when the tram engines visited Stratford works for overhaul, the bodies were removed and sent to the wagon works at Temple Mills for attention. When first introduced in 1883 the 'G15' class body was of varnished teak finish. T.W. Worsdell had introduced the standard ultramarine blue livery for locomotives in 1882 and so the tank side panels below the woodwork was painted in this blue livery with black borders with curved corners and vermilion lining in between. The black border was wider at the ends than at the top and bottom. The buffer beams were of timber, faced with steel plates and were mounted on the upward extension of the frames at either end thus covering much of the lower part of the end tank panels. The remaining portion of the tank above the buffer beam was also blue with a narrower black border and vermilion lining. The letters 'G. E. R.' were painted on the side panels in the small 4 inch pattern lettering used at that time. The letters were gold shaded to the left and below in white, yellow, red and chocolate and counter-shaded to the right and below in black. Curiously the buffer beams were also painted ultramarine blue as were the side sheets protecting the wheels, although the latter had no edging or lining, whilst the cowcatchers were black. The standard elliptical brass number plate with vermilion background was mounted centrally on the bodyside and numbers were painted on the buffer beams probably in yellow with chocolate shading.

When James Holden succeeded Worsdell in 1885 he made minor changes to the black borders on the tram engines so they were of equal width all round. The 'G. E. R.' initials were increased to a depth of 6 inches and spacing was further apart. The coupling rods and also connecting rods and return crank rods on the 'C53' class were painted vermilion. There were no changes in livery until World War I, when in 1915 the blue livery was discontinued and engines were painted lead grey. The tram engines began to appear with wooden bodywork painted carriage brown but the tank sides and ends including buffer beams and casings were in plain grey livery. The side skirts were either grey or black whilst 'G. E. R.' was applied to the tank sides in a simpler style of yellow lettering shaded in vermilion. The wheels were painted black and the vermilion side rods were retained. Later in the war alterations were made to the buffer beam lettering and numerals, which were white instead of yellow. In 1919 the GER adopted crimson lake for its carriage livery and the tram engine wooden bodies were painted in a similar way. A further change came in 1921 when the company introduced its Train Control System, which required the painting of the engine stock number in large plain yellow numerals on the tank sides instead of the initials GER.

After Grouping the LNER painted the bodywork on the tram engines brown, whilst the remainder of the engine was black, with the exception of the buffer beams and casings which were red. To the end of World War II the tram locomotives were classified for secondary passenger engine livery despite the withdrawal of passenger services between Wisbech and Upwell from 31st December, 1927, thus the tank side panels were lined in red with the lettering LNER. The engine number was, however, not carried on the engine sides except for a small brass or cast-iron plate, which replaced the large GER brass pattern. The numbers were carried on the buffer beams which were edged in black and lined in white. Red lining was also carried on the narrow portion of the tank fronts above the buffer beam. Prior to the LNER 1924 renumbering scheme, ex-GER engines were given an 'E' suffix to the running number but in at least one case 'Y16' class 0-4-0T No. 0125E carried the suffix as a smaller 'E' after the 'LNER' on the side tanks as there was insufficient space on the buffer beam. During World War II some of the tram locomotives ran with the abbreviated initials 'N E' on the side tanks with no lining.

After Nationalisation the locomotive bodywork remained brown, the buffer beams plain red and the remainder of the engine was finished in unlined black. Some acquired the title 'BRITISH RAILWAYS' in full on the side tanks, a legend, which was later replaced by the lion and wheel emblem, with the lion facing towards the smokebox end of the locomotive. Smokebox numberplates were not fitted but the number was painted in cream or white on the tank front above the buffer beam on the 0-6-0Ts. Only two of the four-coupled engines survived to be renumbered, but as there was insufficient space on the front of the tank, the numbers were painted towards the top of the buffer beam.

Sentinel Tram Engines

In May 1925 the LNER undertook test runs on the Derwent Valley Light Railway line from York to Cliff Common near Selby using that company's Sentinel four-wheel shunting locomotive. The Sentinel Waggon Works of Shrewsbury had developed the four-wheel shunting locomotive design from their widely used steam road lorries using a similar type of vertical boiler and high speed engine with chain drive to the wheels. The Sentinel proved ideal for use on lightly-laid branch lines or in station yards where the permanent way was of a lower standard than on main lines, and in September 1925 the LNER purchased a similar locomotive for use at Lowestoft Harbour. The new acquisition became the initial member of the 'Y1/1' class and was numbered 8400. Four more were ordered for Departmental use in July 1926 and the last of

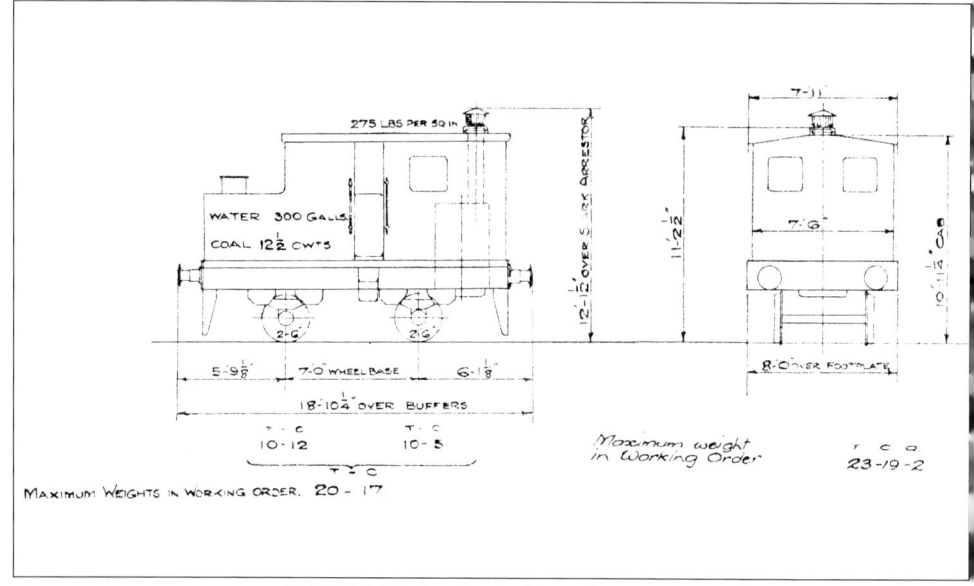

LNER 'Y1/1' class Sentinel 0-4-0 locomotive.

On 4th May, 1927 trials were held to assess the suitability of operating a steam Sentinel locomotive on the tramway. Here 'Y1/1' class 0-4-0 No. 8401 stands at Upwell in the company of a 'J70' class 0-6-0 tram locomotive before departing with the return to Wisbech. The trials were unsuccessful and the locomotive was returned to Lowestoft sleeper depot. The photograph is of further interest as the train is double-headed with a 'J70' class 0-6-0 rostered for a passenger diagram.   *R. Garraway*

the batch No. 8401 (Works No. 6710), was delivered in December of the same year and allocated to work at Lowestoft sleeper depot. In the early months of the following year the motive power authorities considered such locomotives might be suitable for use on the Wisbech & Upwell Tramway, where their steady drawbar pull over a distance could be used to advantage. With the rotary motion imparted to the wheels by the chain drive there was an absence of pounding and reduced tendency to slip compared with a normal reciprocating locomotive. Thus in late April 1927 No. 8401 was dispatched to Wisbech and worked trial trips across the tramway with both passenger and freight services. On 4th May, 1927 she was double-headed on one trip by a 'J70' class 0-6-0. Some sources record No. 8401 being equipped with the Westinghouse brake to work the passenger services but from its earliest days the locomotive was equipped with a train pipe connection but no hose. It was not officially recorded as being fitted with the Westinghouse brake and if equipment was fitted it was of a temporary nature and fitted at Norwich shed whilst *en route* from Lowestoft to Wisbech. The trials on the tramway were inconclusive and No. 8401 was soon returned to Lowestoft sleeper depot.

GER No.	LNER 1943 No.	LNER 1946 No.	BR No.	Withdrawn
8401	7773	8131	*	April 1963

* allocated Departmental No. 39 in August 1953.

The leading dimensions of No. 8401 were:

Cylinders	2 inside	6¾ in. x 9 in.
Motion		Rotary cam with poppet valves
Boiler		
	Diameter at top	2 ft 8½ in.
	Height	4 ft 4⅝ in.
Heating surface	Firebox	26.70 sq. ft
	Water tubes	27.73 sq. ft
Total evaporative		54.43 sq. ft
Superheater coil		9.72 sq. ft
Total		64.15 sq. ft
Grate area		3.97 sq. ft
Water tubes		30 x 1¾ in.
Boiler pressure		275 psi
Wheel diameter		2 ft 6 in.
Wheelbase		7 ft 0 in.
Length over buffers		18 ft 10¼ in.
Weight		20 tons 17 cwt
Max. axle loading		10 tons 12 cwt
Water capacity		300 gallons
Coal capacity		12½ cwt
Sprocket ratio		11:25
Tractive effort		7,260 lb.

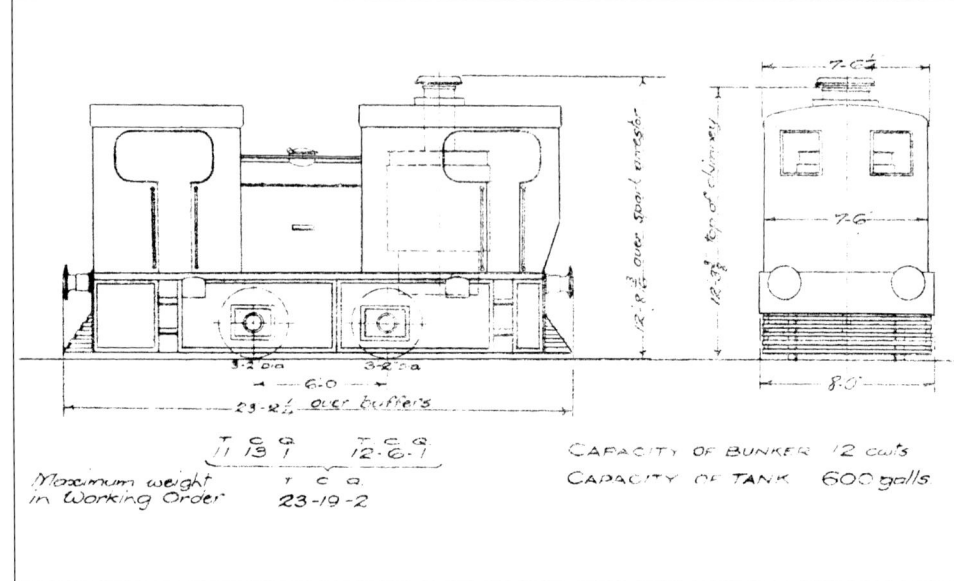

LNER 'Y10' class Sentinel 0-4-0 locomotive.

'Y10' class 0-4-0 Sentinel shunting locomotive No. 8404 standing outside the shed at Wisbech in company with a tram locomotive in January 1931. No. 8404 arrived at Wisbech on 11th September, 1930 to take up duties on the tramway but showed no superiority over the conventional tram locomotives and was transferred away to Yarmouth Vauxhall shed on 8th May, 1931.   *W. Whitworth*

The LNER, finding No. 8401 underpowered but having experienced success with steam railcars and shunting locomotives of Sentinel design, placed an order in November 1929 for two 200 hp double-engine, doubled-geared Sentinel tram engines specifically for use on the Wisbech & Upwell Tramway. Costing £4,720, the pair numbered 8403 and 8404 (Works Nos. 8147 and 8148) were taken into stock on 5th and 26th June, 1930 respectively as LNER 'Y10' class and allocated initially to Cambridge depot. The official works photograph shows one of the locomotives bearing 'Wisbech and Upwell Tramways' in small lettering on the footplate edging. Within six days No. 8403 was transferred to Wisbech and immediately entered service on the tramway, but No. 8404 did not follow until 11th September. To comply with BoT regulations the engines were fitted with cowcatchers, whilst the wheels were concealed behind protective skirting which came within 4 inches of the rail level. As passenger traffic had ceased, Nos. 8403 and 8404 were fitted with steam brakes and hand brakes only and the engines were governed to run at a maximum speed of 10 mph. These Sentinels had two standard Sentinel locomotive two-cylinder engines at the rear end, partly housed in the cab, with a two-speed gearbox. The boiler was located in the cab at the front end and duplicate controls were provided in both cabs so that they could be driven from either end. The water tank was situated between the two cabs. Other features included throated chimneys fitted with spark arresters, two engine-driven feed pumps and twin injectors, hand sanding gear, steam and hand brakes with the automatic governor working on the steam brake, duplicate controls and Delvac cylinder lubricator. A separate blast pipe led from each of the four cylinders into the chimney casing. A horizontally-mounted whistle was located above the cab roof at the front end and a bell was provided in front of the cab at the opposite end. Foot operated warning gongs were also fitted in each cab. Unfortunately the 'Y10s' were found to be totally unsuitable for the Upwell line. When hauling the maximum loads, especially at the height of the fruit season, they had to be worked at full stretch, which resulted in excessive fuel consumption and emission of sparks in the close proximity of the lineside.

Following complaints from footplate crews and the local populace, especially over the smuts on washing hanging on clotheslines adjacent to the railway, the LNER motive power authorities withdrew the engines from the Tramway. No. 8403 was sent to Yarmouth on 3rd October, 1930 and then for trials at Ipswich between 31st December, 1930 and 9th February, 1931, where she met with little success and was reallocated to Wisbech. By May 1931 both had been transferred to Yarmouth where they worked on the old Union Railway quayside line. In February 1934 No. 8404 was sent to Scotland where it spent a few weeks allocated to Kittybrewster shed and worked on the Aberdeen dock lines, followed by a short period at St Margarets, Edinburgh working at the local St Leonard's Yard. By May 1934 it had returned south to Yarmouth and except for a short spell at Norwich, between May and November 1940, caused by the threat of invasion on eastern coastal ports, both locomotives remained at Yarmouth until withdrawal from traffic and they were subsequently cut up at Stratford.

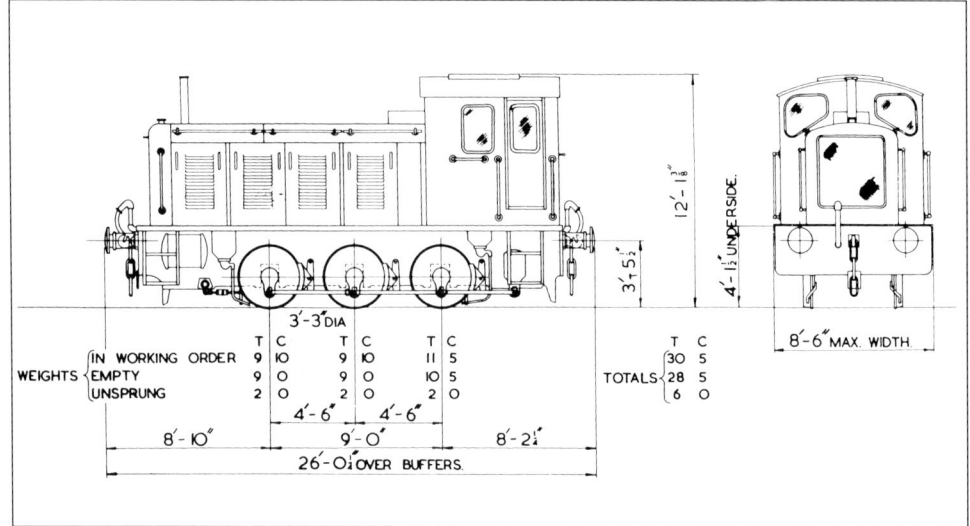

Drewry 204 hp 0-6-0 diesel mechanical shunting locomotive BR class '2/13' later class '04'.

Drewry 204 hp 0-6-0 diesel-mechanical locomotive No. 11101, later BR class '04', has yet to receive her narrow exhaust stack and yellow and black chevron painted ends as she waits at Upwell with the Railway Club brake van special train on 9th July, 1955.   *The late B.D.J. Walsh*

GER No.	LNER 1943 No.	LNER 1946 No.	BR No.	Withdrawn
8403	7775	8186	–	February 1952
8404	7776	8187	–	August 1948

The leading dimensions of the class were:

Cylinders	4 inside	6¾ in. x 9 in.
Motion		Rotary cam with poppet valves
Boiler (vertical)	Diameter	4 ft 6 in.
	Total height	6 ft 5⅜ in.
Heating surface		
	Firebox	51.0 sq. ft
	Water tubes*	108.0 sq. ft
	Total evaporative	159.0 sq. ft
	Superheater†	40.0 sq. ft
	Total	199.0 sq. ft
Grate area		6.5 sq. ft
Boiler pressure		275 psi
Wheels		3 ft 2 in.
Wheelbase		6 ft 0 in.
Length over buffers		23 feet 2¼ ins
Weight in working order		24 tons 0 cwt
Maximum axle load		12 tons 6 cwt
Water capacity		600 gallons
Coal capacity		12 cwt
Sprocket ratio		
	countershaft : wheels	18:31
Tractive effort		
	Low gear (ratio 45:102)	11,414 lb.
	High gear (ratio 57:90)	7,965 lb.

* 90 x 2 inches
† 1½ inch diameter

Diesel Mechanical Shunting Locomotives

After Nationalisation serious attempts were made to reduce the cost of shunting duties by the introduction of diesel shunting locomotives that could replace ageing steam locomotives and which required much less maintenance. At the end of 1951, the Railway Executive, Eastern Region investigated various possible locations where diesel traction might be utilised and with the ancient steam tram engines still operating to Upwell, the tramway from Wisbech was a prime case for renewal of motive power. The Railway Executive subsequently placed an order with the Drewry Car Company Ltd for thirteen 204 bhp diesel-mechanical locomotives 'for service on the Wisbech to Upwell branch and on Eastern and North Eastern Region dock lines where not dissimilar conditions prevail'. The 13 were of Drewry design, although the initial four required for service in East Anglia were constructed by Vulcan Foundry. All four were

The Drewry 204 hp diesel-mechanical shunting locomotives were originally delivered in plain black livery with red buffer beams and black cowcatchers and side aprons. No. 11102 stands on the headshunt outside Wisbech shed before taking up duties on the tramway on 4th June, 1952. Both locomotives allocated to work the Upwell tramway were later equipped with a slender exhaust pipe. *M.N. Bland*

Drewry 204 hp 0-6-0 diesel-mechanical shunting locomotive No. D2201 was one of the pair regularly allocated to March depot to work the Wisbech & Upwell Tramway. She is fitted with the obligatory side aprons and cowcatchers for roadside running, and was originally numbered 11101. She was renumbered to No. D2201 in December 1961 and after the closure of the tramway was transferred to Crewe as works shunter on 15th September, 1966 before withdrawal from traffic on 6th April, 1968. *Author's Collection*

distinctly modified as tram locomotives, being equipped with side valances, cowcatchers and a governor, which put the final drive out of mesh if the speed exceeded 12 mph. The four allocated to East Anglia were numbered 11100, 11101, 11102 and 11103 and were initially allocated as follows: No. 11100 to Ipswich for shunting in the docks, No. 11101 to Yarmouth South Town, No. 11102 to March to work the Wisbech & Upwell Tramway and No. 11103 to March.

Driver H. Potter of Wisbech, was delegated to work No. 11102 over the tramway on trial trips accompanied by several officials, although the journeys were operated without the side skirts being fitted on the locomotive. The declared intention was to concentrate the diesel-mechanical shunting locomotives on the tramway during the soft fruit season and if necessary disperse the class to other work during the winter and the spring, when the 'J70' steam class would again work the line. It was proposed to changeover fully to the new traction on the Upwell Tramway from 4th July, 1952. However, because of teething troubles the starting date was deferred to August. In addition tram locomotive No. 68222 was retained at Wisbech until March 1953 as cover and was frequently utilised. No. 11102, officially allocated to March depot for use on the Upwell services, was normally outbased at Wisbech. When she entered regular traffic on the line she was fully equipped with the skirts. No. 11101 was transferred to March depot in July to share the Upwell line workings whilst sister locomotive No. 11103 was transferred away to Yarmouth Vauxhall to work on the Quay. Thereafter the pair Nos. 11101 and 11102 were the regular locomotives on the Upwell line and were later renumbered D2201 and D2202 respectively. No. 11101 was transferred in March 1955 to Plaistow shed to shunt Dagenham Dock yard with sister locomotive No. 11110, which had been transferred from Parkeston, but within a month she had returned to March to resume her diagram working on the tramway. The locomotives were originally painted in unlined black livery with red buffer beams but after a visit to works, No. 11101 emerged in December 1961 in unlined green livery with yellow and black warning stripes on the front and rear and renumbered D2201. No. 11102 renumbered D2202, had been similarly treated in January 1958. Wisbech drivers were of the opinion that No. D2201 was the more powerful of the two locomotives.

The class later became class '2/13' and March were allocated Nos. D2200, D2201, D2202, plus D2237, D2238, D2239 and D2240 of the class '2/13A'. Nos. D2201 and D2202, later allocated to BR class '04', were the engines regularly allocated to the Wisbech & Upwell Tramway and the locomotives worked the line until closure on 20th May, 1966. No. D2201 worked the last service and the pair remained at March depot until 15th September when it and No. D2202 were transferred to Crewe works as the works shunting locomotives, although for much of the time they were stored out of use. Nos. D2201 and D2202 were withdrawn from traffic on 6th April, 1968 and 20th February, 1968 respectively, both being cut up by private scrap contractors. No. 11103, renumbered D2203, has been preserved as a representative of the class.

The leading dimensions of the class were:

Drewry 204 hp BR class '04' 0-6-0 diesel-mechanical locomotive No. D2202 swings into Elm Bridge depot with the 1.30 pm Wisbech to Upwell freight train on 18th August, 1964. The train is on the main single line with the goods loop running parallel in the foreground.   *Ken Paye*

Drewry 204 hp 0-6-0 diesel-mechanical shunting locomotive No. D2202 hauling the 3.30 pm Upwell to Wisbech train past the trees bordering the Inglethorpe Hall Estate on 18th August, 1964.   *Ken Paye*

Weight in working order		32 tons 4 cwt
Tractive effort	1st gear	15,650 lb.
	2nd gear	9,050 lb.
	3rd gear	6,000 lb.
	4th gear	3,860 lb.
	5th gear	2,070 lb.
Wheelbase		9 ft 0 in.
Wheel diameter		3 ft 6 in.
Width overall		8 ft 7 in.
Length overall		26 ft 0 in.
Height overall		11 ft 11 in.
Minimum curve negotiable		2 chains
Maximum speed	1st gear	3.66 mph
	2nd gear	6.35 mph
	3rd gear	9.60 mph
	4th gear	14.90 mph
	5th gear	27.80 mph
Fuel tanks		280 gallons
Cooling water		20 gallons
Lubricating oil sump		8 gallons
Brakes		Compressed air and hand, also fitted with belt driven vacuum exhauster
Sanding		Compressed air operated
Power equipment		8 cyl. diesel engine - Gardner 8L3 type, 204 hp at 1200 rpm
Transmission		Fluid coupling - Vulcan Sinclair type 23, capacity 8½ gallons. Gearbox - Wilson Drewry C.A.5 type 5-speed epicyclic gearbox, compressed air operated. R.F.11 spiral bevel reverse and final drive unit, compressed air operated, gear ratio 9.82:1

Motive Power Facilities and Staff

When the railway through Wisbech was opened in 1847 some locomotive servicing accommodation was provided on the east side of the Wisbech, St Ives and Cambridge Junction line on the approach to the terminal station. A shed was shown on ECR plans of 1847 complete with turntable, which was provided from the outset on the east side of the approach to the station. The ECR worked the line and with the arrival of the East Anglian Railway from the east in 1848, no additional facilities were provided. By 1852 the ECR was working both routes to Wisbech and the existing facilities served for over 20 years. Six years after the GER was created in 1862, the Directors on a tour of inspection during 11th and 12th September, 1868 were aghast at the state of affairs and questioned whether anything could be done to improve the 'engine house'. The General Manager and locomotive superintendent were instructed to report on the affair. By the early 1880s the earlier facilities had been abandoned and a two-road engine shed was in use on the western side of the line which from 1855 was the approach to the goods yard. A brick water tower stood alongside the structure

Wisbech shed on 2nd July, 1946 with *left to right*: 'J70' class 0-6-0s Nos. 7128 and 8217, 'Y6' 0-4-0 No. 8083 on the back road and 'J70' No. 8218 and 'Y6' No. 8082 outside the shed. The signal to the right was Wisbech Station signal box up starter for the high level tram road serving the back platform.   *A.F. Cook*

Wisbech shed on 25th August, 1950 with 'J70' class 0-6-0 tram locomotive No. 68217 on No. 1 road outside the original 1883 structure and sister locomotive No. 68225 on No. 2 road outside the later 1894 building. Note the neatly stacked coal on the coaling stage.

The late H.C. Casserley

together with a 42 ft, later increased to 44 ft 9 in., diameter turntable near Wisbech Goods Junction which was sometimes used to turn the tram locomotives to prevent uneven flange and tyre wear.

With the opening of the tramway from August 1883 the three tram locomotives were maintained and serviced in the existing shed alongside the goods spur near Wisbech Goods Junction signal box. This was not satisfactory and after consultation with the locomotive superintendent, the Way & Works Committee sought tenders on 21st August, 1883 for the erection of a new engine shed nearer the tramway. On 4th September, 1883 a contract was awarded to R. Girling for a single-road shed after he had tendered at £376 6s. 7d. and this was completed in September 1884 on a site to the south-east of Wisbech passenger station. As the traffic increased and further tram engines were required, the shed became increasingly congested and on 5th September, 1893 the question of additional accommodation was considered, but as the estimate for new structure was a prohibitive £640 the matter was put in abeyance. In the spring of 1894 the locomotive superintendent again raised the issue of increased accommodation and after detailed discussion it was agreed to make additions to the existing shed and tenders were sought. On 5th June, 1894 the contract was awarded to S. Hipwell of Wisbech at a cost of £295; this entailed doubling the size of the shed by having an additional single-road bay constructed on the north side of the original structure. The shed alongside the spur to the goods yard went out of use in 1914 and soon after World War I was abolished. The main line locomotive allocated to Wisbech was then serviced at the tram shed, although more often than not it was stabled overnight near the turntable, which remained by the site of the old shed. At this time Wisbech shed was part of the Peterborough District and was under the charge of a foreman responsible to the district locomotive superintendent. With the abolition of the Peterborough District locomotives were allocated to Kings Lynn. After Grouping, control went to Cambridge but with locomotives allocated from Kings Lynn. This continued after Nationalization with engines carrying the BR allocated shed plate of 31C.

When the Drewry 0-6-0 diesel-mechanical shunting locomotives arrived in 1952 they were initially accommodated in the steam shed but this was an unsatisfactory arrangement and plans were prepared for the reconstruction of the shed to service diesel traction. The newer northern portion of the shed was demolished and the redundant inspection pit was filled in. All the walls on the original section of the shed were made good and new windows installed. A new lintel over the entrance and a reclad roof completed the work, which was finally completed in 1958. Heavier repairs were carried out at March depot and the two locomotives allocated to the tramway carried the shedplate 31B on the back of the cab.

Locomotive watering facilities were available at Wisbech in the engine yard near Wisbech Goods Junction where a jib crane served the shed road and the down goods road. A water crane fed from a water tank provided replenishment for the tram locomotives in the tram siding near Wisbech station and tram engine shed. Initially there were no watering facilities at Upwell, but this was rectified in 1907 when a water tank formed of a GER locomotive tender, with wheels

WISBECH DEPOT

WEEK DAYS.

No. 2.

a.m. arr.		a.m. dep.	
	On Duty	{ 4 0	**S X**
		{ 5 15	**S O**
	Loco'	6 0	**L**
	Wisbech	6 30	**G S X**
8 0	Upwell	9 15	**G S X**
10 35	Wisbech	11 5	**G S X**
p.m.		p.m.	
12 30	Upwell	1 28	**G S X**
2 11	Wisbech	2 15	**G S X**
3 5	Upwell	4 15	**G S X**
5 40	Wisbech		
a.m.		a.m.	
	Wisbech	6 30	**G S O**
8 0	Upwell	8 15	**S O**
8 54	Wisbech	9 30	**S O**
10 9	Upwell	10 15	**S O**
10 54	Wisbech	11 5	**G S O**
p.m.		p.m.	
12 30	Upwell	1 25	**S O**
2 4	Wisbech	2 50	**S O**
3 29	Upwell	3 35	**S O**
4 14	Wisbech	4 25	**S O**
5 8	Upwell	5 15	**S O**
5 54	Wisbech	6 20	**S O**
6 59	Upwell	7 5	**S O**
7 44	Wisbech	9 0	**S O**
9 39	Upwell	9 45	**S O**
10 24	Wisbech		**L**
	Loco'		

Men change at Wisbech Station **SX** 10.50 a.m., **SO** 2.30 p.m. Shunts Loco' 4.0 a.m. to 6.0 a.m. **SX**

No. 3.

arr. a.m.		dep. a.m.	
	On Duty	6 30	
	Loco'	7 15	**L**
	Wisbech	7 30	**S X**
8 9	Upwell	8 15	**S X**
8 54	Wisbech	9 30	**S X**
10 9	Upwell	10 15	**S X**
		p.m.	
10 54	Wisbech	12 40	**S X**
p.m.			
1 19	Upwell	1 25	**S X**
2 4	Wisbech	2 30	**S X**
3 9	Upwell	3 15	**S X**
3 54	Wisbech	6 20	**S X**
6 59	Upwell	7 5	**S X**
7 44	Wisbech	8 30	**S X**
9 9	Upwell	9 15	**S X**
9 54	Wisbech		
a.m.		a.m.	
	Wisbech	7 30	**S O**
8 9	Upwell	9 15	**G S O**
10 35	Wisbech	11 25	**G S O**
p.m.		p.m.	
12 46	Upwell	1 28	**G S O**
2 11	Wisbech		**L**
	Loco'		

Men change at Wisbech Station 2.20 p.m. **SX**

No. 4.

arr. a.m.		dep. a.m.	
	On Duty	10 5	
	Loco'	10 50	**L**
	Wisbech	10 55	
11 34	Upwell	11 40	
p.m.		p.m.	
12 19	Wisbech	12 40	**S O**
1 19	Upwell	1 50	**G S O**
3 33	Wisbech	12 45	**G S X**
2 15	Upwell	3 35	**G S X**
5 20	Wisbech		**L**
	Loco'		

Locomotive and enginemen's diagrams, Wisbech depot 1925.

removed, was erected by the buffer stops of the engine release road. This served a water crane located by the buffer stops at the passenger station run-round loop.

Main line and tram crews at Wisbech had separate links, with two crews for the main line and six sets of men for the tramway workings. Typical diagrams in 1925 involved three tram locomotives and five sets of men for the weekdays-only passenger and goods services. Wisbech diagram 1 was for a main line locomotive working to March and Cambridge. The day-to-day administration was the responsibility of a driver-in-charge and most tramway work was carried out by early, middle and late turn diagrams, although night coal trains offered an opportunity for overtime. A cleaner or acting fireman and shedman were booked on night duty employed on disposing of and preparing locomotives for the next turn of duty as well as unloading coal from wagons on to the coaling stage and then coaling the locomotives. Tube cleaning was carried out on Sundays by the senior fireman who earned half a day's Sunday pay for the work. In 1914 the foreman, William French aged 63 years with 41 years service on the railway, had a staff of two drivers, three tram drivers, two acting drivers, three firemen, four acting firemen and two cleaners. In addition there were fitters and shed labourers about the shed.

The first driver based at Wisbech to take a tram locomotive across the new line was John Whyman, who later transferred to Kings Lynn. He died in March 1896 and was interred at Wisbech where many of his former colleagues attended the funeral. Other tramway drivers in the early years included John Hardman and James Palmer. In 1923 driver Ernest (Ernie) Albert Brooks was in the tramway link with fireman Stephen Culley as his regular mate. Brooks died on 23rd October, 1930. Driver Albert South joined the tramway staff as a cleaner in 1918 and was fireman on the last passenger tram on 31st December, 1927. He remained at Wisbech to work the last train across the branch on Friday 20th May, 1966, with fireman Derek Norman. Other tramway drivers included Frederick Charlesworth who retired in 1926 and died in 1940 aged 78, William Emerson who retired on 6th July, 1934, Robert Henry Morriss, who retired on 11th October, 1934, Charles (Charlie) Rand, Jack Ogden, Harry Potter and in the latter years David Bailey. Fireman on the tram locomotives and later second men on the diesel-mechanical shunting locomotives included Percy South (no relation of driver Albert South), Stephen Culley, Arthur Banyard, Edward Nichols, Tom Kirby, Bert Beales and Jim Dowling. Kings Lynn and later March men were allocated to assist on tramway work and accordingly 'signed the road' to Upwell when traffic was heavy and also to cover for sickness and holiday absence.

In the event of a mishap or derailment the March breakdown crane was used to cover the Wisbech & Upwell Tramway. From 1908 this was GER 20 tons capacity steam crane No. 4A. However after World War I a breakdown van was retained at Wisbech shed for use on the line, but soon after Grouping the March breakdown crane reverted to cover the tramway. In 1938 the crane was renumbered 961602 by the LNER and later No. 134 by British Railways. The crane was withdrawn from service in 1964 and for the remaining period the branch was open to traffic, March 35 tons capacity steam crane No. 135 covered any emergency. This crane was built by Ransomes & Rapier in 1919, numbered 961600 by the LNER and was subsequently withdrawn as No. 135 in 1968.

Two 'Y6' class 0-4-0 tram locomotives Nos. 07125 and 07126 waiting to depart from Upwell with trains of covered vans laden with fruit traffic on 25th June, 1929.   *The late H.C. Casserley*

The coal stage at the tram shed was conveniently situated alongside No. 1 shed road where driver John Ogden is coaling his tram locomotive in 1937. A trio of tram engines and a Great Western Railway open wagon are stabled on back road formerly occupied by the covered shed erected for passenger tram coaches.   *Author's Collection*

The 13th August, 1960 marked the retirement of Ernie Gretton who had served for 30 years as depot foreman at Outwell Village. From the cab of Drewry 204 hp 0-6-0 diesel locomotive No. 11101 driver Charles Rand shakes hands with Gretton whilst fireman Edwards Nichols looks on. Charles Barton, the new foreman is on the footsteps of the locomotive and guard Arthur Blake holds the shunting pole.   *Lilian Ream Gallery*

The undermentioned statement showing expenses of Locomotive and Carriage operation on the Wisbech & Upwell Tramway for the year ending 31st December, 1914 makes interesting reading, when compared with receipts for the same period of £6,125 14s. 4d.

Working Stock	Locomotives	6
	Cars	10

Train miles	Passenger	23,136
	Goods and Coal	16,522
	Total	39,658

Mileage of cars	No. 1	4,620
	No. 2	4,168
	No. 3	3,420
	No. 4	6,576
	No. 5	9,672
	No. 6	14,560
	No. 7	10,444
	No. 8	8,020
	No. 16	19,976
	Ordinary brake vans	3,180
	Total	84,636

General Repairs and Maintenance of Locomotives and Cars:

	£	s.	d.
Engines	258	12	0
Cars	164	12	0
Total	423	4	0

Cost of Traction Power:

	£	s.	d.
Fuel	392	12	4
Drivers and Firemen	674	14	5
Lubricants	23	17	10
Cleaners, Coalmen etc.	73	2	5
Other stores	17	14	6
Water	53	1	6
Total	1,235	3	0

Depreciation:

	£	s.	d.
Engines	165	5	4
Tram cars	99	3	2
Total	264	8	6

Total Expenditure and Depreciation:	1,922	15	6

Chapter Eleven

Coaching Stock and Wagons

The initial coaching stock provided for the passenger service from Wisbech to Outwell was originally built for use on the Millwall Railway by George Starbuck of Birkenhead, where they were hauled by both horse and steam locomotive. The four vehicles transferred to the Tramway, GER Nos. 1 and 2 were probably first/third composites, whilst Nos. 3 and 4 had second class accommodation. The four-wheel stock was unpopular and uncomfortable and all four vehicles were withdrawn in June 1890 on the introduction of new Tramway vehicles. The leading dimensions were:

GER Diagram	None issued
Type	Four wheel
	First/third composite
	or full 2nd
Length over body	20 ft 1 in.
Body height	7 ft 1½ in.
Wheelbase	12 ft 0 in.
Weight empty	4 tons 8 cwt

For the opening of the line through to Upwell, five new vehicles were built at Stratford works specifically for the tramway. The first two were four-wheel vehicles, GE No. 5 to diagram 600 and order Z16 was a composite with a second class saloon measuring 11 ft 6 in. and seating 14 passengers, with a smaller first class saloon measuring 5 ft 7½ in. and seating six passengers. In the same order but to diagram 601 was vehicle No. 6, an open second, later third seating 22 passengers. Both were completed in July 1884. The principal dimensions were:

GER diagram		600	601
Type		Four wheel composite	Four wheel second open
Length over buffers		27 ft 1 in.	27 ft 1 in.
Length over headstocks		23 ft 7 in.	23 ft 7 in.
Length over body		17 ft 11 in.	17 ft 11 in.
Body height		7 ft 0½ in.	7 ft 0½ in.
Max. width		8 ft 0 in.	8 ft 0 in.
Max. height		10 ft 2½ in.	10 ft 2½ in.
Wheelbase		10 ft 0 in.	10 ft 0 in.
Wheel diameter		2 ft 9 in.	2 ft 9 in.
Seating	1st	6	–
	2nd	14*	22#
	3rd	–	–
Total weight empty		6 tons 5 cwt†	6 tons 2 cwt†

* 20 x 3rd class from January 1893
† later increased to 7 tons 14 cwt
# 22 x 3rd class from January 1893

Diagram Nº 1

3ʳᵈ Period 1871 to 1875

Tram Cars

Second class & Composite

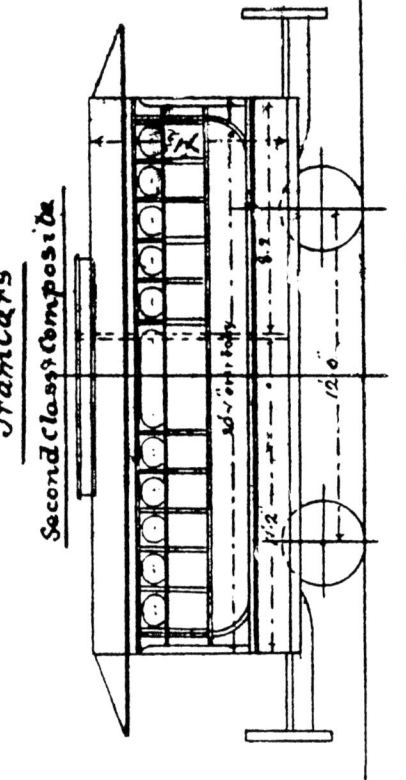

Total weight empty 4.8 T. cwt

No built to this between 1871+1875 = 2

" " " " " " = 2

Nºˢ 1 to 4.

To Seat Passengers Nºˢ 1+2

" " " 2ⁿᵈ class Nºˢ 3+4

GER diagram for original 4-wheel tramcar vehicles transferred from the Millwall line.

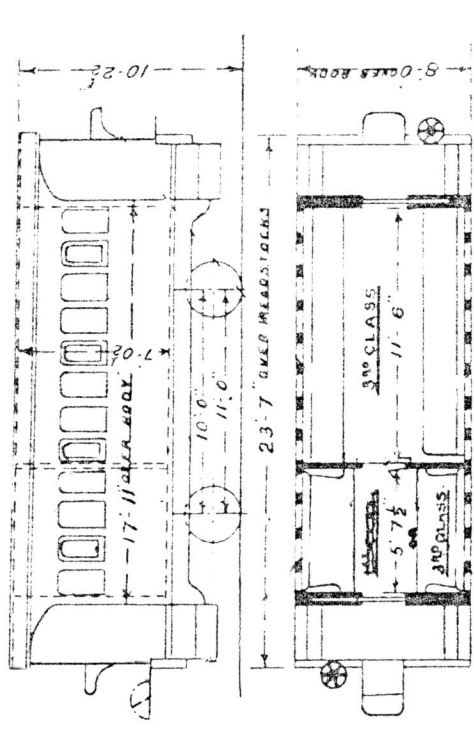

GER diagram 600 four-wheel composite tramcar.

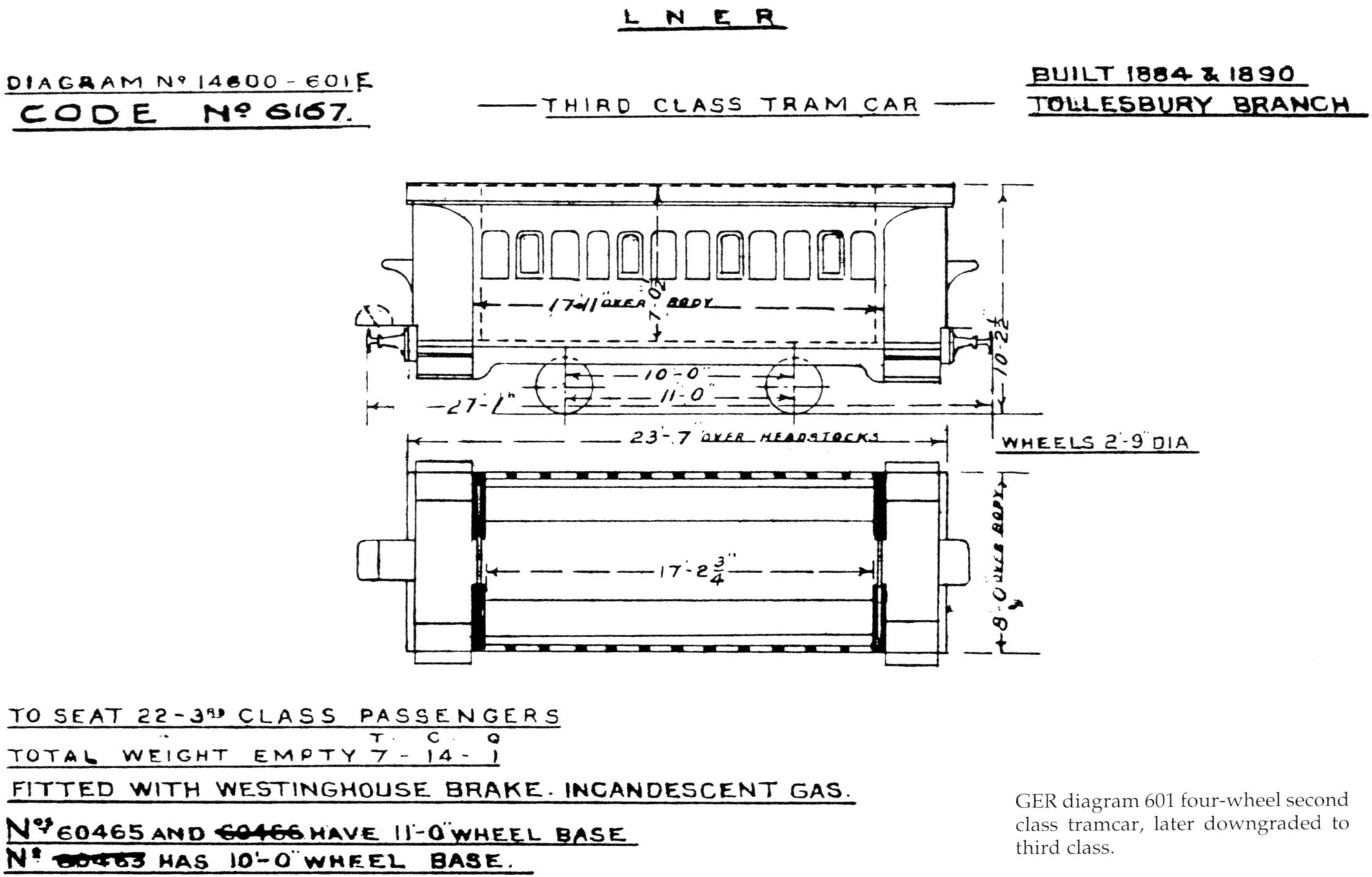

L N E R

BUILT 1884 & 1890
TOLLESBURY BRANCH

DIAGRAM Nº 14600-601E

CODE Nº 6167.

—— THIRD CLASS TRAM CAR ——

WHEELS 2'-9" DIA

22-0¼

10-2¾

23-7 OVER HEADSTOCK

17 OVER BODY

10-0

11-0

27-1½

17-2¾"

8'-0" OVER BODY

TO SEAT 22-3RD CLASS PASSENGERS

TOTAL WEIGHT EMPTY 7-14-) T C Q

FITTED WITH WESTINGHOUSE BRAKE. INCANDESCENT GAS.

Nº 60465 AND 60466 HAVE 11'-0" WHEEL BASE

Nº 60463 HAS 10'-0" WHEEL BASE.

GER diagram 601 four-wheel second class tramcar, later downgraded to third class.

Order A17 completed in September 1884 included coach No. 7 to diagram 602, a bogie composite tramcar with a 17 ft 5 in. second class saloon seating 22 passengers and a 10 ft first class saloon seating 10 passengers. The balance of order A17 was a second, later third class bogie tramcar No. 8 to diagram 603, which seated 34 passengers.

GER diagram		602	603
Type		Bogie composite	Bogie second
Length over buffers		37 ft 4½ in.	37 ft 4½ in.
Length over headstocks		33 ft 10½ in.	33 ft 10½ in.
Length over body		28 ft 2½ in.	28 ft 2½ in.
Max height		10 ft 2½ in.	10 ft 2½ in.
Body height		7 ft 0½ in.	7 ft 0½ in.
Max width		8 ft 0 in.	8 ft 0 in.
Bogie wheelbase		4 ft 6 in.	4 ft 6 in.
Wheelbase		23 ft 0 in.	23 ft 0 in.
Wheels diameter		2 ft 9 in.	2 ft 9 in.
Seating	1st	10	–
	2nd	22*	34#
	3rd	–	–
Total weight empty		10 tons 10 cwt†	10 tons 10 cwt†

* altered to 24 x 3rd in January 1893
† later increased to 12 tons 5 cwt
\# altered to 34 x 3rd class in January 1893

Just after the turn of the century the Wisbech & Upwell Tramway services were experiencing overcrowding, especially in the summer months. The Directors were not in favour of providing additional coaching stock as the existing vehicles were adequate for most periods of the year. In March 1907, however, a plan was prepared at Stratford to provide seating on the roof of the bogie tramcars to give greater accommodation at peak periods. The modification was considered too costly for it required considerable strengthening of the roof and extra costs for maintenance. Had the work been carried out it would have provided an additional 40 seats per bogie car.

The fifth new vehicle also completed in September 1884 under order 'Y16' was four-wheel luggage van No. 9 to diagram 604.

GER Diagram	604
Type	Four wheel luggage van
Length over buffers	15 ft 6 in.
Length over body	12 ft 0 in.
Max. height	10 ft 2 in.
Body height	7 ft 0 in.
Max. width	7 ft 7 in.
Wheelbase	6 ft 0 in.
Wheel diameter	2 ft 9 in.
Luggage	
Total weight empty	4 tons 3 cwt

72

Diagram No. 4

5th Period 1881 to 1885

Third Class Tram Car

& Composite   "   "

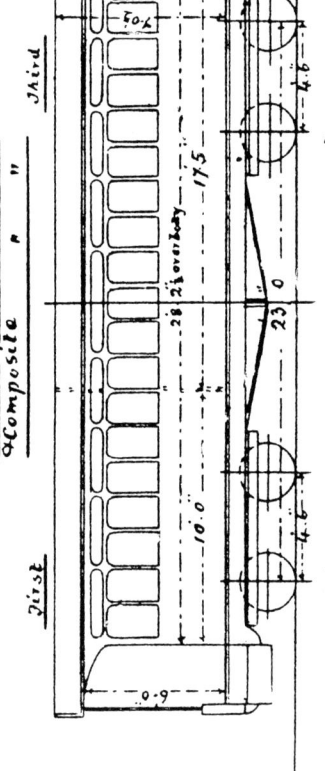

First

Third

Third

9·0

10·0

28'2 over body

17·5

23·0

4·6 right empty

4·6 right empty

5·0½

Total weight empty 10·10

No. built to this between 1884 & 1885 = 1

"   "   "   "   "   "   "   = 1

"   "   "   "   "   "   "   = 1

No⁵ 4 & 8

To Seat 36 Passengers 3rd Class

"   "   10 1st Class . . 24 3rd   "

Copied from D.B. No. 6847

GER diagram 4 second, later third class and composite bogie tramcars. The diagrams were later altered to 603 and 602 respectively.

'G15' class 0-4-0 tram locomotive No. 132 waiting to depart Upwell on 10th March, 1923. Driver Ernest Brooks and fireman Stephen Culley are on the footplate. The leading vehicle is composite bogie tram No. 7, which many years later appeared in the film *The Titfield Thunderbolt* and has since been preserved. Locomotive No. 132 later became LNER No. 7132 and was withdrawn from traffic in October 1931. *Author's Collection*

Former Wisbech & Upwell composite bogie tramcar No. E60461 at Kelvedon on 29th July, 1950. After withdrawal from service the vehicle was used in the Ealing comedy film *The Titfield Thunderbolt*, which was located on the former Great Western Railway Camerton branch. The coach has since been renovated and restored to its former GER condition. *LCGB/Ken Nunn Collection*

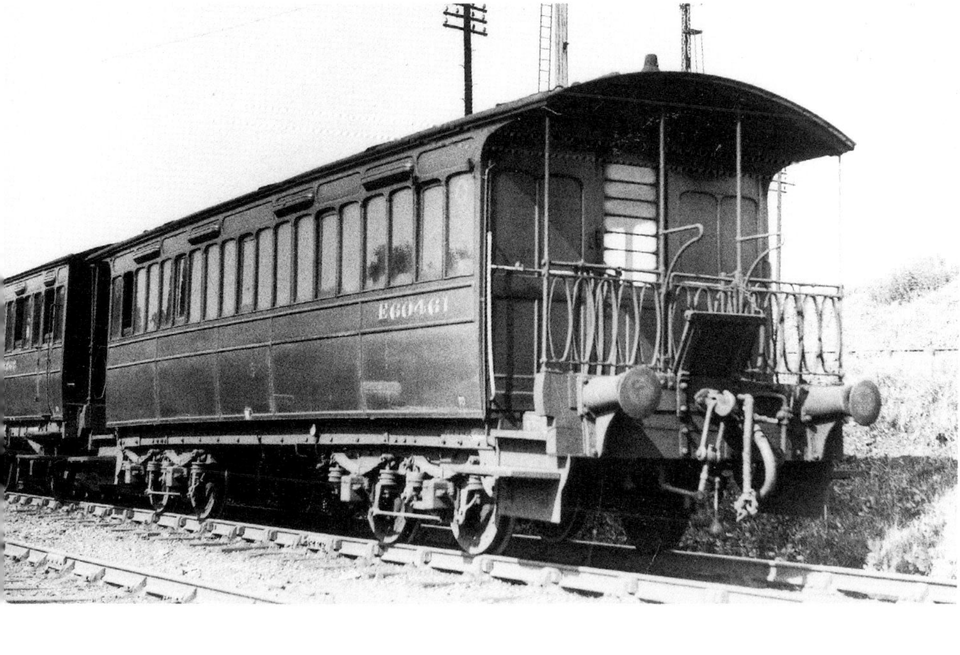

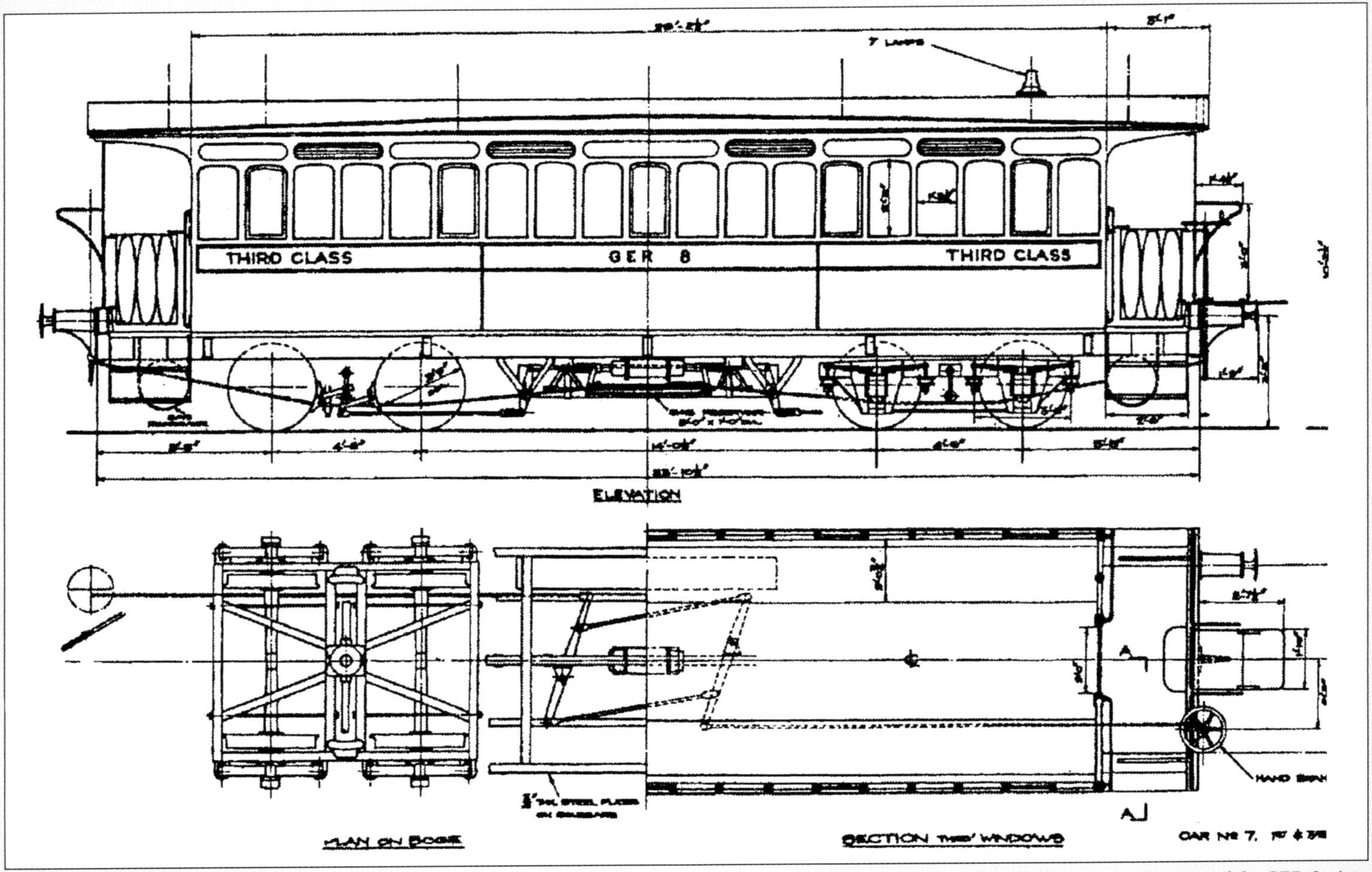

THIRD CLASS

GER 8

THIRD CLASS

ELEVATION

SECTION THRO' WINDOWS

PLAN ON BOGIE

CAR No 7, 10 & 8.

HAND BRAKE

Plan of GER bogie tramcar No. 8.

Courtesy of the GER Society

GER diagram 603 second, later third class bogie tramway coach No. 8 at Upwell showing the end balcony and step arrangement to enable passengers to alight from and join the train at the roadside stops. The other vehicles on the train are a four-wheel composite to diagram 600 and four-wheel brake van No. 16 to diagram 611 specially converted for tramway use in October 1903. *Author's Collection*

Former Wisbech & Upwell bogie tramcar GER No. 8, LNER No. 60462 was transferred to the Kelvedon &Tollesbury Light Railway in Essex in September 1928 and is seen at Tollesbury in January 1949. *John H. Meredith*

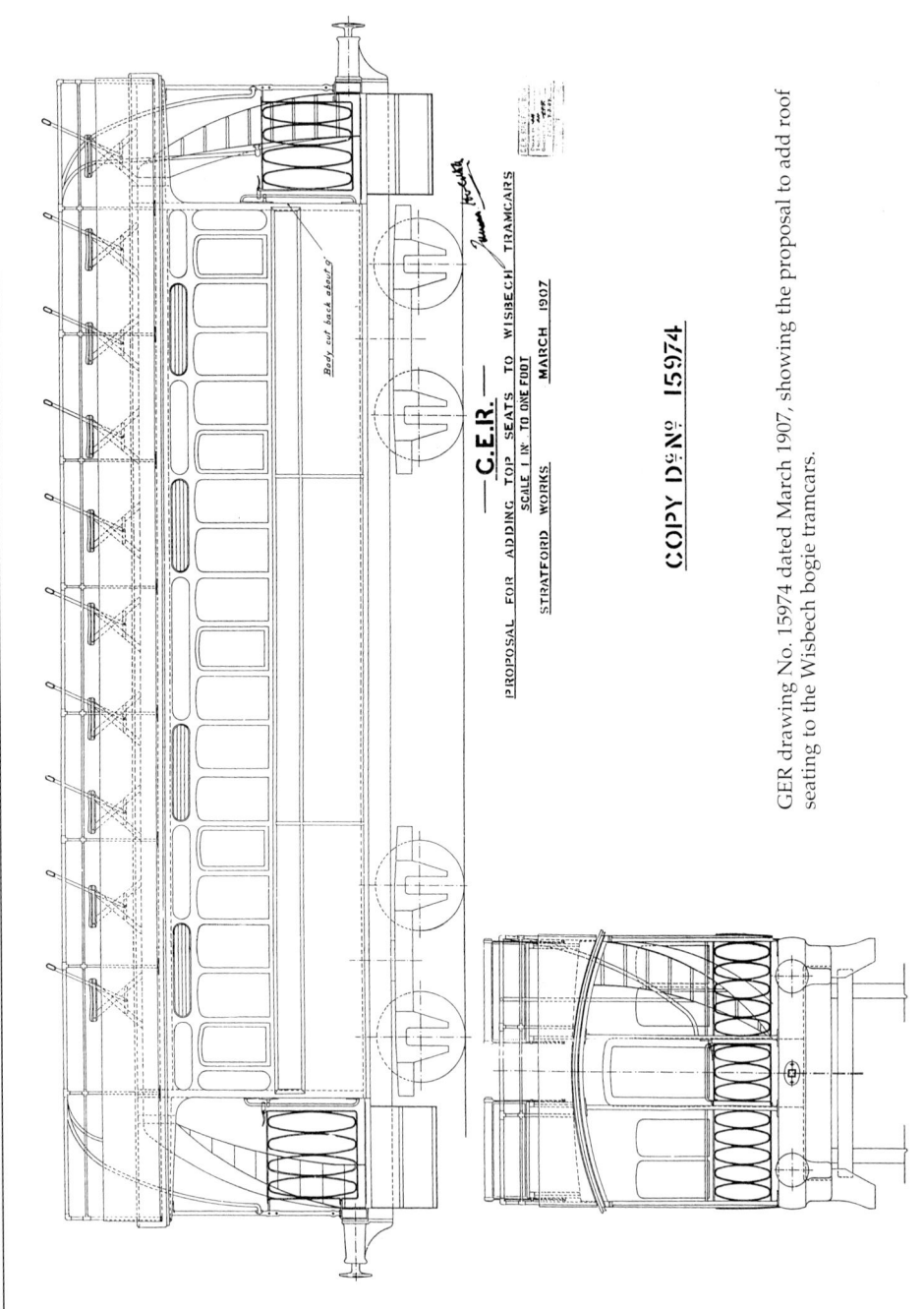

— C.E.R. —

PROPOSAL FOR ADDING TOP SEATS TO WISBECH TRAMCARS

SCALE 1 IN TO ONE FOOT

STRATFORD WORKS   MARCH 1907

COPY D^G N^O 15974

Body cut back about 9"

GER drawing No. 15974 dated March 1907, showing the proposal to add roof seating to the Wisbech bogie tramcars.

Two former Stoke Ferry branch six-wheel vehicles and former Wisbech & Upwell third class bogie tramcar No. E60462 form a passenger train for Tollesbury at Kelvedon Low Level station in September 1939. All three coaches were sent for further use on the Tollesbury Light Railway after the closure of their respective branches and survived until closure of the Essex light railway in 1951. The side steps on the vehicles can be seen to advantage as can the raised drop plate position by the wrought-iron work. Whilst the train was in motion passengers were not permitted to ride on the end balconies of the Wisbech tramcars, an instruction often ignored.

Author's Collection

Internal view of former Wisbech & Upwell bogie coach showing the longitudinal seating along the side of the vehicle at Tollesbury on 19th September, 1950.   *Ian L. Wright*

GER diagram 604 four-wheel luggage van No 9.

By the late 1880s the original Millwall vehicles were showing signs of age and, with increasing traffic, it became imperative to introduce replacement tramcar vehicles. These were built to order T25 in June 1890 and received the same numbers as the Millwall tramcars, which were withdrawn. Strangely, instead of introducing additional bogie tramcars, the four new vehicles were four-wheel tramcars. Nos. 1 and 2 were first/second composites to diagram 600 whilst Nos. 3 and 4 were full seconds to diagram 601. The chief alteration from the 1884 build was the increase in wheelbase from 10 ft to 11 ft. From January 1893 the second class accommodation on diagram 600 and 601 vehicles was converted to third class.

The usefulness of four-wheel van No. 9 was limited by the lack of guard's accommodation and so in 1903 the GER authorities decided a replacement was necessary. A four-wheel suburban brake/third No. 16, originally built as a suburban brake third by the Metropolitan Railway Carriage & Wagon Company in September 1875, was duly withdrawn for conversion to a full brake for use on the tramway in October 1903. The transformation to diagram 611 included an end door and step plates provided for the guard's use. It retained its original GE running number 16 and was not included in the tramway series. The leading dimensions, as converted were:

GER diagram	611
Type	Four wheel brake van
Length over buffers	26 ft 4¼ in.
Length over body	22 ft 8¾ in.
Body height	6 ft 8 in.
Max. height	10 ft 11 in.
Max. width	8 ft 0 in.
Width over guard's ducket	9 ft 0 in.
Wheelbase	13 ft 0 in.
Wheel diameter	3 ft 6½ in.

On the arrival of No. 16, the minute No. 9 was put into store for some months before being transferred to the Downham to Stoke Ferry branch, where it provided additional luggage accommodation. As parcels traffic increased on the Norfolk branch, its usefulness was again considered inadequate and it was replaced by an ordinary covered van. After the opening of the Elsenham to Thaxted Light Railway in March 1913, No. 9 was transferred to the Essex branch on 23rd December of the same year, where it was occasionally used as a general parcels and milk van when the normal brake was full. The van was withdrawn from traffic on 29th December, 1929 without being renumbered by the LNER, and was sent to Stratford for further use as an internal service vehicle, stock No. EX044, where it is believed to have survived until the mid-1950s.

The Wisbech & Upwell Tramway became part of the LNER on and from 1st January, 1923 and the new owners subsequently renumbered the surviving passenger stock as under:

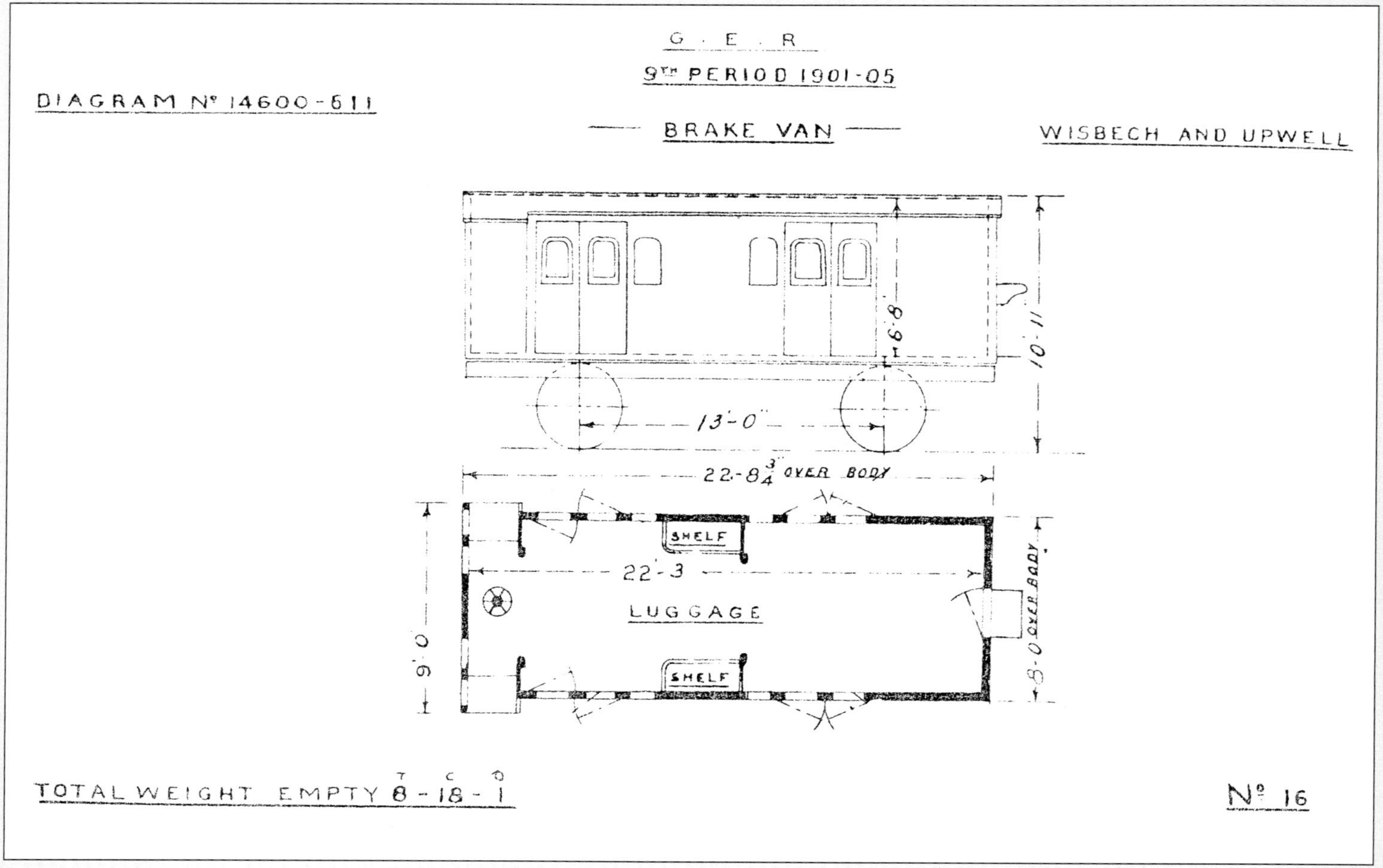

G. E. R

9TH PERIOD 1901-05

WISBECH AND UPWELL

BRAKE VAN

DIAGRAM No 14600 - 611

No 16

10·11

8·9

13·0"

22·8¾ OVER BODY

8·0 OVER BODY

22·3

LUGGAGE

SHELF

SHELF

6·0

TOTAL WEIGHT EMPTY 8 - 18 - 1

GER diagram 611 four-wheel brake van No 16.

'G15' class 0-4-0 tram locomotive No. 125 eases along Elm Road, Wisbech with a passenger train from Upwell on a wintry day. The train is formed of 4-wheel luggage van No. 9, composite bogie van No. 7, four 4-wheel tramcars and third bogie tramcar No. 8. No. 125 later became GER No. 0125 then LNER No. 07125 before withdrawal from traffic in February 1940. The local authority has dumped a quantity of roadstone for highway repairs on the canal bank. *Author's Collection*

An Upwell to Wisbech passenger train hauled by a 'G15' class 0-4-0 tram locomotive running along Elm Road beside the Wisbech canal. The train is formed of the entire passenger stock of the tramway with the leading vehicle 4-wheel passenger brake van No. 16 followed by a bogie tramcar, then three 4-wheel tramcars, the second bogie vehicle and bringing up the rear three 4-wheel tramcars.
Author's Collection

Diagram	GER No.	LNER No.
600	1	not renumbered
601	2	60464
601	3	60465
601	4	60466
600	5	not renumbered
601	6	60463
603	7	60461
603	8	60462
611	16	not renumbered

After the withdrawal of the passenger services on the Wisbech & Upwell Tramway from 31st December, 1927, the remaining tramcars were put into store until it was realised replacement vehicles were required on the Kelvedon & Tollesbury Light Railway, in Essex. Six of the nine vehicles were actually transferred, bogie tramcars Nos. 60461 and 60462 on 30th September, 1928, the former being down-classed to a full third and reclassified to diagram 603 before transfer. Four-wheel brake van No. 16 was also withdrawn on the same day without being renumbered, and the body was used as a coal yard office at Dovercourt until 1963. On 9th December, 1928 four-wheel tramcars Nos. 60463, 60465 and 60466 to diagram 601 followed the bogie tramcars for further use on the Essex light railway, whilst No. 60464 had its hand brake removed and steps altered before being down-classed to third class only, and was transferred to the Tollesbury branch on 12th January, 1929. No further use could be found for the remaining two vehicles, ex-GER Nos. 1 and 5 and they were withdrawn from stock on 21st June, 1930.

Three of the four-wheel tramcars, Nos. 60463, 60464 and 60466, were withdrawn on 16th May, 1936, whilst No. 60464 survived World War II before being withdrawn on 20th March, 1948. The bogie tramcars Nos. 60461 and 60462 soldiered on until the withdrawal of the Kelvedon to Tollesbury passenger services on 5th May, 1951. The pair remained at Kelvedon for a short while before having the side steps removed for transit to Stratford, and even then they were not removed from capital stock until 1st October, 1951. In 1950 Ealing Studios were planning a comedy film based on the fight by local people to save their local branch railway from closure. During the course of the search for a suitable line, the Kelvedon to Tollesbury line was inspected but found unsuitable. The former Wisbech & Upwell tramcars were, however, noted and subsequently No. 60461 was purchased and used in 'The Titfield Thunderbolt', filmed on the former Great Western Railway Camerton to Limpley Stoke branch in 1952, where it was one of the star attractions. After the conclusion of filming it was sold on 24th January, 1953 and finished up as an onion store on a farm near Huntingdon. It remained in this condition for nearly 20 years before being rescued for preservation by the Rutland Railway Museum, Cottesmore. In the meantime sister vehicle No. 60462 was restored to GER livery as No. 8 for preservation, the main attraction being the end balconies with wrought-iron railings. It was initially stored at Bounds Green carriage depot from 22nd March, 1952 and then Stratford but, unfortunately, through lack of storage space and later misunderstanding, the vehicle was scrapped on 9th March, 1957 and the body burnt. No. 60461 returned to its old haunts, albeit minus wheels and on a low loader *en route* from Cambridge to the Rutland Railway Museum on Saturday 10th July, 1982 and then again during centenary celebrations for the tramway held at Wisbech and across the route to Upwell on Saturday 20th August, 1983. It has since been moved to the North Norfolk Railway and restored to its former glory as GER No. 7 but with modern day embellishments.

The tremendous increase in fruit traffic generated at the tramway depots especially in the summer months brought an equally serious problem with the associated paperwork, which could not be satisfactorily dealt with in the limited space of the depot offices by the resident foreman. The GER and later LNER thus contrived to send clerks from Wisbech Goods to the respective depots in vehicles equipped with desks to handle the consignments notes and other correspondence whilst the depot foremen and other staff supervised the loading and unloading of wagons and vans. Once at the depots, staff waybilled the consignments and labelled wagons and vans for onward transit before being picked up on the return working, when they completed their documentation. This method saved considerable time and obviated congestion of rolling stock at Wisbech Goods thereby ensuring early connections for onward destinations.

From the early 1920s the GER was operating a pair of their sundry vans built in 1897 to diagram 34 to convey staff to depots. But it was not until 1937 that the LNER converted three of these vehicles as fruit traffic office vans and these were used during the fruit growing season to convey goods clerks from Wisbech to each of the depots. The three vehicles were built by the GER October 1897 and their subsequent history is shown below:

GER No.	LNER No.	Withdrawn from traffic	Converted to fruit traffic office van	Departmental No.	Withdrawn
1871	6201	February 1937	1937	962351	1950
1873	6203	August 1933*	1937	962352	1950
1874	6204	February 1937	1937	962353	1950

* It is possible that this vehicle was used experimentally from this date as a fruit traffic office van on the Upwell tramway but was not officially transferred to Departmental stock until 1937.

The leading dimensions of the vans were:

GER diagram	34
Type	Sundry van
Length over buffers	25 ft 1½ in.
Length over body	22 ft 0 in.
Body height	7 ft 4 in.
Max. width	8 ft 0 in.
Max. height	11 ft 7 in.
Wheelbase	13 ft 6 in.
Total weight empty	8 tons 7 cwt

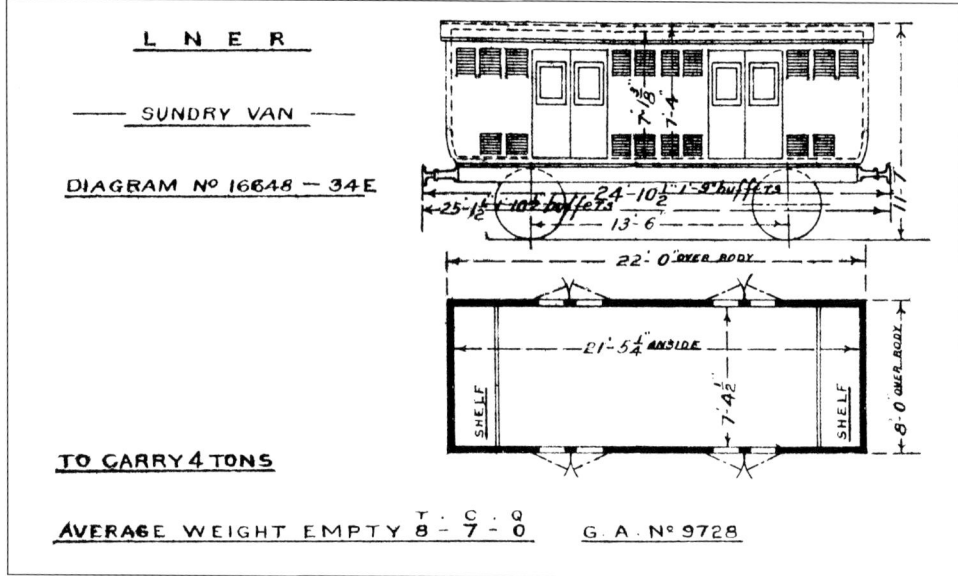

GER diagram 34 four-wheel sundry van converted to fruit traffic office van.

Looking towards the buffers stops from the former passenger platform at Upwell with the station building to the left and fruit traffic office van No. 962353 to the right. By the buffer stops is the locomotive water tank formed of an ex-GER locomotive tender body mounted on timber trestles. This fed the water column located by the run-round loop headshunt.

Author's Collection

LNER fruit traffic office van No. 962353 standing at Wisbech. It was one of three vehicles used on the tramway at the height of the fruit harvesting campaign to convey goods clerks to the tramway depots to handle consignments notes, thus obviating delays at Wisbech. The vehicle was built by the GER in 1897 as a sundry van and was converted to a fruit traffic office van in 1937. It was finally condemned in 1950.   *A.F. Cook*

In the late 1920s the LNER also utilised a diagram 505 four-wheel brake third vehicle No. 62085 as a fruit traffic office van. It was built in March 1903 as a six-a-side suburban five-compartment carriage, one of 254 constructed at Stratford works between 1898 and 1905. In late 1927 and during the course of 1928 the LNER converted 12 of the carriages to brake thirds to diagram 505, No. 62085 being converted in October 1927 when it received its LNER running number. One of the three compartment doors nearest the guard's compartment was stopped up to incorporate the section into the guard's compartment thus reducing the passenger accommodation to two compartments. It is a mystery as to why a London suburban brake third carriage was being used on the Wisbech and Upwell Tramway but it can only be assumed it was a temporary replacement for a diagram 34 van. No. 62085 was withdrawn from traffic in September 1935, in line with the remaining 11 vehicles which were withdrawn between September 1935 and March 1936.

The principal dimensions of the No. 62085 were:

Diagram No.		505
Type		Brake/third
Length over buffers		30 ft 7½ in.
Length over body		27 ft 0 in.
Body height		7 ft 4 in.
Max. width		9 ft 0 in.
Max. height		11 ft 7 in.
Wheelbase		15 ft 6 in.
Seating	*3rd class*	24

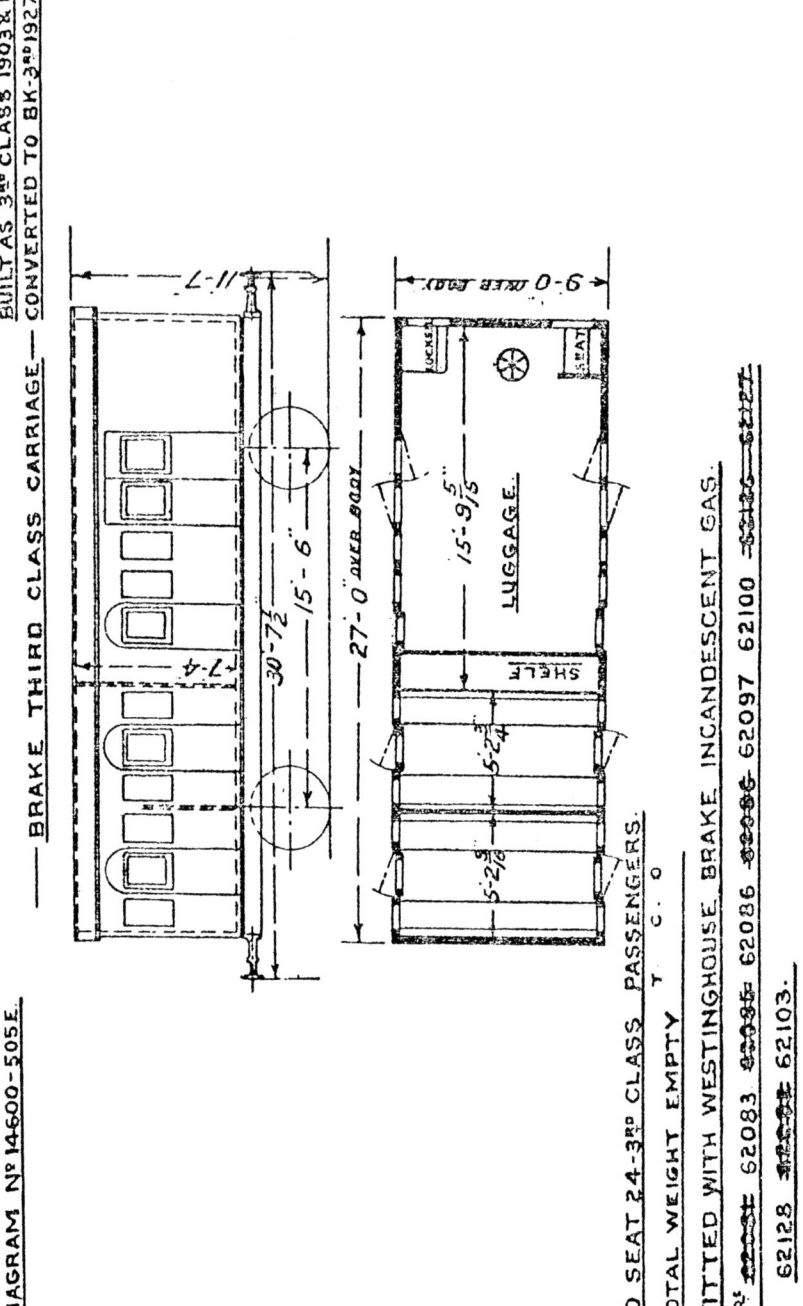

L. N. E. R.

DIAGRAM Nº 14600-505E.

BUILT AS 3ᴿᴰ CLASS 1903 & 1905

CONVERTED TO BK-3ᴿᴰ 1927 & 1928

BRAKE THIRD CLASS CARRIAGE

11'-7"

15'-6"

30'-7½"

7'-4"

27'-0" OVER BODY

9'-0" OVER BODY

15'-9⅝"

5'-5"

LUGGAGE

SHELF

5'-2¾"

5'-2⅜"

LOCKER

SEAT

TO SEAT 24-3ᴿᴰ CLASS PASSENGERS.

TOTAL WEIGHT EMPTY T.C.0

FITTED WITH WESTINGHOUSE BRAKE INCANDESCENT GAS.

Nᵒˢ 62081 62083 62085 62086 62097 62100 62101 62127
62128 62181 62103.

GER diagram 505 four-wheel brake third converted to fruit traffic office van.

Freight Stock

The initial wagons used on the tramway were wooden open vehicles with side doors and some were fitted with dumb buffers. Where grain, straw or merchandise was susceptible to wet weather, a tarpaulin sheet was utilised to protect the contents of the wagon. The brakevan at the tail of the train would have been a 10 ton vehicle. In the years prior to the turn of the century the GER utilised four-plank bodied, open wagons with wooden frames, dating from 1882, for conveyance of general merchandise and minerals. From 1887, these wagons were gradually superseded by five-plank, 9 ton capacity (later 10 ton) opens, to diagram 16 with 9 ft 6 in. wheelbase and measuring 15 ft 0 in. over headstocks. Later 10 ton, five-plank open wagons to diagram 17, with a length of 15 ft 0 in. over headstocks and 9 ft 0 in. wheelbase, were also used. Another variation was the use of 10 ton, seven plank opens to diagram 55, measuring 17 ft 0 in. over headstocks and 9 ft 6 in. wheelbase for vegetable and root traffic. Fruit and perishable traffic were conveyed in 10 ton ventilated vans to diagram 15, measuring 16 ft 1 in. over headstocks, with 9 ft 0 in. wheelbase and overall height of 11 ft 0¾ in. Later covered goods vans to diagram 47 were also utilised. They measured 17 ft 3 in. over headstocks, had a wheelbase of 10 ft 6 in. and were 11 ft 2 in. in height. A third variation was the 10 ton capacity covered goods wagon to diagram 72, which measured 19 ft 0 in. over headstocks whilst maintaining a 10 ft 6 in. wheelbase.

The small amount of cattle traffic generated from the Upwell tramway would have brought three types of cattle wagons to the branch, and indeed such vehicles were pressed into traffic to convey fruit traffic at the height of the harvesting season. The first of 8 tons capacity to diagram 5 was 18 ft 7 in. over headstocks, had a 10 ft 6 in. wheelbase and was 10 ft 10¾ in. in height. The second to diagram 6 was of 9 ton capacity and measured 19 ft 0 in. over

An up freight working departs from Outwell Village depot in 1950. The weed-covered Wharf or Water siding terminates by sleepers short of the main single line at one time bisected the track and continued curving along the bank of the waterway.

Author's Collection

In the latter years traffic was light and the 1.30 pm Wisbech to Upwell train is formed of a 16 ton all-steel mineral wagon and a former LMS goods brake van hauled by Drewry 204 hp 0-6-0 diesel-mechanical locomotive No. D2202 shown crossing the Wisbech to Littleport/Ely A1101 main road at Horn's Corner level crossing No. 11 at 4 miles 51 chains.   *Ken Paye*

Outwell Basin depot with the main single line in the foreground showing the steeply rising gradient culminating in a short 1 in 30 to Outwell Basin Bridge No. 2336. Two covered van wait in the loop siding for collection whilst the yard is filled with Aluminium Wire & Cable Company cable drums.

headstocks, with a 10 ft 6 in. wheelbase and overall height of 10 ft 10½ in. The third GER variant to diagram 7 was of 10 tons capacity, 19 ft 3 in. over headstocks with 10 ft 6 in. wheelbase and overall height of 11 ft 2 in. At the tail of the train was usually a 20 ton four-wheel brakevan to GER diagram 56, measuring 17 ft 6 in. over headstocks, a 10 ft 3 in. wheelbase and 3 ft 1 in. diameter wheels. In addition many wagons owned by other railway companies were used to deliver and collect agricultural and horticultural traffic, whilst coal and coke supplies came in private owner coal wagons. These fell into two categories, those belonging to the collieries consigning the coal, and merchants and coal factors wagons, which were loaded at the collieries.

After Grouping the GER wagons continued in use but gradually LNER standard design wagons made an appearance. The most numerous were probably the 12 ton, five-plank opens with 8 ft 0 in. wheelbase to code 2, and 12 ton, six-plank open with 10 ft 0 in. wheelbase to code 91 built after 1932. Later types included the 13 ton, seven-plank open wagons to code 162 measuring 16 ft 6 in. over headstocks and with a 9 ft 0 in. wheelbase. All were used on vegetable and sugar beet traffic. Fitted and unfitted 12 ton, 9 ft 0 in. wheelbase vans to code 16 conveyed perishable goods and fruit and later some were designated for fruit traffic only. From 1934 12 ton capacity vans to code 171, with steel underframe and pressed corrugated steel ends, were introduced, whilst at the same time the wheelbase was extended to 10 ft 0 in. These specific fruit vans saw much use on the tramway. Agricultural machinery destined for local farms was delivered on 12 ton Lowfit wagons, with 10 ft wheelbase and overall length over headstocks of 17 ft 6 in. Larger machinery would have arrived and departed on one of the GER 14 ton, 25 ft 6 in. 'Mac K2' machinery wagons to diagram 75 and later LNER builds. LNER brakevans provided for the branch included 20 ton 'Toad B' to code 34 and 'Toad E' to code 64 vehicles with 10 ft 6 in. wheelbase and measuring 22 ft 5 in. over buffers. Later 'Toad D' brake vans to code 61 with 16 ft 0 in. wheelbase and measuring 27 ft 5 in. over buffers were employed. After Nationalisation many of the older wooden-bodied vehicles were scrapped, and much of the traffic conveyed in open wagons was carried in the standard 16 ton all-steel mineral vehicles.

In GER days the body, solebars and headstocks of the open wagons were painted slate grey, whilst the ironwork below solebar level, buffer guides, buffers, drawbars, drawbar plates and couplings were black. Lettering was white. Brake vans had vermilion headstocks. The LNER wagon livery was grey for non-fitted wagons and covered vans, whilst all vehicles fitted with automatic brakes, including brakevans were painted brown red oxide, which changed to bauxite around 1940. Similar liveries were carried in BR days.

The maintenance of wagon stock used on the tramway was carried out by the wagon repair shops at March. In the event of the failure or defect of a wagon on the branch, a wagon repairer travelling from Wisbech attended the casualty.

(Much of the freight rolling stock operating on the Upwell tramway was used on other East Anglian lines. For this reason the plans published in the author's earlier titles for the Oakwood Press – *The Framlingham Branch*, *The Hadleigh Branch*, and *The Snape Branch* – have not been repeated in this volume.)

Appendix One

Level Crossings

No.	Location	M. from Tramway Junction	Ch.	Local Name	Status
Main Line					
32	Wisbech Jn & Wisbech Station	93	44 ½	Victoria Road	Public
1	Wisbech & Emneth	0	13	Prospect Place	Footpath
2	Wisbech & Emneth	0	22	Milner Road	Occupation
Tramway					
1	Wisbech & Elm Bridge Depot	0	31	Elm Road	Public
2	Wisbech & Elm Bridge Depot	0	50	Ramnoth Road	Public
3	Wisbech & Elm Bridge Depot	1	28	Duke of Wellington	Public
4	Elm Bridge Depot & Boyce's Bridge	3	22		Occupation
5	Outwell Basin & Outwell Village	4	21		Public
6	Outwell Basin & Outwell Village	4	26	Back Lane	Public
7	Outwell Basin & Outwell Village	4	32	Diggle	Occupation
8	Outwell Basin & Outwell Village	4	37	Harslip	Occupation
9	Outwell Basin & Outwell Village	4	39	Wardrop No. 1	Occupation
10	Outwell Basin & Outwell Village	4	43	Edgett	Occupation
11	Outwell Basin & Outwell Village	4	51	Horn's Corner	Public
12	Outwell Village & Upwell	5	02	Church Terrace	Public
13	Outwell Village & Upwell	5	26	Goodman's Corner	Public
14	Outwell Village & Upwell	5	41	Wardrop No. 2	Occupation
15	Outwell Village & Upwell	5	48	Pingle Bridge Road	Public
16	Outwell Village & Upwell	5	50	Small Lode	Public

There were numerous other occupational level crossings which were un-numbered. These mileages are used in Chapter Six.

Elm Road, Wisbech, tramway crossing No. 1, in March 1966 with a gate across the single line. The protecting stop signal can be seen in the background. *R. Powell*

This revised list issued by BR gives an example of great discrepancies made by various railway departments in calculating the tramway mileage!

No.	*Location*	*M.*	*Ch.*	*Local Name*	*Status*
		from Tramway Junction			
Main Line					
32	Wisbech Jn & Wisbech Station	93	47 ¾	Victoria Road	Public
1	Wisbech & Emneth	0	06	Prospect Place	Footpath
2	Wisbech & Emneth	0	17	Milner Road	Occupation
Tramway					
	Wisbech & Elm Bridge Depot	0	52 ½	Elm Road	Public
	Wisbech & Elm Bridge Depot	0	59	Ramnoth Road	Public
	Wisbech & Elm Bridge Depot	1	30 ½	Duke of Wellington	Public
	Wisbech & Elm Bridge Depot	1	40 ¼		Public
	Elm Bridge Depot & Boyce's Bridge	2	36 ¾		Public
	Boyce's Bridge & Outwell Basin	3	48 ¼		Public
	Boyce's Bridge & Outwell Basin	3	48 ¾		Public
2	Outwell Basin & Outwell Village	4	20 ¼		Public
3	Outwell Basin & Outwell Village	4	26	Outwell Basin Bridge	Public
4	Outwell Basin & Outwell Village	4	30 ¾	Outwell Back Road	Public
5	Outwell Basin & Outwell Village	4	33 ¼	Cousin's	Occupation
6	Outwell Basin & Outwell Village	4	36 ¼	Naylor's	Occupation
7	Outwell Basin & Outwell Village	4	39 ¾	Diggle's	Occupation
8	Outwell Basin & Outwell Village	4	46 ¾	Harslip	Occupation
9	Outwell Basin & Outwell Village	4	49 ¼	Edgerson's No. 1	Occupation
10	Outwell Basin & Outwell Village	4	53	Edgerson's No. 2	Occupation
11	Outwell Basin & Outwell Village	4	57	Horn's Corner	Public
12	Outwell Village & Upwell	5	09 ½	Outwell Village	Public
13	Outwell Village & Upwell	5	33 ¼	Goodman's	Public
14	Outwell Village & Upwell	5	41 ¼	Blunt's	Occupation
15	Outwell Village & Upwell	5	55 ¾	Small Lode Drive	Public
16	Outwell Village & Upwell	5	56 ¾	Small Lode	Public

Altogether there were 16 official numbered level crossings on the Wisbech and Upwell Tramway but many other occupational level crossings remained unnumbered. On this section of line one such crossing bisects the railway near the site of Outwell Sluice siding. *Author's Collection*

Appendix Two

Bridges

Bridge No.	Location	Mileage m. ch.	Local Name	Under or Over	Type	Spans	Square Span between abutments or supports ft in.	Skew Span between abutments or supports ft in.	Width ft in.	Depth of construction ft in.	Distance from road or surface of water to rail ft in.	Construction
2335	Wisbech & Elm Bridge	0 48	Newcommon bridge	Under	Canal	1	25 0					Replaced 1932 by concrete culvert.
2336	Outwell Basin & Outwell Village	4 20	Basin bridge	Under	Canal	3	10 6 30 6 10 6	11 6 over Basin 32 1 over Canal 10 11 over Bank	14 9	2 0	11 0	Cast-iron cylinders for abutments and piers, side girders, corrugated cross troughing, ballast LR. Used also as entrance to goods yard.
2337	Outwell Basin & Outwell Village	4 79	Outwell bridge	Under	River	3	10 0 28 0 12 9	13 7 over Bank 36 6 over Canal 17 0 over Bank	14 9	1 10	8 0	Cast-iron cylinders for abutments and piers, side girders, corrugated cross troughing, ballast LR.
2338	Outwell Village & Upwell	5 49	Small Lode	Under	Culvert	1	9 3	9 6		2 2	6 6	Timber pile crossheads, longitudinal running timbers, cross sleeper timbers TR. Rebuilt 1953 2 ft 6 in. diameter concrete pipe, concrete surrouds and headwalls.

Acknowledgements

The publication of this history would not have been possible without the help of many people who have been kind enough to assist. In particular I should like to thank the late A.R. Cox, the late W. Fenton, the late G. Woodcock, the late Dr I.C. Allen, the late K. Townroe, the late Peter Proud, the late Geoff Pember, John Watling, R.H.N. Hardy, Dave Hoser, Mike Brooks, Peter Webber, the late B.D.J. Walsh, the late R.C. (Dick) Riley, John Petrie, also staff of the former March, Cambridge, King's Lynn and Wisbech motive power depots, and the many other active and retired railway staff, some of whom worked on the tramway. I am also extremely grateful to Robert Powell who read through the draft of the manuscript and made many useful comments and Chris Cock who rendered sterling assistance on the finished work.

Thanks are also due to the National Archives, Kew, British Railways, Eastern Region, House of Lords Record Office, the British Library Newspaper Library, Cambridge Record Office, Cambridge Collection and members of the Great Eastern Railway Society.

Bibliography

General Works

Aldrich C.L.	GER locomotives
Allen C.J.	*The Great Eastern Railway* (Ian Allan)
Gordon D.I.	*Regional History of the Railways of Great Britain* Volume 5 (David & Charles)
Gordon W.J.	*Our Home Railways* Volume 1
RCTS	LNER Locomotives

Periodicals

Bradshaw's Railway Guide; *Bradshaw's Railway Manual*; *British Railways, Eastern Region Magazine*; *Buses*; *East Anglian Magazine*; *Great Eastern Railway Magazine*; *Locomotive Carriage & Wagon Review*; *Locomotive Magazine*; *LNER Magazine*; *Railway Magazine*; *Railway World*; *Railway Year Book* and *Trains Illustrated*.

Newspapers

Cambridge Chronicle
Wisbech Advertiser
Wisbech Observer
Wisbech Telegraph

Also Minute Books of the Eastern Counties Railway, Great Eastern Railway, London and North Eastern Railway.

Working and Public Timetables: Great Eastern Railway, London and North Eastern Railway and British Railways, Eastern Region.

Appendices to the Working Timetables: Great Eastern Railway, London and North Eastern Railway and British Railways, Eastern Region.

Index

The tramway remembered (I). Road sign on the approach to Outwell Village depicting a steam tram locomotive, September 2006. *Author*

The tramway remembered (II). Village sign at Upwell depicting tram locomotive and covered vans, September 2006. *Author*